To Susan
Happy Cooking!
Jill Sheeley

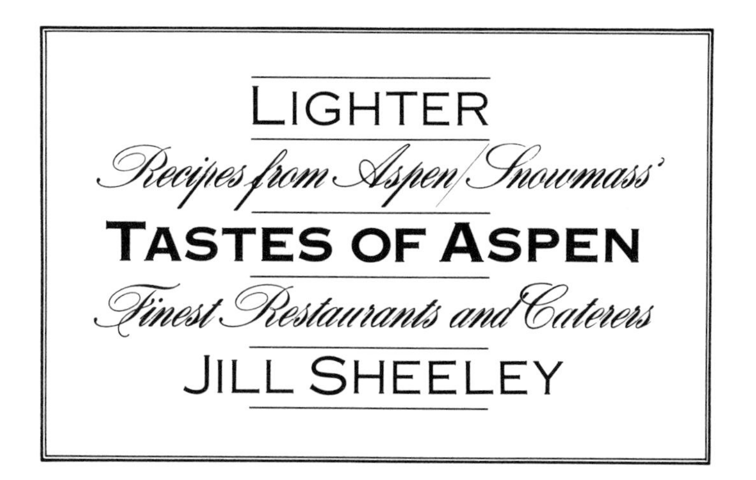

LIGHTER

Recipes from Aspen/Snowmass'

TASTES OF ASPEN

Finest Restaurants and Caterers

JILL SHEELEY

Illustrated by

RUTH STERN

COURTNEY PRESS • ASPEN

First edition published in 1994 by Courtney Press, Aspen, Colorado.

Printed in U.S.A.

ISBN 0-9609108-2-4

DEDICATION

This book is in memory of Stuart Mace, who passed away August 4, 1993 in his mountain home.

Those lucky enough to have visited the Maces' Toklat Lodge in the 60's or 70's will remember enjoying a wonderful meal of wild mushroom soup, homemade bread and Alaskan king crab legs in their homey dining room by a roaring fire. After coffee and dessert, the lights would dim and Stuart would entertain you for hours with his marvelous adventure stories and poems. He truly had a gift for storytelling. Then, he would take you outdoors, under the most magnificent starlit sky, to see his beloved Husky dogs who howled with happiness. Those were the days!

Stuart was dedicated to preserving and protecting the land at any cost. He loved and understood nature. He possessed an uncanny awareness known to few. He spoke of harmony, balance, empathy, humility, frugality and gentleness. He once wrote, "Let them explain that Life is a Gift; that we are guests at that Banquet. Then your spirit will propel you to action, not talk. Only then will others listen with their hearts and change."

Stuart now lies next to his son, Greg, at the base of Castle Peak, in peace.

ACKNOWLEDGEMENTS

I would like to express gratitude to the many people who helped make this book a reality:

All of the restaurant owners, chefs and caterers *who gave so generously of their time.*

To the following friends who helped test recipes either at home or at one our numerous, ever-popular recipe-testing parties:

Fiona
Sam
Nancy
Lisa
Di
Linda
Jennifer
Carol
Krys
Gwyn
Martha
Barbara
Gretl
Jane
Polly
Gail
Joy
Muffy
Sunny
Kay
Carlyn
Ann
Sherri
Bobbi
Mari
Dottie
Becky
Katie
Sonya
Nancy & Betts
Madeleine

Ruth *for her wonderful drawings.*

Ed and Bland *for their editing advice.*

Fiona *for all her invaluable help testing.*

Karen Keehn *for her Guide to Wine and Food.*

Curt *for his creativity.*

Susan *for her advice on nutrition.*

Bland and Scott *for their computer help.*

My family and friends *for their support.*

And to Don and Courtney *for their understanding.*

TABLE OF CONTENTS

PART I • Aspen Restaurants

PART II • Snowmass Restaurants

PART III • Mountain Restaurants

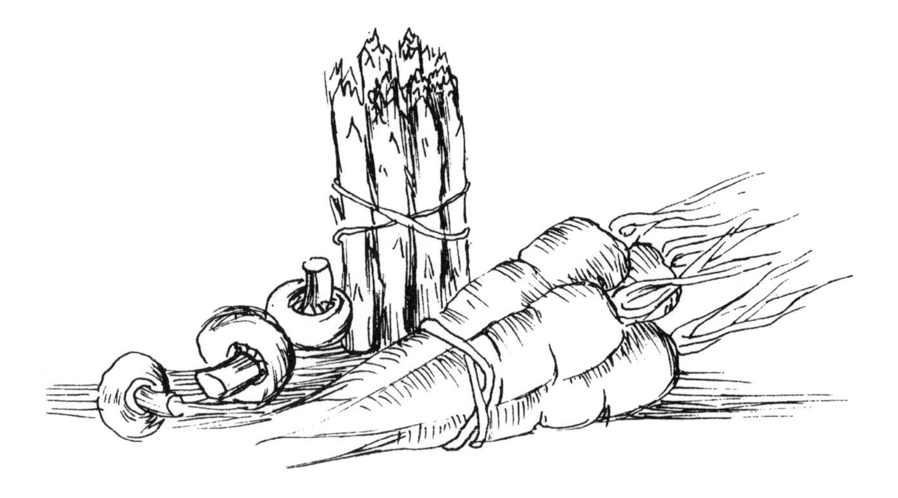

INTRODUCTION

Aspen is like none other. Besides the spectacular mountains that play host to so many sports and activities, we are fortunate to enjoy an abundance of unusually superior restaurants. The superb mountain cuisine served here is complemented by a unique charm.

Lighter Tastes of Aspen is a collection of favorite recipes from Aspen and Snowmass' best restaurants and caterers. The emphasis these days is on lighter, yet satisfying fare. Because of the demand for lower fat, lighter cuisine, I have asked the chefs to choose recipes that reflect this trend. Most of the chefs eagerly contributed delicious, lower fat recipes resulting in an incredible spectrum of dishes from Garbanzo and Couscous Soup to Warm Balsamic Marinated Salmon with Orange Ginger Sauce. You will find that not all the chefs complied with this request.

However, I have a theory about desserts—most people adore them. They are an integral part of a meal. They're tempting, beautiful and comforting. Whether it be a platter of imported cheeses or a low-fat sorbet, diners desire one more taste before truly finishing a meal. Because I believe in moderation, I also believe that three or four bites of a rich dessert are well-deserved. Denial can only go so far! When requesting dessert recipes, I gave the chefs total freedom of choice. Some chefs do give advice on how to lower the fat. Just look for the ♥ symbol.

If you already have my first book, *Tastes of Aspen*, you'll be happy to know that I have gathered all new recipes for this cookbook. Due to popular demand, I have included *Tastes of Aspen's* most popular recipes in the *Old Favorites* section. I have also included an *Aspen Specialty Foods* section.

Each and every recipe has been tested and re-tested to ensure successful results. They are calculated for Aspen's altitude of 7,900 feet. In Appendix I, you will find a helpful explanation for conversion to low altitude.

Trying new food is one of life's pleasures. I hope you'll enjoy these wonderful and innovative recipes as much as I have.

Bon Appétit!

PREFACE

I have had a love affair with food my whole life. It was only natural for me to create food as well as to eat it. And as it turned out, I was good at the creative part and formed a career for myself. I have been working with food professionally for over twenty years and during that time, I have seen a lot of changes.

There are thousands and thousands of recipes, many ways to use the same ingredients with an entirely different result. The more I work with food and the more I learn about it, the more I realize how much more there is to learn. That's the wonderful part of being a chef; it is never boring!

Of course, food is basic to life and how people want to eat dictates what chefs create. Eating is very personal and at the same time, there are clear societal guidelines. As a chef, I must always be aware of what people are interested in eating.

There was a time when the only really good restaurants were French. Today, we have a very eclectic cuisine in America and especially in Aspen. Chefs create incredible food from international cuisines and as a result, we are beginning to see an "American Cuisine" emerge. The tastes of the American public are more sophisticated than ever before. Americans are more concerned with health and physical fitness. The result is a very healthy, nutritious cuisine that is interesting, creative and sensual.

So how does one create food that tastes great and is good for you? Many of us believe it is impossible. But I've learned that all one really needs to do is look at food in a different way. Usually we only consider taste in our experience with food, but that experience is made up of all the senses. The first thing we do is *see* food; color and presentation become very important. Perhaps we *smell* the food before we ever taste it; aroma becomes important as well. Texture, sound, the *feel* of finger foods—all of these senses add to our experience. Being creative, we want to consider all of these sensations when we cook.

If we would like to eat food that nourishes us, provides fuel for our bodies and is low in fat and sugar, then we want to use everything available to us when creating our meals. Spices and herbs are wonderful little gifts. They accentuate the flavor and aroma of any dish. Using beautiful garnishes such as creatively cut vegetables or edible flowers can create a feast for the eyes. Using natural water-based stocks can make soups and sauces lighter and more flavorful. And creating a beautiful ambiance with table setting and music completes the experience!

I believe it is very important that we make eating a nourishing experience. If we say "no" to ourselves when we eat, we will not feel satisfied. When we cook for ourselves, we can say "yes" to exquisite aromas, interesting flavors and unusual beauty. Our bodies are satisfied through all the senses.

A great deal of research is being done these days on nutrition and health. It is important to be aware of the findings. For instance, we find that the mono-saturated oils like canola and olive are not only high-quality oils, but they cling to cholesterol and carry it out of our bodies. The Omega-Three oils found in large cold-water fish such as salmon and swordfish do much the same thing. If we choose to create a dish using olive or canola oils rather than poly-unsaturated or saturated oils, we have made a choice to nourish our bodies. I find these oils lighter, tastier and a wonderful background for herbs and spices.

Glucose is an important source of fuel to human beings. To try to create a "sugarless" diet is dangerous and absurd. What is important is to fuel our bodies from the most natural source of glucose we can find: the complex carbohydrates such as grains, potatoes and beans. Complex glucose sources fuel us like time-released capsules, a little at a time over a long period of time. This is just what the body needs to be energetic all day. And, if we want to "sweeten" our food, it is better to use whole sugars from a natural source, such as maple syrup. The more processed a sugar is, the less valuable it is to the body.

Our planet is bountiful with natural resources. We were meant to eat fresh, flavorful, nurturing foods all the time. It is up to us to learn to cook that way. We must agree to take more time and become more educated, because we are worth it. In return, we will feel better about ourselves in every way.

In the nine years I have lived in Aspen, the complexion of the restaurant business has changed constantly. In some ways, Aspen is on the cutting edge of the new cuisine because of our emphasis on health and exercise. The chefs in Aspen create dishes out of an awareness of health. On the pages of *Lighter Tastes of Aspen*, you'll find lots of ideas for creating healthy, delicious food. Use these recipes as a guide and create from them. Notice the alternatives for lower-fat ingredients; substitute them when you need to and indulge when you can afford the luxury.

You are your own best chef because you know your body better than anyone!

Good eats!
Susan Sinnicks
Aspen Chef

Author's Note:
♥ This symbol denotes recipes that are lower in fat or include a lower-fat version. With a few exceptions, these recipes are not designated *heart healthy* and are not endorsed by the American Heart Association. Please use your own judgement if you're on a special diet.

PART I

Aspen Restaurants

Aspen boasts some of the finest restaurants in the world. Known for their atmosphere and superb cuisine, Aspen's restaurants are as popular as our ski mountains. The variety of dining experiences is impressive. Diversity, service, pride and charm are the ingredients for success. Gourmands come back yearly for a dose of Aspen hospitality. Travel these pages and you'll find stories and recipes from Aspen's favorite restaurants.

Abetone Ristorante

THIS CHIC, NEW YORK-STYLE RESTAURANT IS NAMED FOR a ski resort in Italy.

Northern Italian cuisine is the fare you'll find here. The food is prepared to individual order. It's light and they cook with only the freshest ingredients. The menu is extensive and each evening you'll delight in the chef's innovative specialties. Favorites among customers include: prime veal, homemade pastas and fresh seafood. Health-conscious diners appreciate the lighter, less fattening sauces. Lobster Fra Diavolo is a delicate mixture of fresh Maine lobster, cognac, crushed red pepper, garlic, oregano and a fresh tomato sauce. Devotees love this enticing dish.

The kitchen staff is thoroughly professional and take pride in what they prepare.

Abetone is owned by Dan Surin and Ermanno Masini, two restauranteurs who met in New York City. Skiing and the desire to own their own restaurant lured them to Aspen. They merged their talents and opened Abetone, which became an instant success. Masini is originally from the Abetone area, where his family owned and operated the restaurant, Casina Rossa.

Authenticity exists here. Perhaps that's why so many Europeans frequent Abetone and feel at home.

The decor is Italian contemporary. It's comfortable and spacious with two large dining rooms separated by tinted glass panels. The walls are covered with a gray wool fabric and strips of mirrors in between for a totally different look.

It's not uncommon to find both locals and visitors meeting for a drink, cappuccino or appetizers in Abetone's large mirrored bar area. It has just the right atmosphere.

"Spaghettini All' Ortolana"

SERVES 4

1 Box (16 oz) De Cecco Spaghettini
1¼ C Extra Virgin olive oil
2 Cloves Garlic, peeled and chopped
1 T Parsley, chopped
½ C Broccoli florets
½ C Carrot sticks, 2 inches long
½ C Mushrooms, sliced
½ C Peas, shelled
¼ C Onions, chopped
½ C Zucchini sticks, 2 inches long
½ C Tomatoes, diced
Salt & pepper to taste
¼ C Parmigiano Reggiano cheese

In a large sauce pot filled with salted, boiling water, add the Spaghettini and cook until "al dente" firm to the bite, about 12 minutes in Aspen. Meanwhile, place the oil, onions, mushrooms and garlic in a sauté pan and cook at medium heat for 2 minutes. Add all the other vegetables, salt and pepper and sauté for an additional 5 minutes, mixing well. Strain the pasta and reserve one cup of the liquid. Add the pasta to the vegetables and mix, adding the cheese and reserved liquid and serve immediately. Add parsley for garnish.

♥ *The kicker:* if you skip the cheese, this recipe is cholesterol-free!

Wine suggestion: Sauvignon Blanc, Poggio Alle Gazze, Marchese Loeovico Antinori, 1989.

Spuma Al Choccolato (Chocolate Mousse)

Whip the eggs, sugar, Kahlua and cream until firm. Mix in the chocolate until entirely amalgamated. Place in individual goblets and refrigerate until ready to serve. You can make this mousse 2 days in advance.

SERVES 6

1 C Chopped bittersweet chocolate, melted in a double boiler (warm)
2 C Heavy cream
½ C Sugar
1 oz Kahlua
¼ C "Second Nature" egg product or 2 raw egg yolks (we prefer to not serve raw eggs)

Aspen Grove Café

CAN A RESTAURANT HAVE A SPLIT PERSONALITY? The Aspen Grove Café does. It leads two lives and has two distinct moods. "The Grove" is a bustling, fast-paced, dynamic café by day; but when evening falls, it transforms into an intimate, dimly-lit environment. Jazz music and candlelight invite quiet conversation.

Owner Wes Cantrell built the restaurant in 1985 with the intention of creating a contemporary-style café. He and his wife Lynne came together with both restaurant and business experience, fulfilling a dream to run their own restaurant. Currently, they've continued to remain owner-operated which is why "The Grove" is such a success.

At breakfast, you'll find a mix of "regular" locals and tourists enjoying traditional American fare. The breakfast burritos are their most popular item. Lunch offers creative sandwiches, pasta dishes and homestyle specials. As in any European café, they offer espresso and cappuccino.

The dinner menu was described to me as "eclectic cuisine," combining the traditional with nouvelle cuisine. The menu has evolved and offers interesting, varied dishes. Examples include: Pheasant Quesadillas, Montrachet Salad (macadamia-breaded goat cheese and pinenuts on meadow greens with raspberry vinaigrette), and Elk Forestière (grilled elk loin with a fresh forest mushroom/Dijon sauce).

They serve quite a bit of game, accommodating their customers who choose to eat leaner, healthier meats. They try not to use butter, but rather olive and canola oils. They use only the freshest ingredients and strive to keep the flavors light. They offer a nice selection of French and California wines to complement any meal.

They are proud of the fact that customers can choose an affordable meal from their à la carte menu. They are available for private parties and weddings and are more than happy to assist with menu planning and decorating.

Decide on which personality you prefer, but definitely put The Aspen Grove Café on your list of places to dine.

Ginger Peach Crème Brûlée

CREATED BY
GRANT WEBB

SERVES 8

1 Large ripe peach: peeled, seeded and sliced
3 C Milk (whole, 2% or heavy cream)
¼ C Sugar
½ t Vanilla extract
⅔ C Eggbeaters or 3 whole eggs plus 3 yolks
1 inch Fresh ginger, sliced thin or 1 t ground ginger
Confectioners' sugar for dusting

Line the bottom of eight, ½ cup ramekins with peach slices and set aside. Preheat oven to 300 degrees. Heat milk in a heavy sauce pan with ginger over medium-low heat just to the boiling point. Meanwhile, whisk the sugar and eggbeaters (or eggs) together in a large bowl until the mixture is light and frothy. Slowly whisk the hot milk into the egg mixture and mix thoroughly. Strain and stir over low heat until it just coats the back of a spoon. Add the vanilla. Divide the custard among the 8 ramekins and set in a baking dish and add water two-thirds to the top of the ramekins. Bake about 35-40 minutes (until a toothpick in the center comes out clean). Cool and cover. Chill for 2 hours or up to 3 days. To serve: preheat your broiler and sift a light layer of Confectioners' sugar over the ramekins. Place under the broiler until the sugar caramelizes, 2-4 minutes. Serve immediately.

♥ *The kicker:* this is a wonderful, light dessert and different from the usual crème brûlée; a lovely treat for a warm, summer evening. It's low in cholesterol if you use low-fat milk.

Grilled Salmon on Polenta with Juniper Citrus Sauce

CREATED BY
GRANT WEBB

SERVES 8

4 lbs Fresh salmon fillets (½ lb per person)
Canola oil

POLENTA
1 Package polenta
2 T Sherry
¼ C Parmesan cheese, grated
1 t Fresh basil, chopped
1 Egg, beaten
Flour

SAUCE
1½ C Milk
5 Juniper berries, (found at specialty or health food stores), crushed and chopped fine
1 Lime, zested, and the juice
1 Orange, zested, and the juice
¼ t Fresh garlic, minced
¼ t Parsley, chopped
1½ oz Sherry
1 t Cornstarch

Prepare the polenta according to the directions, but add the sherry along with the water. Cook a bit longer until a spoon stands up in the polenta. When cooked and very thick, add the next 3 ingredients. Pour into a paper-lined loaf pan and chill. This can be made 2 days in advance.

■ Make the sauce: add all the sauce ingredients (except the juices) into a cold saucepan and bring to a simmer. Then, add the juices and bring to a boil and allow to thicken to a medium-light thickness. Brush the salmon fillets with canola oil and place face down on a hot grill turning once. Cook about 8 minutes on each side for 8 ounce portions, or to a desired consistency.

■ While the salmon grills, sauté slices of polenta. Dredge the slices first in flour, then sauté in a hot skillet with a non-stick surface (or use small amounts of canola oil) until crisp.

To serve: place the grilled salmon on top of the polenta with approximately 2 ounces of sauce over the top.

The kicker: this is a wonderful dish with many delicious tastes. We made extra polenta and served it the next day—we topped it with fresh mozzarella and fresh basil.

Wine Suggestion: Sonoma-Cutrer Chardonnay, 1990.

Bentley's at The Wheeler

BENTLEY'S CLAIMS THE CORNER SPOT OF THE RECENTLY renovated Wheeler Opera House. This historic red brick building is a landmark in Aspen dating back to 1889. It was built at the height of the silver boom by mining entrepreneur Jerome B. Wheeler.

Aspen enjoyed four glorious years of performances in The Wheeler before the silver panic hit in 1893. The Opera House also survived two fires in 1912. Walter Paepcke and Herbert Bayer transformed the damaged Wheeler into Aspen's premier theatre once again in 1960. One final, historic face-lift took two years to complete with a gala opening in May 1984. It closely resembles The Wheeler of yesteryear.

Bentley's interior was designed with visions of keeping it harmonious with the Aspen Victorian style. It also fits the old/new image of the Opera House. Victorian curtains and lamps, green velvet chairs and English pictures on the walls help to create a warm ambiance. It has the feeling of an English pub. The large mirror behind the bar reads "Bentley's Yorkshire Breweries, Ltd."

Bentley's serves lunch, dinner and late-night snacks. Lunch features fish and chips, a steak sandwich, soups, barbecue baby back ribs, a chicken sandwich and a large 20-item salad bar. Dinner includes prime rib, salmon, steak, pasta and shrimp scampi. A variety of imported beers is served.

Bentley's is frequented by both locals and tourists alike. After a concert, play or dance performance at The Wheeler, Bentley's is a must. They go together.

Crawfish Salad

CREATED BY
PATRICK O'ROURKE

SERVES 2

Mixed greens
Tomato wedges
Cucumber slices
Pepperoncinni (little green peppers)
2 Six oz Crawfish tails
2 t Canola oil

DRESSING ♥
8 oz Red wine vinegar
2 oz Dijon mustard
1 t Cajun spice
Pinch fresh tarragon
Pinch fresh parsley
Pinch fresh thyme
Pinch fresh chives, and for garnish

Heat a skillet and add the canola oil, crawfish tails and salt and pepper to taste. Toss lightly for 2-3 minutes.

■ Make the dressing by whisking all the ingredients together.

■ Arrange the mixed greens, the tomato wedges, the cucumber slices and the peperoncinni around the plate and add the hot crawfish. Add the fresh chives for garnish and drizzle with dressing.

♥ *The kicker:* the dressing in this recipe contains no fat and no cholesterol.

Wine Suggestion: Chateau St. Jean, Chardonnay.

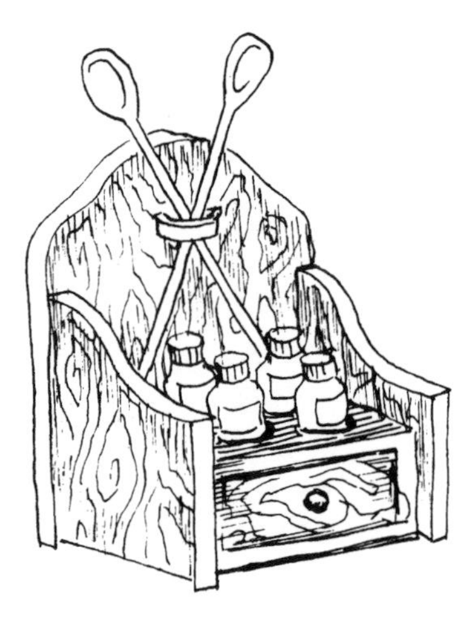

Oriental Tuna Salad

CREATED BY
PATRICK O'ROURKE

SERVES 2

Mixed greens
Tomato wedges
Carrots, julienne
Cucumber, julienne
Caramelized red onion
2 Six oz Tuna filets
1 T Sesame oil
1 T Butter
1 T Canola oil

DRESSING
4 oz Yakatori sauce
4 oz Soy sauce
1 Level T Fresh ginger, chopped
1 Medium Shallot, chopped fine
Pinch toasted sesame seeds

Preheat your oven to 350 degrees. Mix the dressing ingredients together. Cube each tuna filet into six pieces. Add to a small bowl with ½ of the dressing and let stand for 2 minutes. Heat an oven-proof skillet and add the sesame oil, the contents of the bowl and toss. Put into the preheated oven for 2-3 minutes.

■ Caramelize the onion: place the onion in a combination of the butter and canola oil in a sauté pan. Start on high heat, but cook on low until the sugar cooks out of the onion. Stir with a fork. Be careful not to burn the onion.

■ Arrange the mixed greens on a plate with the tomato wedges, carrots, cucumber and caramelized onion as a border. Add the finished tuna to the center of the plate with the remaining pan sauce. Garnish with the toasted sesame seeds.

Wine Suggestion: Raymond, Chardonnay.

Boogie's Diner

SERVING GOURMET DINER FARE, BOOGIE'S IS BY FAR THE most *fun* place in town to dine. It's a wild spot and it's fast-paced. They play great "oldies but goodies" and don't be surprised if your waiter sits down with you and breaks into song. If your kids are bored to tears with gourmet, glitzy restaurants, take them to Boogie's for a burger and fries—waiter "Biff" will entertain them with jokes and jive all night!

"There are only 2 places to eat meat loaf—Home and Boogie's." They said it and they mean it. Famous for delicious meat loaf, Boogie's offers so much more. Who would ever think a place like this has a chef? Well, in order to turn out such specialties as grilled yellow fin tuna with a pineapple salsa relish and New Zealand rack of lamb in a Burgundy tarragon sauce, a real chef comes in handy. "Reggie" Barbour has been adding more to the menu each year. "I like to add items that I can be creative with; we're constantly upgrading and expanding so as not to be close-minded. We're perfectionists here."

Boogie's was the first restaurant to have their recipes approved by the "Dine to Your Heart's Delight" program of the American Heart Association. It was a smart move since almost everyone is cutting down on their fat and cholesterol intake.

Who is Boogie? Lenny "Boogie" Weinglass became a success in the fashion industry, but fell in love with Aspen and moved here. There's a boutique downstairs, but he wanted to feed people, too. And since Boogie's character was portrayed by Mickey Rourke in the 1982 movie "Diner," it seemed fitting to operate as a diner, yet serve something for everyone. Kids will be happy to see squeeze bottles of ketchup on the tables instead of the olive oil you so often find in the chic restaurants. Each member of a family can get what they want: the kids can devour a thick milk shake, a hot dog and fries; dad can have a rib-eye steak and mom will be delighted with Pep's Power Plate (brown rice, steamed vegetables and tofu).

Manager Bernie Mysior recalls a great quote from a happy customer, "I'm a General and I've never seen more organization in a state of chaos in my whole life." That's how Boogie's operates best. Mysior is quick to credit his entire staff, "We're like a family here. Everyone from the dishwasher to the bus boys to the waiters and waitresses—I trust them. They make Boogie's the success that it is!"

Not to be overlooked are Donna Mysior's award-winning desserts. She makes everything from scratch. Patrons love her brownies, chocolate cake, rum cake and pies. The servings are large—"diner portions."

Kids love it, celebrities love it and you'll love Boogie's, too!

Grilled Chicken Salad with Fresh Basil & Sun-dried Tomato Vinaigrette

SERVES 6

SALAD

6 Six oz Skinless chicken breasts, grilled or broiled
Leaf lettuce
Fresh spinach
2 Carrots, julienne
2 Hearts of palm, julienne
1 Red pepper, julienne
1 Yellow pepper, julienne
1 Cucumber, sliced
1 Tomato, sliced
Red Cabbage, thinly sliced

Reconstitute the tomatoes in 1/3 cup warm water for 1 hour and drain. Chop the tomatoes until they are semi-fine diced. Mix all the vinaigrette ingredients in a bowl and chill for 2 hours.

■ Put the greens mixture on serving plates and arrange all the other vegetables around the rim of the plate. Cut the chicken in very thin strips and place in the center, on top of the salad. Pour some vinaigrette over the chicken and serve the remainder on the side.

♥ *The kicker:* this is a delicious salad. For those who are watching your fat intake, use only a tiny bit of dressing and squeeze a fresh lemon on top of the salad.

Wine Suggestion: Newton, Chardonnay.

VINAIGRETTE

2 C Olive oil
3/4 C Balsamic vinegar
1 oz Sun-dried tomatoes, dry
4 t Fresh basil, chopped fine, lightly packed
3 Green onions, diced thinly
2 t Fresh parsley, chopped fine
2 t Dijon mustard
2 t Sugar
1 t Garlic, freshly minced
3/4 t Black pepper
1/3 t Salt

Smoked Chicken & Wild Rice Salad

SERVES 7

Seven 5 oz Chicken breasts, immersed in water with Liquid Smoke to taste for 1½ hours
Red & gold bell peppers, julienne
2-3 Bananas, sliced (optional)

CURRIED YOGURT CHUTNEY DRESSING
2 Garlic cloves, chopped & minced
3 T White wine vinegar
4 T Lemon juice
1½ T Curry powder
1 Jar (8 oz) Major Grey's Chutney
¾ C Olive oil
2 C No-fat yogurt
½ C Fresh coriander, finely chopped
3 T Water

Make the dressing in a blender or food processor. Blend the garlic, vinegar, lemon juice, curry powder, chutney and salt and pepper to taste, until the mixture is smooth. With the motor still running, add the oil in a steady stream, add the yogurt and the water and blend it until it's sufficiently combined. Transfer the dressing to a bowl and stir in the coriander. The dressing may be made a day in advance, covered and chilled.
■ In a large heavy sauce pan, combine the wild rice with the water and salt and simmer it covered for 45-50 minutes, or until it's tender and all the water is absorbed. Transfer the wild rice to a bowl and add the vinegar, oil and salt and pepper to taste. Toss the mixture well and let it cool completely. Stir in the scallions.
■ Grill the chicken breasts until done, then cool. Line a large cooled plate with leaf lettuce. In the middle, add a mound of salad lettuce, then some wild rice topped with sliced chicken. Ladle some dressing over the chicken. Garnish with the peppers and bananas.

The kicker: this is a great summer salad.

Wine Suggestion: Clos Du Bois Chardonnay.

WILD RICE MIXTURE ♥
2½ C Wild rice
6½ C Water
2 t Salt
1 T White wine vinegar
2 T Olive oil
1 Bunch scallions, chopped

Cache Cache

CACHE CACHE MEANS "HIDE AND SEEK" IN FRENCH. Hidden away, on the lower level of the Mill Street Plaza, you'll find one of Aspen's finest and most popular restaurants. Patrons definitely seek out this Provençal, cozy eatery that turns out healthy, rustic-flavored adventurous dishes.

Chef-owner Philippe Mollicchi has an impressive culinary background. His family owned an inn in Senlisse, a 17th century town catering to vacationing Parisians. His mother was the chef and taught her son well. He then moved to Houston, Texas, where he owned a chain of French Delis. Ironically, he met Marie, a Parisian, in Houston!

They married and moved to Aspen after ski-vacationing here. As it often happens, Philippe and Marie's talents complemented each other well when they decided to open Cache Cache. Philippe is the chef and Marie helps manage, hostess and does the day-to-day book-work. Jodi Larner co-owns the restaurant with the Molliccis and is a welcome presence at the door.

The soul of their menu is varied; the rustic flavors from Southern France mixed creatively with the bold Mediterranean style of cooking from Spain and the healthy, wholesome foods from Italy.

Mollicci uses only a small amount of butter and cream in his creations. He utilizes extra virgin olive oil to let the true flavors come out. He grills most of the fish and vegetables instead of frying or sautéeing. Herbed olive oil replaces butter on the tables. Patrons who haven't already tried lightly dipping homemade bread in olive oil will be delighted at its satisfying and distinctive taste.

Mollicci uses no thickeners in his soups. He believes in using just the right amount of vegetables and accents the flavor with lots of fresh herbs. The result is incredibly innovative, delicious and lower-fat cuisine.

Vegetarians love the grilled polenta, Shiitake mushrooms and fresh mozzarella-zucchini cakes for a light main meal. Lamb Loin Tian, marinated in sage and grilled, is served over spinach and ratatouille for an innovative alternative. Devotees love the grilled salmon, on sautéed spinach topped with tomato fondue, olive purée and basil.

Summer lends itself to dining outdoors in their garden café. What could be nicer than to enjoy a balmy Aspen evening, sipping great wine, listening to a quartet from the Aspen Music School and savoring Cache Cache's lighter, adventurous cuisine?

Almond Polenta Pound Cake

¾ C Butter
½ C Almond powder, if you can't find, put raw almonds in a blender
1¼ C Sugar
1t Vanilla
6 Eggs, separated
1½ C Flour
¾ C Corn meal
1 t Baking powder
1 C Heavy cream

Cream the first 4 ingredients until creamy and light. Add the egg yolks, one at a time. Sift together the flour, cornmeal and baking powder. Add to the butter mixture. Whip the cream and add to the mixture. Whip the whites with ½ cup of sugar to form peaks. Fold into the mixture. Bake at 350 degrees in greased ramekins or a cake pan for 20 minutes or until it tests done. Allow to cool for 15 minutes before unmolding.

Tester's notes: we enjoyed this delicious, not-too-sweet cake with Dudley's Chili (see page 180).

Tartare D'Aubergine

AN APPETIZER

1 Eggplant
2 T Horseradish
1 Shallot, chopped
3 T Champagne vinegar
Salt & pepper
½ C Extra virgin olive oil
Caviar
Roasted red peppers

Roast the eggplant in a 400 degree oven until very tender (about 40 minutes—ovens vary). Peel and chop the eggplant. Make the vinaigrette: place the horseradish, shallots, vinegar, salt & pepper and oil in a blender. Mix the eggplant and some vinaigrette (save some for the plate) and mold in a ramekin. Coat a cold plate with a layer of the vinaigrette and place the mixture (in the ramekin) on top. Garnish with caviar and red peppers.

Manicotti Farci Aux Poivrons Rouges

MAKES 8 CRÊPES

CRÊPES
2 Eggs
1¼ C Milk
1 C Flour
Salt & pepper

FILLING
½ Red pepper, puréed
1 C Ricotta cheese
2 oz (⅓ cup) Chèvre
1 Egg
2 T Basil chiffonade (thinly chopped fresh basil)

TOMATO FONDUE
6 Whole, blanched, peeled, seeded and chopped fresh tomatoes
2 T Shallots, chopped
½ C White wine
2 T Lemon juice
2 T Olive oil

Make the crêpes: whisk all the ingredients together. Strain to remove lumps. Let rest for 2 hours before making the crêpes. In a caste iron skillet, lightly butter the pan using a paper towel. When the pan is hot, use a cup with a spout to pour the batter into the pan. Swirl it all around and quickly pour out any excess. Whatever batter sticks to the pan will make a perfectly thin crêpe. Cook until just before the edges turn crispy.
■ Mix all the filling ingredients together in a food processor. Then, make the tomato fondue. Sweat the shallots in half the oil. Once tender, add the remaining ingredients. Bring to a boil and simmer for 10 minutes. Season with salt and pepper.
■ Stuff each crêpe with some filling and bake for 10 minutes with some tomato fondue on the bottom and mozzarella slices on top. Once hot, add the sun-dried tomatoes, chopped basil and some more tomato fondue on top.

Wine Suggestion: Antinori Chianti Classico Riserva.

GARNISH
6 oz Mozzarella slices (fresh)
3 T Sun-dried tomatoes, julienne
3 T Basil, chopped in strips

Napoleon de Saumon

AN APPETIZER

Puff pastry rectangles, 2 x 4 inches (found in the frozen food department of grocery stores), cooked
4 oz Norwegian smoked saumon
1 European cucumber, sliced
Lemon, sliced thin
Fresh dill

YOGURT-DILL DRESSING ♥
¼ C Fresh dill, chopped
½ T Fresh garlic, minced
1 T Shallots, chopped fine
1 C Yogurt, plain, low-fat
¼ C Champagne vinegar
Salt & pepper

Slice the cooked puff pastry in thirds, horizontally. Place the cucumber slices and saumon slices on the bottom half, add puff pastry, more saumon slices and cucumber slices. Cover with puff pastry. Make the dressing: combine all the ingredients in a blender. To assemble: pour some dressing on a plate, place the Napoleon on top. Garnish the top of the Napoleon with a small piece of saumon, dill and lemon segments.

The kicker: this is an appetizer that makes a beautiful presentation. Don't be surprised when guests won't want to be the first to cut into it. Once they do, it'll be gone in no time!

The Century Room at The Hotel Jerome

STEEPED IN HISTORY AND TRADITION, THE HOTEL JEROME epitomizes the Aspen spirit. Jerome B. Wheeler, former president of New York City's Macy Department Store, originally came west in the 1880's for health reasons and fell in love with Aspen's beauty and potential. Ore and silver were plentiful and Aspen flourished. An oppor-tunity gave Wheeler the chance to finance a new hotel with the intention that it would rival the Ritz in Paris and the grandest hotels in the world.

No expenses were spared and they installed one of the first elevators in the west. The interior was exquisite. Imagine the warmth and gaiety at their grand opening the eve of Thanksgiving 1889. After this gala event, the word spread and the Jerome became *the* place to stay while in Aspen. Rooms rented for $3.00! It thrived until the devaluation of silver in 1893 that sent Aspen into an economic depression. Somehow, the Jerome survived the lean years.

After World War II, the Jerome experienced a rejuvenation with the introduction of skiing as a viable industry in Aspen. The Jerome once again resumed its role as the center of the town's exciting social life.

Badly needing a new facelift, the Jerome underwent a major restoration and renovation in the 1980's. The interior was refurbished in the true Victorian style. Once again Aspenites had a significant part of their heritage preserved.

You can experience the charm and romance of the past by dining in the Jerome's Century Room; offering a tantalizing, savory American menu featuring foods of substance. Many are heart-healthy, catering to a 'growing demand from customers for lighter fare. Interesting variations include: Grilled Baby Sturgeon on Avocado Purée with a warm black bean-corn relish; Gratin of Colorado Bass and Dungeness Crab with asparagus and roasted tomato coulis; Cavatapi Pasta with a grilled vegetable medley and sun-dried tomatoes, pesto and bruschetta and Peppered Cervena Venison Loin with sweet corn spoonbread and blackberry sauce.

The desserts are delectable. Particular favorites are: Lemon-Lime Tart with a raspberry coulis, White Chocolate Crème Brûlée and Angel Food Cake with a strawberry-rhubarb compote.

Linger over coffee, savor the evening, reminisce over the past and hope the Hotel Jerome lives on forever.

Grilled Lemongrass Chicken Salad

CREATED BY JEFFREY TROIOLA

SERVES 6–8

One 3 lb Fryer, cut up

MARINADE
- *2 Bunches lemongrass, cleaned & chopped coarsely*
- *1 Lemon, cut into 8 wedges*
- *6 Cloves Garlic, unpeeled, cracked*
- *5 Slices ginger, smashed (3 T)*
- *1 T Chile sate*
- *1 t White pepper*
- *¼ C Oil*

Rinse and dry the chicken well, then score pieces with a knife so that they will absorb the marinade. Combine all the marinade ingredients except the oil and process medium fine. Stir in the oil and rub the marinade into the cuts on the chicken. Marinate overnight.

■ To cook, wipe the marinade off the chicken pieces. Combine the oil and fish sauce and toss with the chicken pieces to coat. Place the chicken on a prepared grill and cook slowly until done, turning occasionally.

■ Cool and shred the grilled chicken and toss with the salad ingredients. Combine the dressing ingredients and toss with the salad.

Wine Suggestion: Trimbach, Gewürztraminer.

FOR GRILLING
- *2 T Olive oil*
- *2 T Thai or Vietnamese Fish Sauce*

SALAD
- *1 C Carrots, shredded*
- *1 C Jicama, shredded*
- *1 C Basil, shredded*
- *1 C Red onion, shredded*
- *1 C Cabbage, shredded*
- *½ C Toasted, chopped peanuts*

DRESSING ♥
- *1 C Brown sugar*
- *½ C Fresh lime juice*
- *6 Cloves Garlic, chopped*
- *2 T Fish sauce*
- *1 T Chile sate*
- *2 T Sesame oil*

Lemon-Lime Tart

CREATED BY
JEFFREY TROIOLA

TART DOUGH
8 T Sugar
4 oz Butter, softened
1 Egg yolk
1 Vanilla bean, scraped
1 t Lemon zest, finely chopped
2½ C Cake flour, sifted

TART FILLING
5 Eggs
1 Egg yolk
1 C Sugar
6 oz Heavy cream
2½ Lemons, zested & juiced
1 Lime, zested & juiced

Mix the sugar, butter and egg yolk. Add the vanilla bean and zest and fold in the flour. Grease a removable-bottom tart pan and dust with flour. Roll out the dough and line the pan. Chill the pan and dough for 15 minutes. Bake the shell lined with vanilla beans for 10-15 minutes.

■ To prepare the filling, combine the eggs, egg yolk and sugar thoroughly. Then add the cream. Just before baking, add the lemon juice, lime juice and peels. Fill the shell and bake at 325 degrees for 15-20 minutes. Do not brown. Cool on a rack.

The kicker: this is a wonderfully refreshing summer dessert.

Chart House

THE ORIGINAL CHART HOUSE WAS LOCATED ACROSS from Little Nell's—where the Aspen Square presently is situated. Now, you'll find the Chart House on the corner of Durant and Monarch.

It was started by two ski/surf bums who wanted something to do to support their life-styles. They developed the nautical theme for their decor. All of the handmade tables have an authentic nautical chart laminated into the tabletops and are trimmed with teak to enhance their beauty. Many customers enjoy following a previously-traveled route.

The photos on the walls also help to set the mood for this California-style restaurant. They depict a variety of sports from sailing, windsurfing and skiing to climbing, kayaking, rodeo roping and skateboarding. They express the owners' enthusiasm for excelling in sports.

The Chart House is now owned by Pacific Ocean Enterprises which also own 69 other Chart Houses in 17 states. Their premise is based on this motto, "We are friendly people serving quality food in a clean atmosphere." And, indeed they do.

The Aspen Chart House is known for its wonderful warm homemade bread and enormous salad bar with over 60 items to choose from. It's a meal by itself. The menu ranges from seafood to beef to fowl. I was told their most popular items are Teriyaki Chicken, Baked Scallops and Prime Rib. They also offer lobster, Sante Fe Shrimp, teriyaki steak, swordfish, top sirloin, Filet Mignon and pepper steak.

The Chart House is famous in Aspen for serving huge pieces of their rich and delicious Mud Pie.

Jicama Salad

SERVES 4-5

2-3 lbs Jicama, trimmed, peeled, julienne cut
1/8 C + 2 T Fresh lime juice
1 C Orange juice
1 C Fresh cilantro, roughly chopped
1 C Mandarin oranges, well drained

Combine and toss all of the ingredients. Refrigerate for a minimum of 2 hours before serving.

♥ *The kicker:* this healthy salad accompanied fried chicken and was served at a concert picnic. The diners concurred that it was a crisp, delicious salad; perfect for a warm summer's evening.

Poppy Seed Dressing

MAKES MORE THAN ONE QUART

2 Eggs
½ C Sugar
2 T Dijon mustard
1½ C Red wine vinegar
1 t Salt
½ C Grated white onion
1 qt Canola oil
½ C Poppy seeds (you'll use a small bottle)

Beat the eggs in a Cuisinart or blender until frothy. Slowly add the oil in a continuous stream. Dissolve the salt in the vinegar. Add the sugar, mustard, salted vinegar and onion and blend. Add the poppy seeds and blend. Keep refrigerated.

The kicker: this dressing is wonderful on any salad, but the Chart House recommends it for spinach salads!

Key Lime Pie

MAKES 1 PIE

6 Eggs, separated
One and one half 14 oz Can sweetened condensed milk
¾ C Key Lime Juice (preferably Nellie & Joe's, found in most grocery stores)
¾ t Cream of tartar
1 Graham cracker crust (made from crushed graham crackers and enough butter to moisten it)

Use a large pie pan or quiche pan. In a bowl, beat the egg yolks at high speed. Add the milk and mix on slow speed until well mixed. Add half of the lime juice, the cream of tartar and then the remaining lime juice. Mix well. Ladle into the crust and bake at 325 degrees for 10-15 minutes. Set in the freezer for 3 hours and then refrigerate. Serve with a dollop of fresh whipped cream and add lime zest or twists for garnish.

The kicker: this pie is very easy to make and is well appreciated.

Santa Fe Chicken or Shrimp

DRY SEASONINGS

1 t Salt
1 T Whole oregano leaves
2 T Chili powder
½ T Ground cumin
½ T Ground paprika
½ t Onion powder
½ t Garlic powder

BARBECUE BUTTER

8 oz Butter
½ T Whole oregano leaves
1 T Chili powder
1 t Ground cumin
1 t Ground paprika
½ t Salt
¼ t Onion powder
¼ t Garlic powder
¼ C Any good quality barbecue sauce
1 t Worcestershire sauce (use Lea & Perrins ONLY*)*
dash Tabasco sauce

In a mixing bowl, place all the dry seasoning ingredients and stir well. Place in a plastic container, cover tightly and store at room temperature.

■ Place the butter in a cuisinart. Mix until smooth and creamy. Add the dry spices, the barbecue sauce, worcestershire sauce and tabasco. Allow the ingredients to be absorbed and blended into the butter. Blend for 5 minutes. Store in a container in the refrigerator until needed. Before using, allow the butter to soften first.

♥ Lower fat version: simply season the barbecue sauce and eliminate the butter.

■ Season either chicken or shrimp with approximately ½ - 1 tablespoon of the dry seasoning mix, place in a covered pan in the refrigerator until ready to cook. Char-grill the chicken or shrimp and baste often with the softened Santa Fe butter or barbecue sauce. The Chart House serves these entrées with a ramekin of bleu cheese dressing and rice.

Wine Suggestion: 1989 Raymond Chardonnay.

Crystal Palace

THE MOOD IS GAY AND LIVELY. THERE'S EXCITEMENT IN the air. It's a show from the moment you walk in the doors of the Crystal Palace.

It's packed with patrons dressed in their finest, waiting to hear owner Mead Metcalf and his staff sing and entertain you.

You become mesmerized by the decor. The Crystal Palace lives up to its name—stained glass surrounds you. The crystal chandelier that hangs in the main dining room is magnificent. The atmosphere of this restaurant and theatre is striking, it's vibrant and it's harmonious. From the moment you walk in, you know it's going to be a special evening.

The waiters and waitresses are all in costume, running around taking customers' orders and smiling. In 30 minutes, all 200 guests are served a delicious dinner of prime rib, roast rack of lamb, Duck Bigarade or Shrimp Hoisin (made with a tangy Chinese barbecue sauce).

As soon as coffee and dessert are offered, the lights dim and magically, the show begins. Presented is a satirical cabaret revue performed by the waiters and waitresses who just served your meal!

Religion, politics and famous people are all topics for this lively, entertaining show. Many of the numbers will make you laugh hysterically, others will touch you. It's witty and professional.

If you've ever been to the Palace, you'll remember such classics as *The Peanut Butter Affair*, *Old Farts on Wheels* and *Fairy in the Firehouse.*

Mead Metcalf first came to Aspen as a ski bum and played piano at the Hotel Jerome. He opened the Crystal Palace 36 years ago. The building is over 100 years old and was originally an old mining commission. Metcalf remodeled the restaurant himself. "The whole place is for fun. It's all tongue-in-cheek. It's decorated with crazy old junk from the mining days. The railing is from old wrought iron beds and the wainscoting is from doors of old hotels. The old Maxwell and Model T cars, they're for fun, too!"

It all fits together beautifully. The result is a splendid environment, complemented by excellent food and a wonderfully funny show you'll tell your friends about.

Brazilian Black Bean Soup

SERVES 4

4 C Black beans, soaked overnight
8 Cloves garlic
1 Medium onion
3 Green bell peppers
2 Carrots
½ C Fresh parsley
½ Gallon Chicken stock
1 Ham hock

SPICE BAG
¼ T Whole cloves
¾ T Whole mustard seed
3 Bay leaves
½ T Cracked peppercorns

Chop and sauté the garlic, onion, peppers, carrots and parsley. Add the stock, beans, veggies and the ham hock. Bring to a boil. Wrap all the spice bag ingredients in cheesecloth and put into the stock. Simmer for 4-5 hours. Let cool and remove the spice bag and the ham hock. Purée the soup in a blender. Pick the meat off the ham hock, chop and add to the soup. Reheat and serve.

Eastern Winds

ARE YOU IN THE MOOD FOR AUTHENTIC CHINESE cuisine? Eastern Winds is the place to go. It's conveniently located in the very center of Aspen on Cooper Street.

You'll find the owners, Sue and David Han, always involved in the many facets of their busy, popular restaurant. Both are pure Chinese. They rejected the traditional red and gold interior of most Chinese restaurants and instead have created a more simple atmosphere in which to dine. Adorning the walls are large-as-life photographs taken by Jeffrey Aaronson, a local photographer. They depict images of the Orient and its people.

The menu is extensive with over 100 Mandarin and Szechwan items. Sue explains, "You can get any combination, because we don't premake any of our dishes. It's a very healthy way to eat. With the nature of our cooking, we can accommodate people who have special diets."

These sumptuous dishes are just a few of their many specialties: Crispy Duck, Peking Duck, Volcano Shrimp, Treasures of the Sea and Kung Pao Chicken.

Enjoy one of their many exotic, blended cocktails. A favorite on a snowy evening in Aspen is Tiki Coffee, a delectable combination of Tia Maria, banana liqueur, Amaretto, coffee and whipped cream.

Hunan Beef

SERVES 2

½ lb Top sirloin, cut into cubes
½ Red bell pepper, cut into strips
½ Green pepper, cut into strips
1 t Fresh garlic, minced
2 Scallions, chopped
1 t Fresh ginger, minced
½ Yellow onion, cut into strips
1 Bunch Broccoli, for garnish
1 T Vegetable oil

SAUCE
¼ C Water
1 t Cornstarch
½ t Sesame oil
1 t Sugar
2 t Light soy sauce
1 T Oyster sauce
½ T Tomato sauce
2 t Sherry rice wine

Combine the sauce ingredients in a small bowl. Cook the broccoli florets in boiling water until tender. Set aside.

■ Warm the vegetable oil in a wok or sauté pan. Throw in the garlic, ginger and scallions. Add the onion and peppers and stir until softened. Add the meat and stir briskly.

■ Stir the sauce ingredients and tip into the wok. Stir it all until thickened. Turn the contents of the wok onto a serving platter and garnish with the broccoli.

♥ *The kicker:* Served alone or with a healthy brown rice, this recipe is nutritious and because it uses only 1 tablespoon of oil, it's lower in fat than most Chinese dishes.

Moo Shu Vegetables

SERVES 2

⅓ Of a Cabbage, cut into strip
¼ C Bean sprouts
¼ C Black mushrooms (soak in warm water for 30 minutes if using dried shiitake mushrooms), cut into strips
¼ C Bamboo shoots, cut into strips
¼ C Broccoli, cut into strips
¼ C Carrots, cut into strips
¼ C Pea Pods, cut into strips
¼ C Baby corn, cut into strips
2 T Hoisin sauce
1 T Soy sauce
Package of Wei-chuan Moo Shu Shells (found in Asian markets)

Heat a wok to 240 degrees and place all the ingredients into it. Stir around for 2 minutes, then pour the Hoisin and soy sauce into the vegetables. Cook another one and a half minutes. Follow the instructions on the package of moo shu shells for steaming them. Serve the mixture rolled up in the shells with the Hoisin sauce on the side.

♥ *The kicker:* this is a very healthy meal and if you cannot find the moo shu shells, you can serve the vegetables over a healthy rice or noodles.

Explore Coffeehouse

WHILE SAILING THE COAST OF MAINE SEVERAL YEARS ago, I had the pleasure of spending a glorious morning in a charming bookstore-coffeehouse. Sitting on their flower-filled terrace overlooking the ocean, I sipped a hot cappuccino and browsed through local books. Ever since that delightful day, it was my hope that someone in Aspen would be inspired to duplicate the same lovely concept of a bookstore-coffeehouse.

When Katharine Thalberg renovated Explore Booksellers, which is located in a historic Victorian home, she created a coffeehouse on the second floor. Locals and tourists alike are fascinated with the idea of choosing books in a quiet atmosphere and yet being able to enjoy a meal.

Explore Coffeehouse is the only vegetarian restaurant in Aspen and serves gourmet vegetarian cuisine that even non-vegetarians will love. Explore features international specialties prepared with the highest quality ingredients available. The produce is organic and all dairy and eggs are free-range. Most of the entrées are made without using eggs and dairy; instead they rely heavily on whole grains, beans, tofu, tempeh, seitan and vegetables. Using fresh herbs and unrefined ingredients, they do not sacrifice taste; on the contrary, the results are wonderful—exotic flavors that are immensely satisfying.

The very nature of these vegetarian products lends itself perfectly to the demand for lower-fat, lower-cholesterol foods. Specials change daily and include: Thai Red Curry Mushrooms, Seitan Teriyaki, Mu Shu Vegetables and Apricot Glazed Tofu.

Served on beautiful china plates, Explore believes the aesthetics are just as important as the meal. The only salad bar in town with organic mixed greens is accompanied by two low-fat soups daily.

Many book lovers come to read and partake in afternoon tea with deliciously sinful desserts, although many of the desserts are made with no dairy and no sugar—yet devouring a delicious fruit pie or strawberry short cake, you'd never know it! Unique to Explore is their French press coffee presentation which allows customers to brew the strength they desire. The coffees are organic and the French press system produces the freshest cup imaginable. The Coffeehouse also features espresso, cappuccino and lattés.

A well-utilized fireplace makes the coffeehouse warm and convivial in the winter. The prevailing spirit is calm and serene. Since they're away from the mainstream of busy Aspen life, often one can hear the sound of distant music in the summer from their lovely outdoor patio.

You feel a strong sense of commitment here. Their goal is to give people the experience of healthy eating without sacrificing taste or enjoyment. And based on their loyal clientele, the Coffeehouse manages to do just that. The restaurant is open late into the evening every day of the year.

Explore's enchanting coffeehouse is truly a must while in Aspen.

Dairy-less Banana Walnut Muffins

MAKES 12 SMALL MUFFINS

1 C Whole wheat pastry flour
1 C Unbleached white flour
2½ t Baking soda
Pinch sea salt
½ t Ground cinnamon
½ C Unrefined canola oil
½ C Real maple syrup
3 Ripe bananas
2 t Real vanilla extract
2 t Natural apple cider vinegar
½ C Soy milk
½ C Toasted & chopped walnuts

Sift the dry ingredients together and mix all the wet ingredients together except the bananas and walnuts. Mix the wet into the dry ingredients and fold in the mashed bananas and walnuts. Scoop into a pre-greased muffin tin (use either a vegetable oil or spray) and top with a little chopped nuts. Bake at 350 degrees for about 30 minutes or until golden in color and a knife or toothpick inserted into the center of a muffin comes out dry. Remove from the oven and let them cool for 5 minutes. Remove from the tins and finish cooling. Wrap individually with plastic wrap for longer shelf life.

♥ *The kicker:* these are very healthy and yet delicious muffins. You can use other nuts such as pecans or almonds and add orange zest if desired.

Parmesan Wild Rice Crêpes with Silky Porcini Mushroom Sauce

SERVES 6

12 Crêpes (see Cache Cache's recipe on page 19)

CRÊPE FILLING

2 C Cooked rice (½ cup of raw rice will make 2 cups of cooked rice)
½ C Re-hydrated sun-dried tomatoes, chopped
½ C Red bell peppers, chopped
½ C Leeks, finely chopped
2 T Rice vinegar
Salt, pepper
1 Clove garlic, chopped
¼ t Ground caraway seed
½ t Dry tarragon

PORCINI MUSHROOM SAUCE

1 oz Dried Porcini mushrooms
1 Red onion, finely chopped
6 T Butter
4 T White flour
1½ C Heavy cream
2-3 T Dry sherry
2 C Veggie broth, homemade stock or 1 veggie cube plus 2 cups water
Salt & pepper

Make the crêpes or use a good quality of packaged crêpes. Make the filling: sauté the peppers in olive oil until they begin to tenderize. Deglaze with the rice vinegar and add to the cooked rice. Do the same for the leeks and add to the rice. Add the sun-dried tomatoes to the rice and toss with the seasonings to taste.

■ Make the sauce: re-hydrate the mushrooms in just enough boiling water to cover. Let sit until the mushrooms are completely soft, then strain through a cheesecloth or a coffee filter. Reserve the mushroom stock and rinse the mushrooms in cold water to remove the grit.

■ Chop the cleaned mushrooms into small pieces. Melt 2 tablespoons of the butter in a sauté pan and sauté the onions until they are translucent. Add the mushrooms and veggie broth and simmer on a low flame until most of the liquid is absorbed. In a separate sauté pan, melt the remaining butter and stir in the flour to make a roux, continue whisking the roux over a medium flame until it begins to brown. Then slowly add the cleaned mushroom stock, whisking rapidly to incorporate. When the stock/flour mixture is smooth, add the sherry, salt, pepper, mushroom/onion mix and the cream. Let the sauce simmer on low heat for at least ½ hour and adjust the seasonings to taste.

To serve: roll the warm crêpe stuffing into however many crêpes you want, top with parmesan cheese and bake at 350 degrees until the cheese begins to turn golden and the ends of the crêpes brown. Remove from the oven and top with the mushroom sauce.

The kicker: this is an incredibly wonderful dish—not exactly low-in-fat, but very popular at Explore. If you're concerned with the fat content, either put very little sauce on top or simply top with some yogurt mixed with a little low-fat sour cream and some freshly grated parmesan.

Wine Suggestion: Chateau St. Jean, Sonoma, Chardonnay.

Snow Pea Sesame Udon

SERVES 6

1 lb Firm tofu
1½ lb Udon noodles (traditional Japanese pasta)
1 Red bell pepper, julienne
2 C Fresh shiitake mushrooms, sliced (or 12 dried)
½ lb Snow peas

TOFU MARINADE
¼ C Tamari (naturally brewed soy sauce)
2 Cloves chopped garlic
1 T Chinese 5-Spice Powder

BROILING SAUCE
⅓ C Toasted sesame oil
2 T Hot pepper oil
2 T Tamari
3 T Freshly squeezed ginger juice
3 T Real maple syrup
2 T Rice vinegar

Slice the tofu into ½ inch cubes. Mix the marinade ingredients together and marinate the tofu for at least 4 hours or preferably overnight in the refrigerator. Bake the tofu on a lightly oiled tray in the oven at 375 degrees for 40 minutes or until browned. Cook the udon noodles according to the directions and rinse with cold water. Place the sliced shiitake mushrooms, red pepper and baked tofu cubes on a broiling pan.

■ Mix the broiling sauce (reserve ½ of it for later) and brush onto the vegetables and the tofu and broil 2½ inches from the broiler for about 5 minutes. While this is broiling, de-stem the snow peas and lightly steam them until they're bright green.

■ Re-heat the pasta in a strainer in a pot of boiling water briefly and drain well. Put into a mixing bowl, add the remaining broiling sauce, the vegetables, tofu and the scallions and mix well. Dish onto individual plates and top them with the steamed snow peas like spokes on a wheel. Top with sesame seeds, Nori strips and serve immediately.

♥ *The kicker:* this is a wonderful vegetarian meal and naturally low-in-fat. The flavors meld together beautifully. For a variation, you can use buckwheat noodles instead of udon and asparagus instead of snow peas.

GARNISHES
2 T Toasted black sesame seeds
1 Bunch scallions, chopped
2 Sheets toasted Nori seaweed, cut into thin, 1 inch pieces

Yucatan Cha Cha Cha with Pineapple-Mango Salsa

CREATED BY
SUSAN SINNICKS

SERVES 4

MOLE SAUCE
1 C Dry black bean flakes
3 T Cocoa powder
2 T Very finely ground espresso coffee
1 T Cinnamon
1 T Vanilla extract
1 C - 1¼ C Pineapple juice
½ Vegetable stock cube
Salt, garlic and cayenne, to taste
1½ C Boiling water

Make the mole sauce: put everything in a saucepan and whisk to combine. Bring to a boil, then turn the heat to low and simmer for ½ hour to allow the flavors to meld. Keep warm while preparing the remaining steps.
■ Make the salsa by combining all the ingredients in a bowl. Quickly sauté all the vegetables in the Cha Cha Cha in olive oil. Deglaze with the vinegar. Fill the warm tortillas with the vegetables, like an ice cream cone, so one end is larger than the other. Line the bottom of each dinner plate with the mole sauce. Decorate with curves and dots of sour cream (be creative). Place 2 tortillas on each plate with some rice. Top the tortillas with salsa. Garnish with the mint and lemon twists.

♥ *The kicker:* using low-fat sour cream or yogurt makes this recipe low-fat.

PINEAPPLE-MANGO SALSA
1 C Pineapple, chopped
1 Large mango, chopped
Finely diced jalapeño, to taste
¼ C Finely diced red pepper
1 T Mint leaves, chopped
Lemon juice to taste

THE CHA CHA CHA
2 C Red bell pepper, sliced in crescents
2 C Red onion, sliced in crescents
2 C Mushroom caps, quartered
4 C Corn kernels
¼ C Red wine vinegar
8 Flour tortillas, warmed in oven
2 C Cooked rice
Sour Cream
Mint sprigs & lemon twist

Friedl's

FORMERLY DUDLEY'S DINER, FRIEDL'S IS LOCATED AT the Aspen Airport Business Center. It's named for Friedl Pfeifer, a skiing legend who helped launch Aspen Mountain and Buttermilk as premier ski resorts. He was Aspen Mountain's first ski school director. A ski racer, a coach and a member of the prestigious 10th Mountain Division, Pfeifer has contributed much to the skiing industry. Peter Affolter, the chef and the driving force behind the entire operation told me, "We wanted a name that would embody the Aspen spirit."

Affolter has been in the Aspen area for over 19 years, loves to cook and has been a chef at Chez Grandmère, the Peppermill and Chefy's, to name a few. Affolter offers an International menu with foods from around the world. They serve breakfast, lunch and dinner and describe their menu as hearty food for hearty people, served in a traditional Aspen style.

Breakfast consists of a variety of omelettes, biscuits and gravy, burritos, Huevos Rancheros and Eggs Sardoux—2 poached eggs on spinach with Swiss cheese and tomato slices on a toasted English muffin topped with Hollandaise. Lunch offers 6 salad entrées, a kids' menu and entrées that vary from veal bratwurst to veggie stir-fry to crab cakes. Fresh seafood, pork, beef and pasta dishes are the items you'll find for dinner, along with nightly chef specials.

Upon entering Friedl's, you get the feeling of being in a European café. Owner Peter McBride's wife, Laurie, has decorated the restaurant with Bavarian-style curtains and tablecloths. It's light and airy with windows surrounding the dining area. There are fabulous black and white photographs from the 30's, 40's and 50's on the walls, taken by local photographers Miggs and Dick Durrance. They capture the spirit of the times. There's a wonderful photo of Bingo, Elli Iselin's St. Bernard, riding the original 1A single chairlift, and another of Aspen in the 40's. The mountain somehow looks bigger and bolder and the town looks peaceful.

Locals enjoy Friedl's, but when visitors discover this out-of-the-way eatery, they'll tell their friends about the delicious food and European atmosphere. Take some time to study the photographs. In this modern world, it's nice to sit back, relax and enjoy these fond old memories.

Chinese Chicken Salad

SERVES 6-8

SALAD
1 Head shredded iceberg lettuce
1 C Slivered almonds
2 C Crispy Chinese noodles
2 Pieces grilled chicken, julienne
1 C Parsley, chopped
Fresh tomatoes
Olives, chopped
Artichoke hearts

SOMEN SALAD DRESSING
½ C Light soy sauce
1 T Rice vinegar
1 T Brown sugar
1 t Sesame seeds
1 T Vegetable oil
1 T Sesame oil

Mix all salad ingredients together. Make the dressing by mixing all the ingredients and lightly toss just before serving. Garnish with the tomatoes, olives and artichoke hearts.

♥ *The kicker:* if you use skinless chicken, this recipe will be low in fat.

Wine Suggestion: Hess Select Chardonnay, 1989.

The Golden Horn

THE OWNER AND CHEF OF THE GOLDEN HORN IS AN energetic, talented man. Klaus Christ has owned The Golden Horn for 21 years. Originally, The Horn was a "hell-raisin'" bar where famous stars and our own local favorite, Freddie Fisher, played. Presently, The Horn is an Aspen favorite known for its superb Continental cuisine with a Swiss flair, and its European atmosphere.

The golden horn, for which the restaurant was named, hangs in the dining room by the fireplace. It's actually a French horn made in the 1890's in Russia. The horn, amazingly, was used in the first Aspen High School Band.

It's a tradition that during the famous World Cup ski races held in Aspen, Klaus feeds the Swiss team. Nourishing the athletes these days is a science. Klaus told me, "I consult with the team's coach. It's very important to feed these skiers properly, especially before the actual races." The team is most appreciative and takes Klaus skiing when he visits Switzerland.

Klaus, who is originally from Davos, Switzerland, received his training there by apprenticing in a famous restaurant for three years.

The Horn is well known for its extensive wine list. The present wine cellar has over 8,000 bottles. This is the result of 18 years of studying and collecting wines. "I want to provide my customers with the finest selection of wines that they can find." Klaus has a passion for wine and has invested in rare wines over the years. He points out that a customer should not be intimidated. "I have wines ranging from $14.00 a bottle, to $1,200.00!"

He credits his sommelier Stephen Reiss as being, "the most knowledgeable wine steward in this town. Wine is his love." Reiss has the advantage of first being a chef and then becoming interested in wine. He is in the process of taking rigorous exams in the hopes of holding the coveted title of "Master of Wine"—currently held by only 5 people in the U.S. The Horn received an award for having one of the top 100 best wine cellars in the country.

I enjoyed reading Klaus' guest book, with comments from both local and famous people. This quote stood out from the others and sums up The Golden Horn, "More than artistry in food, a beauty in consistency."

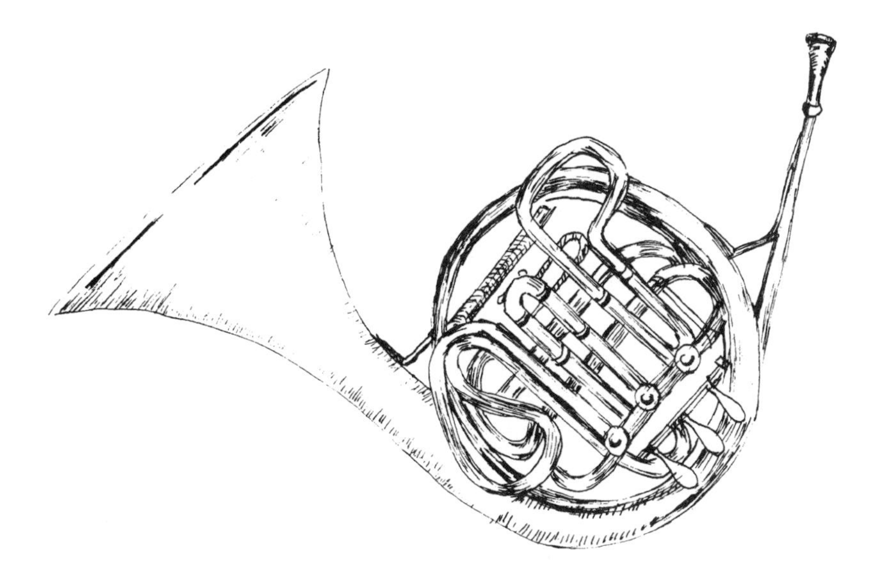

Blackberry Sorbet

1 lb Fresh blackberries
¼ C Water
¼ C White wine
¼ C Orange juice
⅔ C Sugar
Whites of 2 eggs

Cook the first 5 ingredients together for 15 minutes. Let cool and pass through a sieve (so you end up with liquid). Beat the egg whites until stiff. Put the liquid fruit mixture into an ice cream maker. As it turns, slowly add the beaten egg whites. Leave the ice cream maker going until the mixture is firm.

♥ *The kicker:* If you're concerned with raw eggs, this recipe was tested without the egg whites and turned out just fine. It's a no-fat dessert and wonderful on a summer's evening.

No-Fat Vegetable Soup

SERVES 6

2 Yellow squashes
2 Zucchinis
½ Onion, diced
3 Cloves garlic, chopped
1 C White wine
Fresh herbs: ½ bunch cilantro; 1 twig fresh marjoram, plucked; ½ twig rosemary, plucked & 1 twig fresh thyme, plucked
3 C Water
Pinch cayenne pepper
Whole cilantro leaves

Cut up the squashes and zucchinis into chunks. Simmer the onion, garlic, zucchinis and squashes in the white wine for 3 minutes. Add the water, the cayenne pepper and the fresh herbs. Cook for 10 minutes (do not overcook). Place this mixture into a blender and purée. Garnish with the cilantro. This soup is best served hot.

♥ *The kicker:* This no-fat soup has a tremendous amount of flavor from the fresh herbs. This is the perfect soup for anyone on a diet. Soup makes a hearty meal—health conscious eaters will love Klaus' variation!

Fresh Vegetable Salad

SERVES 10

2 Medium yellow squash, sliced
2 Medium zucchini, sliced
1 lb Snow peas
4 Medium carrots, sliced
2 Bunches of broccoli, florets
½ Cauliflower bunch, florets
½ lb Fresh green beans
1 Bunch fresh cilantro
½ Green pepper, sliced
½ Red pepper, sliced
½ Yellow pepper, sliced

DRESSING
⅓ C Balsamic vinegar
⅔ C Extra virgin olive oil
1 Clove garlic, chopped
1 Bunch fresh cilantro, chopped

Put the first 7 vegetable ingredients in boiling water for 4 minutes. Remove and cool off immediately under cold water. Make the dressing by mixing all the ingredients together. Toss the vegetables with the dressing. Serve on top of fresh lettuce.

♥ *The kicker:* We tasted this wonderful and healthy salad at a testing party. Everyone loved the colors of the salad and the crunchiness of the vegetables. If you're concerned with your fat intake, put less dressing over the vegetables.

The Grill on the Park

THIS CALIFORNIA-STYLE RESTAURANT LOOKS OUT AT Wagner Park and has a great view of Aspen Mountain. If you happen to be walking around the Mall and smell the exotic scent of mesquite, it's coming from The Grill. Unique to Aspen, this eatery features Exhibition Cooking and serves ribs, fish and chicken cooked over large logs of mesquite wood.

Owned by Howard and Barbara Gunther, The Grill fills a gap in Aspen's restaurants. You'll find Chicago-style food in a casual, relaxed atmosphere. It's bright inside, with bold purple tables and chairs complemented by beautiful green plants.

Barbara decided on their menu after choosing her favorite dishes from restaurants she loves most in Chicago.

The Grill's chef is Michael Dietrich who is a native Californian. Barbara boasts, "Michael is an innovator with fabulous ideas. And, he's my son-in-law!"

Specialties of the house include: barbecued ribs, steaks—aged prime and served rare, mesquite-grilled seafood, angel hair pasta (with garlic, tomatoes and basil), herb-roasted chicken and a great selection of fresh salads. The famous Charlemagne salad (greens tossed in a warm Brie dressing) also appears on their menu. All of the sauces are homemade and they use only fresh herbs.

Baked Goat's Cheese & Field Green Salad

SERVES 4-6

1 lb Assorted mixed greens: arugula, radicchio, mache, baby red oak, frisee, baby romaine, Belgian endive, etc.
2 T Toasted pine nuts
12 Niçoise olives
½ C Fresh tomatoes, diced
One 11 oz log Montrachet cheese, cut in 8 pieces
2 T Olive oil
1 C Bread crumbs

BALSAMIC VINAIGRETTE DRESSING
1 t Shallots, minced
1 t Garlic, minced
1 T Dijon mustard
¼ C Balsamic vinegar (the best you can buy)
¾ C Extra virgin olive oil
1 t Fresh lemon or lime juice
Kosher salt & freshly ground pepper, to taste

Wash the greens. Make the dressing: whisk together the shallots, garlic, mustard and vinegar. Slowly whisk in the oil so that the dressing is emulsified. Finish with the lemon or lime juice and salt and pepper. Reserve the dressing until needed.

■ Cut the goat cheese into 8 round disk shape pieces and brush each piece lightly with olive oil and dip in the bread crumbs to coat evenly. Bake the goat cheese in a very hot oven (500 degrees) or under a salamander or broiler for approximately 2 minutes, until the cheese is lightly browned and warmed throughout.

■ Toss the field green mixture with the dressing and arrange it beautifully on 4 plates. Sprinkle each salad with the pine nuts and garnish with the Niçoise olives and fresh tomatoes. Top with the goat cheese disks and serve immediately.

The kicker: this is an easy, delicious salad and can be topped with grilled chicken breast or grilled shrimp for a complete meal!

Crème Brûlée

SERVES 4-6

2 C Heavy cream
½ Vanilla bean, split
1 T Orange zest
1 T Lemon zest
5 Egg yolks
½ C Granulated sugar
Brown sugar
Berries of your choice
Fresh mint

Scald the cream with the vanilla bean and citrus zest, being careful not to scorch. Take off the heat and allow the mixture to stand for at least 30 minutes.

■ Beat the egg yolks and the sugar in a bowl until the yolks are pale yellow and thick and ribbon-like. Strain the cream into the yolk mixture while whisking and mix well. Fill soufflé dishes or ramekins with the cream/egg mixture and bake at 250 degrees in a water bath for an hour and a half to 2 hours, until they are just set, but not bubbled or puffy. Cool, cover individually with plastic wrap and refrigerate until ready to serve.

■ Remove the plastic from the custards. Sprinkle each with a thin layer of sifted brown sugar (or raw sugar). Be sure to coat evenly over the entire surface. Place the custards under a hot salamander or an over-fired broiler for approximately 1 minute until the sugar is melted and caramelized. A hand-held propane torch may also be used for caramelizing the sugar. This works well as many home appliances do not get hot enough to achieve proper results. Serve with fresh strawberries, raspberries or blueberries on the side and garnish with fresh mint.

Hotel Lenado

BREAKFAST IS DIFFERENT AND DELICIOUS EVERYDAY at the Hotel Lenado. The coffee is hot and freshly brewed. The juices are served in wine glasses.

If you aren't staying at the Hotel, you're welcome to come for breakfast. It's a bit of a secret and seating is limited. It's lovely on a summer's morning to sit out on the deck and take in that fresh, Aspen morning air. Enjoy reading a paper and relax to a real country-style meal. There is one special each morning. On any given day you might find: omelettes, French toast, waffles, blueberry pancakes or super scrambled eggs. Coffee, juice and fruit accompany your meal. Somehow, each dish is special and has that delicate, home-baked taste. The smells coming from their kitchen conjure up memories of elaborate Sunday breakfasts at home.

The hotel itself should not be overlooked. It was awarded the prestigious Mobile Travel Guide's Four-Star award for 1986. It's a small, cozy, bed-and-breakfast-type hotel. The lobby has an amazing 28-foot fireplace and is furnished with rustic twig furniture. The view from the unusual, cathedral-like windows is of Aspen Mountain. The library is intimate and well-stocked. On the walls are old pictures of the town of Lenado, for which the hotel is named.

Two of the three owners once lived in Lenado, a former logging town near Aspen. Leñado is Spanish and means wooded. They wanted to incorporate many kinds of wood into their hotel. You'll find hickory, hemlock, fir, pine, cherry, apple, birch and willow used in a unique style that flows and fits together beautifully.

Hotel Lenado's Bar Snacks

2 Packages oyster crackers
1 t Lemon pepper
1 t Dill weed
2 Packages original recipe for Hidden Valley Ranch Dressing
1 C Crisco or canola oil

Heat up the Crisco or canola oil and add to the above mixture and stir.

The kicker: the Hotel Lenado makes this recipe with Crisco, but we tested it with the canola oil and it turned out fine. This snack is great to have around the house for any occasion. It makes a great Christmas gift packaged in a nice glass jar.

Salmon Appetizer

SERVES 8

8 oz Softened cream cheese
1 T Lemon juice
1 t Onion, grated
1 t Horseradish
¼ t Salt
1 t Liquid smoke, found in grocery stores
One 6 ½ oz Can good quality red salmon, de-boned, drained and broken into small pieces

Cream together the first 6 ingredients and fold the salmon in gently. The mixture should be coarse and chunky, not smooth. Sprinkle with freshly chopped parsley and chopped walnuts. Serve with crackers of your choice.

Spinach Quiche Lorraine

SERVES 6-8

1 Pastry shell, deep-dish, homemade or good quality store-bought
½ lb Bacon, sliced
2 C Swiss Gruyère cheese, shredded (about ¾ lb)
8 Egg yolks
2 C Heavy cream
½ t Dry mustard
¼ t Salt
¼ t Pepper
1 C Spinach, either fresh, or use 10 oz of frozen spinach
⅔ t Shallots, diced
2-3 T Butter
¼ t Nutmeg
Salt & pepper

Make and partially bake the pastry shell in a 350-400 degree oven. Then, reduce the oven to 350 degrees. Cook the bacon slowly until crisp and drain. Crumble into the pastry shell. Sprinkle the cheese over the bacon. Sauté the shallots in the butter. Cook the spinach, drain very well and chop. Add the spinach to the shallots and sauté a few minutes longer. Salt and pepper to taste and add the nutmeg. Sprinkle the spinach over the cheese.

■ Combine the egg yolks, the cream, mustard, salt and pepper. Set the pie plate on a baking dish and fill with the egg mixture. Bake for 40-45 minutes in a pre-heated 350 degree oven. The custard in the center should be barely set. Serve hot or at room temperature.

The kicker: this is a delicious quiche, very light and flavorful. It is not low in fat. It makes a wonderful brunch item, best served with a lovely salad and rolls.

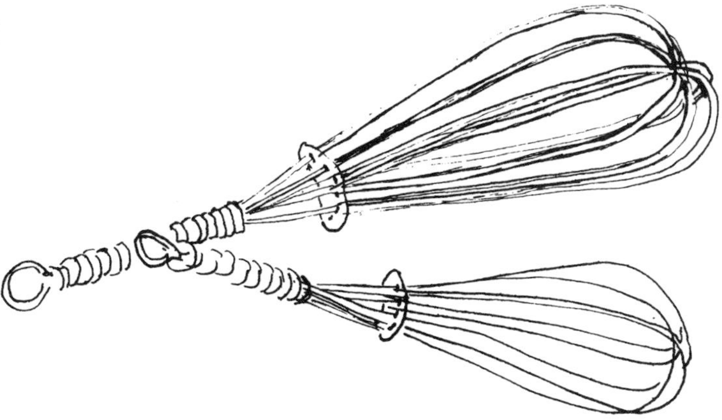

Jour de Fête

JOUR DE FÊTE, LOCATED NEXT TO THE GROG SHOP, IS AN unassuming delicatessen. In French, Jour de Fête means a day of celebration or a holiday. Owner Olivier Mottier wants his customers to "come in and treat themselves."

Mottier is originally from a small resort town in the French Alps where his family has run a popular cheese and wine market for generations. He gained experience working at the market during the summers, but always had a dream to visit America. He came to Aspen in 1983 and worked at Andre's and the Hotel Jerome, knowing that one day he would own a French-style deli. In 1988, he opened Jour de Fête and was delighted with its success. Stocked with 40 imported and domestic cheeses, French patés, meats, dried mushrooms, imported olives, homemade pastas, sauces and New York bagels, Jour de Fête has something for everyone.

When Aspen's only health food restaurant went out of business, customers begged for low-fat, healthy soups and salads. Mottier listened to the locals and it's paid off. Patrons love their hearty sandwiches made on homemade bread, a variety of healthy soups, vegetarian and meat lasagnas and daily delicious specials. Then, of course, there are homemade desserts and the best chocolate chip cookies in town.

It's the 90's and Americans have come to love European espresso and cappuccino. Jour de Fête has a combination espresso and juice bar to please any connoisseur.

Always busy at lunch, you'll see the same faces daily; it's a restaurant's best compliment!

Corn Carrot Chowder

SERVES 6-8

Dash of oil
½ Clove garlic, chopped
2 Small onions, chopped
2 lb Carrots, cut in small pieces
2 Cans Golden corn or 4 fresh corn on the cob (remove kernels)
½ Gallon hot water
Salt & pepper
1 t Chicken bouillon granules (optional)

Pour some oil in a soup pot, on high heat and add the garlic and onions. After 2 minutes, put in the carrots and cook on high heat until the carrots get a little soft. Add the salt and pepper to taste. Add the hot water and when the water boils, lower the heat to medium or low and cook for 40 minutes. Remove from range and run it through the Cuisinart to purée. Put it back in the pot on low heat, add the corn and cook for another 10 minutes. If necessary, add the teaspoon of bouillon granules for more flavor. Garnish with minced parsley or a dollop of sour cream.

♥ *The kicker:* Garnishing this delicious soup with either parsley, or low-fat sour cream makes this soup low in fat.

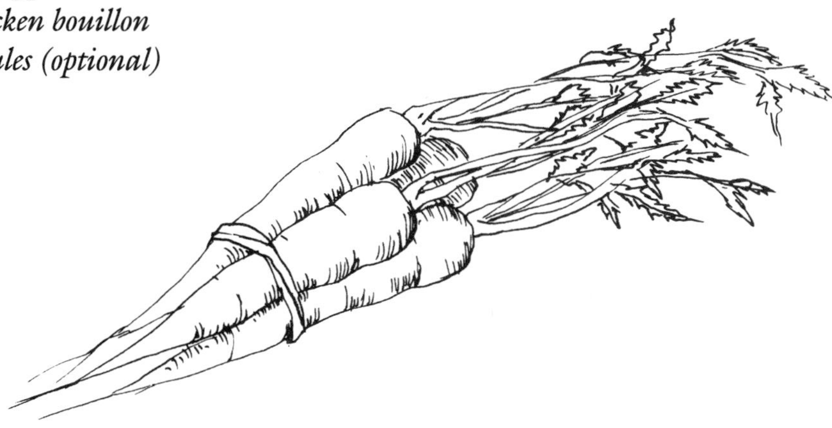

Veggie Chili

SERVES 6 - 8

5 Zucchini, sliced
3 Green peppers, diced
1 Red pepper, diced
2 Yellow onions, diced large
1 Small head broccoli, cut into bite-sized pieces
1 Small head cauliflower, cut into bite-sized pieces
1 Clove garlic, chopped fine
3 Fresh tomatoes, diced
1 16 oz Can tomato sauce
1 Can kidney beans, not drained
1 T Chili powder, or to your liking
Salt & pepper

Steam the broccoli and cauliflower for 5 minutes. Heat olive oil in a large pot until hot. Add garlic and onions and cook a few minutes. Throw in the zucchini and peppers. Let it cook for 10 minutes on high heat. Throw in the tomatoes, salt and pepper to taste and let it cook for another 10 minutes. Throw in the tomato sauce, kidney beans and chili powder. Stir, lower the heat to low and let cook another 30 minutes. Add the broccoli and cauliflower the last 15 minutes. Serve with grated cheese on top.

♥ *The kicker:* This is wonderful served over a healthy brown rice for a nutritious meal.

Vegetarian Lasagna

SERVES 8

WHITE SAUCE
¼ lb Butter
1 C Flour
1 Pint milk
1 lb Ricotta cheese
1 C Parmesan, Reggiano
1 C Romano cheese
Dash of each: Salt, pepper, sweet basil

LOWER-FAT VERSION OF THE WHITE SAUCE ♥
1 lb Low-fat ricotta cheese
2 Egg whites
1 C Parmesan, Reggiano
1 C Romano cheese
Dash of each: Salt, pepper
2 T Fresh basil, chopped

MARINARA SAUCE
Olive oil
1 Clove garlic
1 Yellow onion
3 Sticks celery
1 Large can of peeled tomatoes or 4 fresh tomatoes, remove skin, seeds and dice
1 Large can tomato sauce
1 t Each: Salt, pepper, sugar, rosemary, thyme, bay leaves

VEGETABLES
Olive oil
1 Clove garlic, chopped
1 Large onion, cut in strips
3 Green peppers, cut in strips
6 Zucchinis, cut in bite-size pieces
1 Small head broccoli
1 Small head cauliflower
½ t Each: Salt, pepper, thyme, rosemary, oregano, bay leaves

PASTA
3 Fresh lasagna sheets-8 inches x 20 inches

Recipe continued on following page

Preheat your oven to 375 degrees. Make the white sauce: in a skillet, melt the butter, put in the flour and whisk it. When pasty, slowly pour in the milk while still whisking. Whisk until the texture gets creamy and put it aside. In a bowl, put the ricotta cheese, parmesan, romano, salt, pepper and basil and mix. Add the white sauce and mix together.
♥ Make the lower-fat version: mix all the ingredients together and set aside.
■ Make the marinara sauce: pour some olive oil in a large pot on high heat. Add the garlic, onion and celery and cook for 5 minutes. Add the chopped tomatoes and all the seasonings and cook for 15 minutes. Then, add the tomato sauce and cook for another 30 minutes. Reduce to low heat when the sauce reaches boiling.
■ Make the vegetable layer: pour some olive oil in a sauté pan on high heat. When hot, add the garlic, onions, green peppers and zucchini. Add the seasonings and cook until the vegetables are tender (approximately 15 minutes). Meanwhile, steam the broccoli and cauliflower (about 5 minutes). Then, cut into bite-size pieces.

To assemble: in a deep baking pan, place just enough marinara sauce on the bottom so that the pasta doesn't stick to the bottom. First, place a layer of fresh pasta (it does not need to be cooked), then marinara sauce, white sauce (your choice), and lastly, the vegetables. Repeat this until all your ingredients are gone (save a bit of marinara sauce). Sprinkle the top with parmesan cheese or sliced provolone and add a bit more marinara sauce. Bake for 35-45 minutes and let sit for at least 10-15 minutes before serving.

The kicker: this is a very time-consuming, fairly expensive dish to make, but it is healthy and absolutely delicious. Make it when you have a few helpers!

Wine Suggestion: Macon Village, 1990, White Burgundy.

Little Annie's

BUTCH CASSIDY AND THE SUNDANCE KID WOULD HAVE felt right at home at Little Annie's. It's a "kick off your boots and stay awhile" eatery. This is a fun place. If you're looking for local color, Little Annie's bar has just that. It's always hopping with long-time locals gathering to drink a beer and a shot. It's where the softball teams get together to celebrate their wins or commiserate their losses.

This Western-style saloon is owned by John Hamwi. It's named for the Little Annie's mine which is located on the back side of Aspen Mountain. The environment is Western; it's casual and friendly.

Rob McClanahan, formerly the chef at the famous Parlour Car, explains, "When I first came to Little Annie's, they served mostly hamburgers. They gave me free rein and I expanded the menu. After studying food and traveling around the world to learn more, I enjoy the opportunity to experiment and serve our customers fresher, more appealing items. People trust what we cook here; we've re-educated them and they appreciate it!"

Be sure to check their chalkboard of daily specials including Greek Spanikopita, enchiladas, fresh pasta with different varieties of seafood, herb-roasted chicken, barbecued baby back ribs, to name a few. The wood-burning stove in the dining room always has wonderful homemade soups and chile brewing. The aromas are enticing. Families love Little Annie's. They pride themselves on serving upper-level food at very reasonable prices.

So whether you're coming in for a brew or a fine meal, Little Annie's has it all.

Baked Swordfish with Ginger Lime Sauce

SERVES 4

Four 6-8 oz Swordfish fillets
2 Egg yolks
1 t Dijon mustard
1 T Fresh ginger, finely chopped
1 Bulb garlic
3 Limes, juiced and zested
½ C Gruyère cheese, grated
1 T Thai fish sauce, found in specialty stores
1½ C Canola oil
1 Bunch green onions, chopped fine
Salt & freshly ground black pepper

Roast the whole garlic, unpeeled, at 350 degrees for 25 minutes. When done, peel and chop. Blanch the zested limes in boiling water for 1 minute. In a food processor, whip the egg yolks and mustard for 2 minutes. Slowly add the oil until emulsified into mayonnaise. Add the ginger, lime juice, zest, garlic, onions, fish sauce and salt and pepper to taste and blend for 1 minute. Fold in the cheese.

■ Preheat your oven to 400 degrees. To bake: place fish in an oiled baking dish and space the fish fillets evenly. Pour the sauce over them and bake 8-12 minutes (ovens vary), but do not overcook! Remove from dish immediately and serve.

♥ *The kicker:* If you're concerned with the fat content, delete the cheese from the sauce and simply pour a small amount on each fillet.

Wine Suggestion: Kendall Jackson, Chardonnay.

Red Bell Pepper and Parmesan Soup

SERVES 8

6 Large red bell peppers, washed, seeded and chopped
1 Medium white onion, chopped
8 Cloves garlic, chopped
½ C Flour
⅛ lb Butter
10 C Good quality chicken stock
1½ C Freshly grated parmesan cheese
4 T Oyster sauce, found in grocery stores

In a soup pot, melt the butter, and add the onions and peppers and cover. Stew for 25 minutes over medium heat. Add the garlic and cook uncovered until the liquid is almost evaporated. Add the flour and mix thoroughly. Add warm chicken stock, stir and simmer for 10 minutes. Be careful it does not burn. Purée in blender and strain. Add a bit more of the pepper mixture back into the soup for texture if desired. Add the parmesan cheese (save a little for garnishing each bowl if desired), oyster sauce, salt and freshly ground black pepper to taste.

The kicker: this soup was a hit at our recipe-testing party!

Sautéed Chicken over Linguine with Wild Mushroom Sauce

SERVES 4

- *2 Eight oz Chicken breasts, boneless, without skin, diced 1 inch cubes*
- *1 lb Linguine, cooked al dente & cooled*
- *1 oz Dried porcini mushrooms, soaked in 2 cups water for 1 hour*
- *2 oz Fresh shiitake mushrooms, stemmed & sliced*
- *2 oz Button mushrooms, stemmed & quartered*
- *2 T Shallots, chopped*
- *2 Cloves garlic, chopped*
- *1 C Cream sherry*
- *2 C Chicken stock*
- *2 T Oyster sauce (in the specialty section of most groceries)*
- *½ C Cream*
- *1 T Butter*
- *2 T Olive oil*

Remove the porcini mushrooms from their liquid, squeeze the juice and reserve the liquid. Rough-chop the mushrooms. Melt the butter over high heat, add the shallots, all the mushrooms and sauté for 5 minutes. Add the garlic and cook for 1 minute. Add the sherry and reduce at medium heat for about 5 minutes. Then, add the liquid reserved from the porcini mushrooms, the stock and the cream and simmer for 5 minutes. Add the oyster sauce, salt and freshly ground black pepper. ■ Heat a sauce pan on high heat. Add the olive oil, then the chicken and sauté for 2-3 minutes. Add the mushroom sauce and bring it to a boil, then lower the heat and cook until your desired consistency. *Note:* some ladies at our recipe-testing liked the sauce thicker and some liked it thinner—so you must decide! Add the pasta, toss and serve.

Wine Suggestion: Sterling Chardonnay.

The Little Nell

MANY LOCALS BALKED WHEN THE LITTLE NELL'S Building was torn down in 1988 to make room for the new Aspen Skiing Company-owned Little Nell Hotel. Ironically, many of these same locals now patronize the restaurant at the Little Nell. Known for its contemporary American cuisine in an elegant, yet casual setting, the Little Nell quickly made a name for itself and gained positive recognition.

Serving three meals a day, every day of the year, The Little Nell caters to a wide variety of tastes and requests. Classically trained Executive Chef George Mahaffey came to the Little Nell after six years at the Hotel Bel-Air where he earned the prestigious "Chef of the Year" award. He's quick to point out the fact that he dislikes labeling his style of cooking—he feels it sets up boundaries and suggests limits. "My style," says Mahaffey, "is an interpretation of international cuisine combining the flavors from Asia, South and Central America and the Mediterranean. I strive for a certain level of elegance and style. Colors, flavor and the structure of food are of utmost importance; I like to piece them together to come up with fabulous results."

Mahaffey is a master at presentation. He feels that the food should look as good as it tastes; it's a science. The visual appearance of each plate is impressive and artfully assembled.

The luncheon menu offers unique items such as: Stir-fried Soba Noodles with Swordfish, Scallions, Roasted Peanuts and Snowpeas with a Mango-red Chili Sauce and Shrimp Potstickers with Spicy Mustard and Ponzu Sauces. Salads are a specialty and often incorporate local mixed field greens, fruits and palate-tingling vinaigrettes.

The lights dim in the evenings and the dining room's atmosphere seems to take on a different, more intimate feeling. Diners will find a variety of adventurous entrées: Charred Tuna Steak on a Bed of Wasabi Potatoes and Baby Greens with Lime-Cilantro Sauce, Grilled Beef Tenderloin with Peanut-Cilantro Rice or Roast Rack of Colorado Lamb with Saffron Cous Cous, Braised Vegetables and Mint-Yogurt Sauce.

If you were clever enough to save room for dessert, you'll be well-rewarded. You might have a hard time choosing between the White Chocolate Crème Brûlée, Triple Chocolate Cake with Orange Caramel Sauce or perhaps the Passion Fruit, Coconut and Avocado Sorbets.

The service is unobtrusive, yet prompt and accommodating. Whether you're in your ski suit on a snowy afternoon or sporting a jogging suit after a brisk run, The Little Nell welcomes you.

From spring until the snow falls, enjoy dining outdoors on their flower-filled terrace by the pool with Aspen Mountain as the perfect backdrop. Treat yourself—you only live once!

Lobster Potstickers

CREATED BY GEORGE MAHAFFEY

MAKES 40 POTSTICKERS

1 Large raw chicken breast, skinned
1½ C Raw lobster, diced
4 T Cold press peanut oil
2 C Scallions, roughly chopped
2 C Shiitake mushrooms, roughly chopped
1 T Fresh ginger, grated
2 T Cilantro, chopped
2 T Soy sauce
2 T Sambal paste (found at Clark's)
1 t Sesame oil
40 Egg roll skins (found in oriental section of most grocery stores)

THAI BASIL-PAPAYA SAUCE ♥

2 C Papaya, peeled, seeded & diced
1½ C Orange juice
½ C Seasoned rice vinegar
½ T Sambal paste
¾ T Fresh ginger, grated
1 T Shallots, chopped
½ T Fresh garlic, sliced
½ Piece lemongrass, cut up
½ C Thai basil leaves
1 Bay leaf

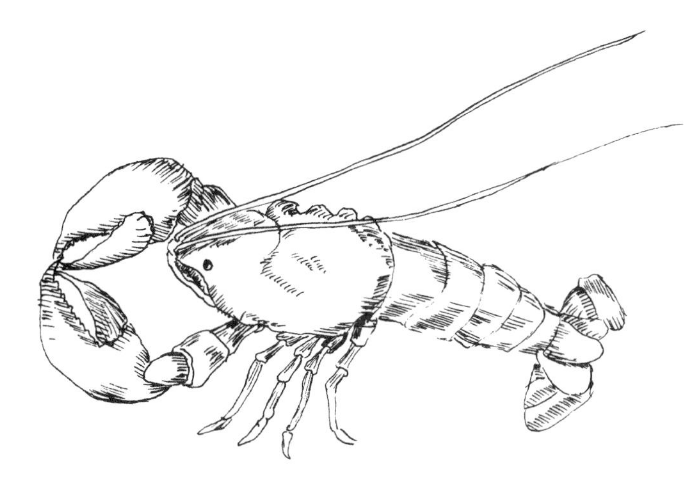

Recipe continued on following page

Purée the raw chicken in a food processor. Heat the peanut oil in a medium size saucepan. Add the shiitakes and cook for 15 seconds. Add the ginger and scallions and cook for 30 seconds longer. Remove from the heat and allow to cool. Add the sambal, soy and cilantro. Combine with the chicken purée and the lobster. Season to taste with a small amount of salt if necessary. Keep on ice.

■ Make the potstickers: cut 4 inch rounds from the egg roll skins and brush with a light egg wash. Place 2 tablespoons of the potsticker mix in the center of the skin and fold into half moon shapes. Brush the edges lightly with the eggwash and make 5 folds along the edge. Poach for 45 seconds, drain and reserve on a lightly oiled, paper-lined container. Refrigerate overnight.

■ Make the sauce: combine the papaya, orange juice, rice vinegar and sambal in a saucepan. Wrap the remaining ingredients in a cheese cloth and add to the pot. Bring to a boil and reduce the heat to a simmer and cook for 15 minutes. Remove from the heat and allow the sachet to remain in the pot until cooled. Remove the sachet and squeeze any excess liquid from it. Purée the sauce and strain.

To serve: in a skillet, heat up a small amount of vegetable oil. Crisp-up the potstickers. Turn them so that all sides get golden brown. Steep a few basil leaves in the sauce when reheating. Serve the potstickers on a platter with the warmed sauce in the middle.

The kicker: these potstickers are loaded with flavor. They'll dazzle your friends.

Lobster Sausage with Sweet Pepper Mustard

CREATED BY RICHARD CHAMBERLAIN

SERVES 6

SAUSAGE
½ lb Lobster meat, cut & diced
½ lb Shrimp, peeled & deveined
½ C Cream
1 t Mustard seed
½ t Chili flakes
1 t Salt
1 t White pepper
½ t Fennel seed
1 Egg

MUSTARD ♥
2 Red bell peppers, roasted, peeled & seeded
¾ C Dijon mustard
2 t Lemon juice
1 T Roasted garlic
½ t Salt

Place all the sausage ingredients (except the lobster) in a food processor and process for 30 seconds. Remove, place in a mixing bowl and fold in the lobster. Roll in plastic wrap to form a 6 x 11 inch log. Place in a steamer and cook 15 minutes longer. Remove and cool. Cut into ¼ inch slices. Refrigerate at least an hour before serving.
■ Place all the mustard ingredients in a blender and process until smooth. To assemble: in a sauté pan over medium-high heat, place 2 tablespoons of olive oil, add the sausage slices and cook until golden brown on each side and remove. On a 12 inch plate, drizzle some mustard, lay the sausage over and garnish with greens.

Wine Suggestion: Murphy Goode, Alexander/ Sonoma, 1990.

Whiskey Braised Venison Osso Bucco with Creamy Garlic Polenta

CREATED BY RICHARD CHAMBERLAIN

SERVES 4

VENISON

8 Venison Osso Bucco shanks
1½ C Onions, diced
¾ C Carrots, diced
½ C Celery, diced
½ C Parsnips, diced
1 T Fresh thyme, chopped
10 Garlic cloves, peeled
2 Bay leaves
1 t Black peppercorns, crushed
2 C Whiskey
¼ C Olive oil
1 Quart Veal or beef stock
1 C Balsamic vinegar

POLENTA

1⅓ C Finely ground yellow cornmeal
1 Quart Chicken stock
½ Quart Heavy cream
2 Ears of corn
2 Garlic cloves
⅓ C Parmesan cheese
2 T Olive oil
1½ T Chives
Salt & white pepper to taste

Make the venison first: in a large sauté pan, over medium heat, add the olive oil, onions, carrots, celery, parsnips and garlic. Sauté until golden brown and add the vinegar and whiskey. Reduce by half. Add the venison, thyme, bay leaves and peppercorns. Simmer for 10 minutes, add the veal stock, cover and simmer slowly for 2-4 hours or until tender. Remove the venison and set aside. Strain the vegetables and set aside. Reduce the broth by three-fourths. Place the venison and vegetables back in the pan and keep warm. ■ Preheat your oven to 325 degrees. Make the polenta: in a small sauté pan, place the olive oil and garlic. Place in the oven until the garlic is soft, but not burned. Set aside. Cut the corn off of the cobs and reserve. In a sauce pot over medium high heat, place the cobs and chicken stock and simmer for 20 minutes. Remove the cobs and add the cornmeal slowly while stirring. Reduce the heat to medium-low and simmer, stirring about 45 minutes. Set aside. In a separate sauce pot, add the cream, corn and roasted garlic with olive oil. Simmer for 6 minutes. Purée in a blender. Add to the cornmeal and stir. Add the chives, parmesan, salt and white pepper to taste. To assemble: spoon the polenta in the center of a plate. Place 2 venison shanks on top. Spoon the sauce and vegetables around.

Wine Suggestion: Cheretto, Dolcetto, an Italian red wine.

Wildflower Honey Cake with Indian Summer Berry Compote

CAKE

½ C + 1 T Butter
1 C Wildflower honey
½ C Whole milk yogurt
½ C Sour cream
1 T Lemon juice
1 C All-purpose flour
1 C Rye Flour
½ t Salt
½ t Baking soda
⅛ t Cloves, ground
⅔ C Walnuts, chopped

INDIAN SUMMER BERRY COMPOTE ♥

1 pint Raspberries
1 pint Strawberries, quartered
1 pint Blueberries
1 pint Raspberry sauce, found at specialty stores
1 T Fresh mint, chopped

For the cake: cream the butter and whisk in the next 4 ingredients. Mix in the next 6 ingredients. Combine the ingredients softly. Do not whip or beat. Butter an 8 inch square pan. Pour the batter into the pan and bake at 350 degrees for 45 minutes until a toothpick comes out clean. Cool and unmold onto a cake rack. Make the compote by mixing all ingredients together. Serve the compote next to the cake for people to help themselves (this way the cake won't get soggy).

The kicker: this cake was a real hit at our recipe testing party. The compote makes quite a bit and is wonderful served over waffles and pancakes, or ice cream and frozen yogurt. It was wonderful on the 4th of July, served over pound cake with a dollop of whipped cream on top!

Main Street Bakery & Café

EVERY SMALL TOWN HAS A PLACE TO MEET AND CHAT, TO hang-out, to drink coffee. In Aspen, it's the Main Street Bakery & Café. Located conveniently on Main Street across from Paepcke Park, the Bakery is a wonderful refuge from a busy day.

History abounds around the Bakery. This historic, 1887 one-story building, owned for three generations by the Conner family, once housed silver miners. The back part of the Bakery was rumored to be a brothel in the 1800's, before the de-valuation of silver sent Aspen into an economic depression.

When owners Bill Dinsmoor and Sally Barnett bought the Bakery in 1989, they hired Linda Conger, who introduced many of the unique items they still serve today: the grilled goat cheese sandwich (served open face on toasted Italian bread with sun-dried tomatoes, roasted red peppers and fresh basil), black bean soup and their herbal iced tea (their own herb blend sweetened with apple juice).

Besides doughnuts, croissants, muffins, scones, cinnamon rolls and homemade bagels, they've added a line of no-fat, no-sugar cookies and muffins. Dinsmoor and Barnett agree that they have a more enlightened clientele. "People nowadays are so much more informed and smarter about the foods they eat; they make healthier choices. We use a lot less sugar in our pies, cakes and baked goods as well." The Bakery serves and sells wholesome 6-grain breads and rolls.

Breakfast at the Bakery is popular, evidenced by the line out their door many summer mornings. Omelettes, French toast, 3-grain pancakes and whole-grain hot cereal are nourishing choices.

Comforting during the winter months are cappuccinos, mochacchinos, vegetarian soups, stews and chile. But when the snow melts, enjoy the sunny patio of the Bakery surrounded by an array of beautiful flowers. Savor a variety of fresh salads, sandwiches and choose a refreshing Italian cream soda. Concentrating on light dinners, simply-prepared, the Bakery serves salads, stews, casseroles and grilled fish.

The Main St. Bakery & Café has a casual and friendly ambiance. It's the kind of place that visitors gladly find and locals call home.

Anicini Anise Biscotti

MAKES 12-14 VERY LARGE SLICES

6½ T Butter
1¼ C Sugar
3 Large eggs
1 T Vanilla
3 C All-purpose flour
½ t Baking powder
⅛ t Salt
4½ oz Almonds, sliced & blanched
3 T Anise seed

Crush the anise in a towel with some weight to release the oils in the seeds. Cream the butter and sugar together until fluffy. Slowly add the eggs, then the vanilla. Sift the flour, baking powder and salt together. Add to the sugar mixture. Don't over-mix! Add the anise and the almonds.

■ Shape the dough into a log on a cookie sheet. The log should be 11 inches long by 6 inches wide, with 1 inch in the middle. Bake at 350 degrees until golden brown (about 25 minutes). Let it cool slightly, then cut into ¾ - 1 inch slices. Lay the slices on their sides. Bake for an additional 10 minutes at 350 degrees.

The kicker: these not-too-sweet biscuit/cookies are delicious with cappuccino or fresh hot coffee. They're softer than the usual biscotti you find; we liked them better!

Main Street Bakery's Stir Fry

SERVES 8 AS AN ENTRÉE

SAUCE
½ Bunch chopped green onions
¾ C Light soy sauce
1½ T Sugar
¼ C Salad oil
¾ oz Grated fresh ginger
½ T Chopped fresh garlic
¼ - ½ t Crushed red pepper
¾ C Dry sherry
½ C Sesame oil

VEGETABLES
1 Head Cauliflower (2 cups), cut in florets
1 Head Broccoli (2 cups), cut in florets
1 C Red peppers, julienne
1 C Green peppers, julienne
1 C Red onions, julienne
1 C Carrots, julienne
2 C Zucchinis, julienne
1 C Daikon radishes, julienne
1 C Baby corn, sliced *
1 C Snow peas, left whole *

2 T Peanut oil
Brown rice
Toasted sesame seeds

Make the sauce ahead of time. In a wok, over medium-high heat, stir-fry all the vegetables, except the starred (*) ones in the peanut oil until just barely cooked. Add 2-3 ounces of sauce (per serving) and the starred vegetables and cook quickly (just until hot). Serve over hot rice and sprinkle with sesame seeds. Serve extra soy sauce on the side.

♥ *The kicker:* this dish takes quite a bit of prep work—-best done when you have some eager houseguests to help. It is delicious and low-in-fat. It's surprisingly filling. Fresh fruit for dessert will keep this meal extremely healthy.

Mezzaluna

MEZZALUNA LITERALLY EXPLODED ONTO THE ASPEN culinary scene. They claimed the busy corner on Cooper Street, one block from Aspen Mountain's gondola. Almost instantly it was discovered—whether by virtue of its reputation in New York or L.A., the location or simply being new—Mezzaluna became a place to dine, have a drink, be seen, see others and hang out. It's loud and open; it's not meant for intimate conversation and a spot of tea.

The original Mezzaluna (there are five in the U.S.) is in New York. The atmosphere, casual style and food is basically the same here as it is in New York. Those in the know, including stars and celebrities, flock to Aspen's sister restaurant. It's definitely a "happening" place and legendary for people watching.

They serve Northern Italian cuisine. Lucky for those who have not learned a second language, the menu lists the items first in Italian and then in English. Patrons enjoy the diversity of dishes. You'll find over 15 varieties of pasta served with unique combinations of interesting sauces, meats, vegetables and fish. All the pastas are homemade on the premises. Ever-popular antipastos include: mixed grilled vegetables, buffalo Mozzarella with tomatoes and basil, goose carpaccio, and polenta with porcini mushrooms. Mezzaluna takes health and nutrition into account. Few dishes are made with cream—instead, they use olive oils, white wine, fresh garlic, the best tomatoes available and fresh herbs. They seek out the finest greens and offer seven delicious and refreshing salads.

The authentic pizza oven, located at the end of the bar, is intriguing with its fire-breathing terra cotta face. Try one of their 14 adventurous pizzas cooked to perfection over an apple wood fire.

Eating Italian food is similar to Chinese and other ethnic cuisines. Customers are encouraged to order a variety of dishes and share. Lots of tastes of wonderful flavors, complemented by their rustic breads and a glass of wine, make for an exciting meal.

The price range is moderate, the food is excellent, the wines are enjoyable and above all, Mezzaluna is a place where you'll have a great time.

Grilled Swordfish with Roasted Red Pepper Relish

SERVES 2

2 Eight oz Pieces of swordfish
1 Red pepper
½ Small red Bermuda onion, chopped fine
1 T Basil, cut in long strips
2 T Balsamic vinegar
2 T Olive oil
½ T Pine nuts, toasted
Salt and freshly ground black pepper
Mixed field greens
1 Lemon, sliced for garnish

Grill the pepper, then peel the burned skin off. Cut in fine strips and add the onions, basil and pine nuts. Mix in the vinegar and oil and season with salt and pepper. Grill the swordfish to desired consistency (do not overcook). Arrange the mixed greens on two plates, top with sliced, grilled swordfish and top with the relish. Garnish with lemon.

♥ *The kicker:* By serving 4-ounce portions of the fish, you'll create a low-fat dish.

Wine Suggestion: Sonoma Cutrer, Russian River Chardonnay, 1990.

Insalata Carita

SERVES 1 PERSON AS A MAIN MEAL OR 2 PEOPLE AS AN APPETIZER

6 oz Rock shrimp
3 oz Fresh pitted cherries
½ Mango, puréed
2 t Olive oil
Pinch salt
Pinch chili powder
½ Shot Tequila
⅛ C Rice vinegar
⅜ C Virgin olive oil
1 Roma tomato, cut into wedges
Mixed greens

Sauté the cleaned rock shrimp in olive oil and add salt and chili powder. Add the cherries and mango purée to the shrimp. Deglaze with the Tequila. Take off heat. Add the vinegar and olive oil to the sautéed shrimp. Toss the mixed greens with the sauce and put the shrimp salad on top. Garnish with tomato wedges.

The kicker: this dish is incredibly quick to prepare. It's a great salad to serve at a summer picnic. At our recipe-testing party, the platter was garnished with edible flowers and made a lovely presentation.

Wine Suggestion: Ferrari Carano Fumé Blanc, 1991.

Pasta Chinoise

SERVES 4

1 Plantain banana
1 Yellow pepper
1 Red pepper
1/8 lb Water chestnuts
1/4 lb Asparagus
1 t Peanut oil or 2 t Sesame oil
1/4 lb Bean sprouts
1/2 C White wine
1/4 C Molasses
1/8 C Light soy sauce
1/4 C Coconut flakes
1/4 C Sundried banana or lightly sweetened banana chips
1 lb Fresh fettuccine
Salt & pepper

Fry the plantain banana in peanut oil, then add the next 4 ingredients, sundried bananas and coconut flakes. Sauté until semi-cooked. Add the bean sprouts at the last minute, so they stay crisp. Cook the pasta in a pot of boiling water with salt until al dente. Add the wine to the sautéed vegetables, then the salt, pepper, molasses and soy sauce. Add the cooked and drained pasta to the hot sauce mixture and serve.

♥ *The kicker:* this is a low-fat dish; an unusual pasta variation.

Wine Suggestion: Matanzas Creek, Sauvignon Blanc, 1990.

Milan's

HAVE YOU BEEN CRAVING ITALIAN FOOD LATELY? Milan's is an intimate restaurant whose reputation rests on its fine food. Proprietors Milan Prikryl and Richard Walbert operate their restaurant relying on each others' talents. They specialize in Northern Italian and Continental cuisine.

A variety of pastas are available—offered in appetizer or entrée portions. Veal and seafood lovers will be happy with ample choices. Also featured are: Chicken Parmesan, New York Sirloin, Pepper Steak and Rack of Lamb. Vegetarians will appreciate the Grilled Tempeh with a tahini basil sauce and stir-fried vegetables. Milan's wild game specialties are extremely popular: Roast Loin of Elk, Fresh Colorado Pheasant, Native Buffalo and Thai Duck are served with creative sauces.

The atmosphere is comfortable and relaxing, yet elegant in design. Large photographs of the Aspen area adorn the walls. Outdoor patio dining is provided in the summer.

I asked Milan why he started this restaurant. He replied with a smile, "I have a family. I love to ski, bike and play tennis. I love Aspen, and this restaurant allows me to share in this beautiful community and make a living."

Milan's has been coined "the best kept secret in town" by an appreciative following.

Grilled Eggplant with Fresh Mozzarella and Basil

SERVES 6

3 Eggplants
Extra virgin olive oil
Fresh: Basil, thyme, parsley & garlic
Crushed black pepper
2 C Roma tomatoes, coarsely diced, seeds removed or any good vine-ripened tomatoes
2 C Fresh mozzarella, coarsely diced

ROASTED RED PEPPER VINAIGRETTE
1 Large red bell pepper, roasted, peeled & cut in strips
1 C Extra virgin olive oil
½ C Balsamic vinegar
2 T Fresh basil, sliced
1 t Fresh garlic, minced
Salt & pepper

Slice the eggplants lengthwise into ¼ inch thick pieces, lay them on a paper towel and sprinkle lightly with salt. Allow them to drain for one hour. Marinate the slices of eggplant in olive oil seasoned with the fresh herbs and pepper. Marinate for 2-3 hours or overnight.
■ Make the vinaigrette by combining the ingredients together and whisking.
■ Drain the eggplant of excess oil and grill over hot coals-approximately one minute on each side. Fan out 3 pieces on a plate and garnish with the tomatoes, fresh mozzarella and fresh basil. Drizzle a small amount of the vinaigrette over the eggplant.

The kicker: this appetizer takes a bit of time to prepare but is definitely worth it for all you eggplant lovers! If you're concerned with the fat content, go lightly when you marinate the eggplants.

Roasted Duck with Plum Sauce

SERVES 6

3 Ducks
2 T Chinese 5-spice
Salt & pepper

PLUM SAUCE ♥
3 Cloves garlic
3 Inches Fresh ginger root, peeled & coarsely diced
Soy salad oil
1½ C Stock (or use canned low-salt chicken broth)
1½ C Oriental plum sauce (Koon Chun or Dynasty work well)
1 T Soy sauce
2 T Fresh basil, sliced
1 T Fresh mint, sliced
3 T Cornstarch plus 3 T cold water
1 T Hot chili oil

Preheat your oven to 400 degrees. Wash the ducks inside and out with cold water. Rub the 5-spice into the skin of each duck, season with salt and pepper and place on a rack in a roasting pan. Roast the ducks for one hour (if using wild duck, cut the cooking time by at least one third). Remove from the oven and let cool enough to handle. Bone each half of the duck leaving the wing, leg and thigh bones intact. Reserve the carcasses for a stock. This may be done well in advance to facilitate easy serving.
■ Make the duck stock: simmer the duck carcasses in enough water to cover them for one to two hours. Make the plum sauce: add the garlic and ginger in a blender and cover with enough oil to blend into a purée. Sauté this mixture for two minutes over moderate heat. Then add the next 5 ingredients. Simmer for 15 minutes and thicken with a mixture of the cornstarch and water. Finish the sauce with the hot chili oil. To serve: heat the duck halves in a 400 degree oven for 10-15 minutes. Finish heating under a broiler to crisp the skin. Serve on top of the sauce and garnish with sliced scallions.

♥ *The kicker:* this is an easy, delicious dish. It would be great served with stir-fried vegetables and either white or wild rice. The plum sauce is low in cholesterol.

Wine Suggestion: 1989 Stag's Leap (Napa), Cabernet Sauvignon.

The Mother Lode

THE ESSENCE OF THE MOTHER LODE IS REFLECTED IN THE large stained glass mural in the main dining room. In the center of this impressive piece is a large mermaid who is symbolic of the mother lode—a mining term used to describe the source of the gold. On either side are men attempting to reach this vision.

The owners, Howard Ross and Gordon Whitmer, originally came to Aspen as ski bums. Both worked at the restaurant and eventually purchased it in 1970. Gordon attributes their success to the good food and the fact that, "People love this old building. It feels good in here."

The Mother Lode is one of the oldest buildings in Aspen, going back to 1886. The interior is what you'd expect from a building this old—it's charming and Victorian, with wooden floors and a wood burning stove in the center of one of the four dining rooms. Hanging from the walls are pictures of racy Victorian women, some whose eyes seem to follow you everywhere. Howard and Gordon have been collecting these wonderful women for the past 23 years.

Chef Buddy Senn described "The Lode's" menu to me as classical Italian cuisine, but on the lighter side. Specialties include: Veal Parmesan, Marinated Grilled Shrimp and Chicken with imported olives and tomatoes. In addition to four different spaghetti items, the menu offers ten pasta dishes from the traditional Fettucini Alfredo to Chicken Farfalle (wild mushrooms, chicken breast and prosciutto served on pasta bows). There are also many appetizers and scrumptious desserts to choose from.

The outstanding food, coupled with authentic Victorian atmosphere, makes The Mother Lode a perfect place to dine while in Aspen.

Insalata con Canestrelli Griglia (Grilled Scallop Salad)

CREATED BY
BUDDY SENN

SERVES 2-4

DRESSING

3 Roma tomatoes, peeled & seeded
½ C Sun-dried tomatoes
½ t Garlic
2 T Balsamic vinegar
¼ C Extra virgin olive oil
Salt & pepper to taste

SALAD

3 Romaine hearts
¼ lb Arugula
2 Leeks
¼ C Olive oil
¼ t Garlic
Pinch crushed red pepper
1 t Dried oregano
12 oz Sea scallops
1 Lemon, zested

Make the dressing: place the sun-dried tomatoes in warm water until soft (about 5-10 minutes), then drain. Place the peeled Roma tomatoes and the sun-dried tomatoes in a food processor, pulsing 10-12 times or until the tomatoes are coarsely chopped. Add the garlic and vinegar with the food processor on. Add the oil a little at a time and the salt and pepper to taste.

■ Clean the Romaine hearts and the Arugula well. Pat dry and tear into bite-size pieces. Mix them together with just enough dressing to coat them.

■ Cut most of the green off, but leave 6-8 inches of the leeks. Cut them into 4 strips, lengthwise and soak them in cold water to clean. Mix together the olive oil, garlic, crushed red pepper and oregano. Place the leeks into the oil mixture, then put them on a hot grill. Do the same with the scallops—grill both sides. When done (taste one to see), put them aside and put the salad together.

■ Take the mixed greens and put them on 4 cold plates. Arrange the scallops around the plate, then put 3 pieces of the grilled leeks on top and garnish with the lemon zest.

♥ *The kicker:* If you're concerned with your fat intake, put less dressing on the salad.

Wine Suggestion: Sanford 1990, Chardonnay.

Linguini alla Crostaceo

LINGUINI WITH FRESH MUSSELS

CREATED BY BUDDY SENN

SERVES 4

1 T Olive oil
1 t Garlic, chopped fine
1 Medium leek
3 Roasted red peppers
1½ C Dry white wine (more if needed)
Salt & white pepper, to taste
2 lbs Mussels
1 T Parsley, chopped fine
⅛ t Crushed red peppers
8 oz Butter, room temperature
2 t Shallots, chopped
12 oz Dry linguini

♥ LOWER FAT SAUCE
1 T Olive oil
½ t Garlic
3 Roasted red peppers
Fresh thyme

In boiling, salted water, cook the linguini for 9-12 minutes (depending on the brand). Drain and place under cold running water to cool. Set aside. Rinse the leeks well, discard the green parts, then cut into ¼ inch slices. Rinse the pieces very well. Peel and seed the peppers.

■ Make the red pepper butter: in a food processor, purée the red peppers, add the softened butter, the shallots, the salt and pepper to taste and let sit at room temperature.

♥ Lower fat version of the red pepper sauce: heat the olive oil in a pan and cook the garlic for 1 minute. Chop the roasted red peppers and add to the garlic. Sauté for 3 minutes. Purée this mixture, then add the thyme, salt and pepper to taste.

■ In a large sauté pan, heat the olive oil on high heat. Add the garlic and the leeks. Cook for 20 seconds, add the crushed red peppers, salt and white wine and bring to a boil. Add the mussels, cover and let simmer until the mussels open (about 4-5 minutes). When the mussels are done, take them out of the pan with a slotted spoon and place into a bowl. Cover and set aside. Add the parsley to the cooked pasta.

To serve: put the pasta in the center of a serving platter, pour the liquid on top, then arrange the mussels around the platter. Spoon the red pepper butter on top of the pasta and serve! If you're using the lower fat version, add that purée mixture on top of the pasta. This dish makes a lovely presentation

Wine Suggestion: Pinot Grigio, Eno Friulia, 1990.

Piñons

ASPEN HAS A REPUTATION FOR BEING ONE OF THE world's premier ski resorts—it's no surprise that this one-time mining town has such wonderful restaurants. Each has its own unique charm and character. Piñons has it all—they serve exceptional, inventive cuisine, tempting wines and superlative desserts in a relaxed yet elegant mountain environment.

Fred Mayerson opened Piñons in the winter of '88 with a vision to be the best. That vision is maintained by current owner Paul Chanin who is very involved with the restaurant activities.

Upon entering Piñons, you'll feel as if you've been invited into someone's home—it's comfortable with soft sensuous colors, lodge pole pine, intimate booths and original Western artwork. The interior embodies the Aspen spirit.

From the beginning, Rob Mobilian was hired as the Head Chef. A Culinary Institute of America graduate and a young man who travels and reads in order to be innovative and keep up with current trends, Mobilian is a crucial link to Piñons' success.

Authenticity is the watchword at Piñons, specializing in American cuisine. Their menu emphasizes Colorado-produced meats and fish. Aware of the growing demand for healthier, lighter meals, they utilize minimal amounts of cream and butter. Favorite entrées include: Elk Tournedos, Blackened Pork Tenderloin, Roasted Colorado Striped Bass and their signature dish—Sautéed Ahi with macadamia nut breading. These creative and delicious dishes are visually appealing as well. There's an overwhelming attention to quality that exists at Piñons—it's one of the many aspects that keep them on top.

Damon Ornowski possesses a great love and knowledge of wine. He can recommend an unfamiliar varietal or vintage to diners who are willing to explore. Pairing fabulous wines to Piñons' cuisine offers the ultimate experience.

For most, the perfect meal ends with something sweet—mediocrity is simply not tolerated by diners when it comes to dessert. Fiona Smollen, Piñons' pastry chef, understands this philosophy. Smollen, a self-taught young Australian woman, has a grand repertoire of desserts. Sweet lovers adore the macadamia nut torte with caramel and shaved white chocolate. She also makes delectable homemade ice cream and sorbets.

When I asked General Manager and Maître d' Frank Chock why Piñons is so successful, he stresses the consistency of the food. "We also have the most mature wait-staff in town. Our employees work as a team, enjoy what they do and consider their job a profession." These crucial components earned Piñons the Dirōna award for "Distinguished Restaurants of North America."

Piñons' popularity is astonishing. Customers lucky enough to have discovered this outstanding restaurant are true devotees.

Grilled Ruby Red Trout with Rock Shrimp & Shiitake Mushrooms

SERVES 2

Enough trout for 2 people, either whole trout or fillets (any variety of trout is fine)
Peanut oil
Salt & pepper
½ t Garlic, chopped
½ t Shallots, finely chopped
2 T Red pepper (about ½ a pepper), roasted, peeled & julienne
2 oz Shiitake mushrooms, sliced
1 T Pickled ginger, chopped
3 oz Rock shrimp (or substitute other shrimp), shelled & deveined
3 T Green onions, julienne
¼ C Sake
¼ C Chicken stock
1 T Butter
½ t Tamari

Brush the fish with peanut oil and season with salt and pepper. Grill (or pan-fry) until cooked through. While the trout is cooking, prepare the topping: in a little oil, gently sauté the garlic and shallots. Add the mushrooms, cook briefly, then add the red peppers, shrimp, ginger and green onions. Cook until the shrimps turn pink, then deglaze the pan with the sake and chicken stock. Simmer for a minute or two to cook off the alcohol, then add the butter and tamari. Check the seasonings and spoon the mixture over the cooked trout.

♥ *Lower fat version:* wrap all the ingredients in foil (except the stock and butter) and bake until the fish flakes. Time will vary depending on the size of the trout.

Wine Suggestion: Sterling, "Winery Lake" Pinot Noir.

Macadamia Praline Chocolate Cake

CREATED BY FIONA SMOLLEN

THIS IS A SOFT, RUM-FLAVORED COCOA CAKE, COATED WITH A CRUNCHY MACADAMIA PRALINE GLAZE

CAKE

½ C Cocoa powder
1 C Warm water
2 T Honey
4 oz Butter, melted
½ t Salt
4 Egg yolks
1 t Vanilla
1 C Sugar
1 t Baking powder
1¼ C Cake flour

SYRUP

½ C Water
¼ C Sugar
3 T Dark rum, preferably Myers's

PRALINE

½ C Sugar
3 T Water
½ C Macadamia nuts

GLAZE

8 oz Good quality bittersweet chocolate
1 C Cream

Recipe continued on following page

Preheat the oven to 325 degrees. Grease a 9" pan. Whisk together the cocoa and water in a large bowl until smooth. Add the remaining cake ingredients and whisk until well combined. Turn the batter into the pan and bake about 25 minutes or until you insert a toothpick and it emerges with a few moist crumbs attached.

■ Prepare the syrup: warm the water a little, remove from the heat and dissolve the sugar in it. Stir in the rum. Pour half of the rum syrup over the top of the warm cake and set the cake aside to cool. If the cake has a peak, flatten it gently by pressing with the palms of your hands. Grease a cookie sheet. Make the praline: briefly toast the macadamia nuts in the oven until golden. Rinse the salt off first (if they're salted). In a small pan, stir together the sugar and water and cook the sugar mixture over high heat until deep golden. Immediately remove from the heat, stir in the prepared nuts and turn the mixture onto the greased cookie sheet. Be very careful—caramel burns are very painful! When the praline is cool, chop it with a heavy knife until the pieces are the size of a grain of rice—or do this in the food processor.

■ When the cake is cool, turn it out of the pan (invert it) and pour the remaining syrup over it. When the cake has absorbed the syrup, turn it right side up and set it on a cake round that is slightly smaller than the cake. You can cut out a piece of heavy cardboard if you don't have cake rounds. Lay a piece of wax paper on the counter to collect the drips. Set a coffee mug on the middle of the paper and sit the cake, with its cardboard round, on top of the mug, up in the air.

■ Make the glaze: finely chop the chocolate. Warm the cream until it almost boils, then pour it over the chocolate. Stir until all the chocolate melts. Stir in the prepared praline. Pour all the praline glaze over the top of the cake, letting the excess drip onto the wax paper below. Lift the cake off the coffee mug, put it on a platter and set in the refrigerator so the glaze firms up.

The kicker: this is a wonderful cake that was thoroughly enjoyed by everyone at a recipe testing. It's a bit time-consuming so prepare it when you have a day off. Your guests will love it!

Onion Cracker Bread

CREATED BY FIONA SMOLLEN

SERVES 6-8

DOUGH
1 T Yeast
1⅓ C Water
1¾ T Sugar
1 t Salt
1 T Vegetable oil
3½ C All-purpose flour

TOPPING
2 Medium onions, diced
1 T Vegetable oil
1 T Poppy seeds
3 Green onions, finely chopped
Coarse Kosher salt
1 Egg white, beaten with 1 T water

Make the dough: dissolve the yeast in the water. Add the remaining ingredients and knead until a smooth dough is formed—knead either by hand or in a food processor. Cover the dough and set aside to rise for 45 minutes. Preheat the oven to 450 degrees.

■ While the dough rises, prepare the topping. Sauté the onions in the oil until soft. Remove from the heat and stir in the poppy seeds and the chopped green onions. In a small bowl, whisk the egg white with the tablespoon of water.

■ Divide the dough into 3 pieces. Pat or roll into rectangles about ⅓ of an inch thick. Rest the dough for 10 minutes (to relax the gluten in the flour and to make the dough easier to stretch). Grease 3 large cookie sheets, about 17 inches by 11 inches. If you only have one pan, just stretch and bake one at a time. Stretch each piece of dough to cover the bottom of the pans. Stretch gently with the flat palm of your hand under the dough. Don't worry about the dough being absolutely even—the irregularities are part of its charm; creating soft and crispy pieces of cracker where the dough is thick or thin.

■ Brush the dough with the egg white. Distribute the onion-poppy seed topping evenly over the dough. Sprinkle very lightly with salt. Bake in the oven until golden, about 10-15 minutes. Cool and break into pieces for serving.

♥ *The kicker:* this low-fat, delicious cracker-bread is a great alternative to bread with a meal.

Poppies Bistro Café

"WE WANT TO PLEASE AND TITILLATE THE PALATE in a pleasing atmosphere with a touch of elegance." This is the goal of owners Michael Hull and Earl Jones.

This charming Victorian restaurant located on the outskirts of Aspen, was formerly a residence and dates back to 1886. You immediately feel the charm of age upon entering Poppies. It has the atmosphere most people seek out when looking for a fine dining experience.

It's very romantic with original Franklin Halofain lamps hanging over each table. The wainscot wood panels on the walls tend to glow and give the dining room a warmer feel.

It's the little things about Poppies that will charm you. There's a different antique vase on each table and the fresh flowers vary. The pictures on the walls are fun and interesting. (Earl likes to move them around.) Lace curtains in the windows, wine bottles displayed around the dining room, tiny candles glowing and classical music are there to visually and sensually please you.

Chef Ed Fertig, a graduate of the Culinary Institute of America, turns out classical cuisine using only the freshest ingredients. He explains, "I like to keep it simple, yet serve dishes with lots of flavor. I use fruit juices in our sauces to keep them on the light side. The wild game we serve is very healthy. I seek out the best purveyors to ensure the highest quality." Fertig enjoys working at Poppie's; it gives him the freedom to create and experiment daily.

Poppies has a basic menu with a "specials" sheet that changes each evening. Patrons' favorites include Steak Au Poivre, Grilled Salmon with Hoisin and Ginger Sauce, Grilled Colorado Lamb Chops and South Carolina Quail with a Raspberry Vinegar and Red Wine Sauce.

Dessert wizard Kent Watts LeBoutillier is self-taught and strives for perfection. Her creations are elegantly presented. She dazzles diners with her Chocolate Double Decadence with a Raspberry Sauce!

Poppies glows in the winter and comes to life in the summer. Live, brilliantly colored orange poppies sprout up by the entrance. Their green lawn and magnificent array of flowers, arranged in pots of all shapes and sizes, make for a perfect setting.

Grilled Colorado Lamb Chops

WITH RED PEPPER MINT JELLY, GOAT CHEESE, ROSEMARY, POMMES ANNA & MIXED VEGETABLES

CREATED BY ED FERTIG

SERVES 4

Rack of lamb, trimmed, split & chined (3 inch French), cut into chops
Goat cheese, crumbled

MARINADE
8 Cloves garlic
10 Sprigs thyme
10 Sprigs rosemary
Olive oil, pure (to coat)

RED PEPPER MINT JELLY
3 Red peppers, de-seeded
2 oz Pickled ginger
1 C Cider vinegar
½ Anaheim pepper, de-seeded
Tabasco sauce
Salt & pepper
4 C Sugar
½ Bunch Mint, chopped
1 oz Knox powdered gelatin

MIXED VEGETABLES
2 Carrots, ½ lb sugar snap peas, 1 head broccoli
4 Shallots, chopped
2 Cloves Garlic, chopped
3 oz Butter
Salt & pepper, to taste

POMMES ANNA
3 Idaho potatoes, peeled & sliced very thin
4 oz Butter
Salt & pepper, to taste

For the marinade: chop the garlic and thyme, then mix with the olive oil. Marinate the rosemary sprigs in this mixture. Make the Mint Jelly: use a food processor to combine the first 6 ingredients. Bring to a boil in a heavy sauce pan and simmer for 5 minutes. Remove from the heat. Stir in the sugar with a wooden spoon. Place back on a high flame. Simmer for an additional 10 minutes. Remove from the heat and slowly stir in the gelatin. Add the mint.

■ For the mixed vegetables: blanch the carrots, peas and broccoli in boiling water so that they remain crisp. Melt the butter in a sauce pan and add the shallots, garlic and salt and pepper, to taste. Add the blanched vegetables and cook until the vegetables are warm, yet remain crisp.

■ For the Pommes Anna: clarify some butter and pour into a black steel pan. Place some potato slices in the pan in 4 layers of overlapping concentric circles. Place the pan over medium-high flame. When the bottom potatoes are golden brown, flip the mandoline of potatoes. When the bottom is partly browned, put the pan into a 400 degree oven for 5 minutes. Place the Pommes Anna on a cutting board. Cut into 8, even-sized wedges.

■ Grill the lamb chops. Garnish with the marinated rosemary sprigs and spoon the mint jelly close to the chops. Arrange a mélange of vegetables, a wedge of Pommes Anna and some crumbled goat cheese into an irresistible presentation on the remainder of the plate.

Wine Suggestion: Silverado, Cabernet Sauvignon.

Grilled Salmon with Hoisin and Ginger Butter Sauce with Tomato, Basil Fettuccine

CREATED BY ED FERTIG

SERVES 2

Two 6 oz Boneless salmon fillets
Olive oil
Salt & pepper
2 oz Oriental Hoisin sauce

GINGER BUTTER SAUCE
¼ C Pickled ginger
3 Shallots, minced
1 C White wine, use good wine
½ C White wine vinegar, use a quality brand
¼ - ½ C Heavy cream
¼ lb Unsalted butter, cold

PASTA
2 Vine-ripened tomatoes, diced
3 Shallots, minced
3 Cloves garlic, minced
Julienne fresh basil
Reggiano Parmesan, grated
Homemade fettuccine or a good quality dried fettuccine

Coat the salmon fillets with olive oil, Hoisin sauce, salt and pepper. Make the ginger butter sauce: in a small saucepan, reduce the shallots, wine and vinegar. When syrupy, add the heavy cream. Mound in the cold butter. Add salt & pepper to taste and the ginger.

■ Grill the salmon fillets, do not overcook!

■ Meanwhile, make the sauce for the fettuccine: sauté the shallots, garlic and tomatoes in olive oil. Add the basil (save some for garnish), salt and pepper. Cook the pasta in boiling, salted water until tender. Drain and toss into the sauté pan with other ingredients. Serve immediately and garnish with Parmesan and fresh basil.

♥ *The kicker:* if you can afford the calories, serve the sauce either on top or underneath the fish with the fettuccine on the side. If you're watching your fat intake, avoid the sauce; the fish is delicious coated with olive oil, Hoisin sauce, salt and pepper and grilled. The sauce in the fettuccine is very healthy. Enjoy it either way.

Wine Suggestion: Cakebread Cellars, Sauvignon Blanc.

Poppie's French Silk Pie

CREATED BY KENT WATTS LE BOUTILLIER

CRUST
½ Box (5 oz) of Famous Chocolate Wafers
¼ C Butter

FILLING
2 oz Unsweetened baker's chocolate
3 Eggs
¾ C Sugar
½ C Unsalted butter, softened
1 t Vanilla

GARNISH (OPTIONAL)
5 oz White chocolate
⅓ C Heavy whipping cream
2 oz Semi-sweet dark chocolate

Make the crust: spray one 9 inch pie pan with a food release. Place the chocolate wafers into a Cuisinart and chop well. Slowly add the butter until moist. Pat this mixture on the bottom and sides of the pie pan. Refrigerate to chill.

■ Make the filling: melt the unsweetened chocolate over a double boiler. Combine the eggs and sugar in a metal bowl and heat over a double boiler until the sugar melts (110 degrees). Remove from heat and beat with an electric mixer until fluffy and doubled in size (about 8 minutes). Beat the butter separately until light and fluffy. Combine the egg mixture with the butter and melted chocolate. Beat together, add the vanilla and beat until fluffy and somewhat firm (5 minutes). If it's too hot outside, and the filling won't air-chill, help it chill by beating the filling over ice cold water until it thickens. Pour into the pie pan, level flat and refrigerate.

■ Garnish (optional): melt the white chocolate and dark chocolate over separate double boilers. Scald the whipping cream in a small sauce pan. Pour scalded cream over the white chocolate and mix well with a wire whip. Cool for a few minutes and then pour over the cooled pie to cover the filling. Dribble the dark chocolate over the top of the white chocolate and swirl with a tooth pick for a personal design. Cool for several hours before serving. Serve with fresh raspberries if desired.

The kicker: this dessert is as beautiful upon presentation as it is totally decadent and well-loved by chocolate lovers!

Poppie's Pecan Pie

One 9 inch pie shell (preferably homemade)
6 Eggs
⅓ C Butter, melted
¼ lb Brown sugar
1 C Light corn syrup
1 T Molasses
1 C Pecans

Preheat your oven to 375 degrees for high altitude or 350 degrees at lower altitude. Combine all the ingredients except the butter and mix well. Then add the butter and mix. Pour into the unbaked pie shell and bake until the center is full and puffed up, approximately 35 minutes. Serve hot with vanilla ice cream and/or fresh whipped cream.

The kicker: this is an incredibly easy recipe. Most men absolutely love pecan pie and this is one of the best!

Sautéed Sea Scallops with Citrus Beurre Blanc, Supremes of Orange & Ruby Grapefruit

CREATED BY ED FERTIG

SERVES 4 ENTRÉES OR 6 APPETIZER PORTIONS

1½ lbs Scallops

SAUCE
¼ C Fresh orange juice
2 t Shallots, chopped
¾ C White wine
¼ C Raspberry vinegar
5 oz Unsalted butter, cold and cubed
2 T Clarified butter or 1 T canola oil plus 1 T butter
2 T Heavy cream
1 Orange, cut in segments
1 Ruby grapefruit, cut in segments
Sprigs of thyme, for garnish
Salt & pepper

♥ LOWER FAT VERSION FOR THE SAUCE
½ C Fresh orange juice
4 T Lemon juice
2 t Shallots, chopped
½ C Water
1 t Sugar
2 t Cornstarch dissolved in 1 T water
2 t Heavy cream
2 T Butter

For the sauce: reduce the wine, vinegar, orange juice and shallots in a heavy saucepan. When it is close to a glaze, add the cream. Bring to a boil. Mound in the 5 ounces of unsalted butter and whisk on a lower heat. Adjust the seasonings; salt and pepper, to taste.

♥ Make the lower-fat version: simply place all the ingredients (except the cornstarch dissolved in water) in a saucepan and bring to a boil. Then add the cornstarch mixture and whisk.

■ Sauté the scallops in a hot sauté pan with the clarified butter (or a combination of the oil and butter). When browned, flip them over and cook on the other side.

■ To serve: make a pool of either sauce on a plate and arrange the fruit segments around the perimeter of the plate. Mound the scallops in the center and garnish with the thyme sprigs.

The kicker: this is my husband's most favorite appetizer!

Wine Suggestion: Grgrich Hills, Chardonnay.

Poppycock's

REMEMBER THE LEMONS IN THE WINDOW? THEY ALWAYS caught my attention. Used to make fresh lemonade, the lemons also served as an eye catcher for anyone passing by. They lured you into Poppycock's, a tiny crêperie that also served cappuccinos, health drinks, soups and home-baked desserts. From 1971-1986, it was located in the Brand Building. With only seven stools inside, you could always walk up to the outside window to order.

They were famous in Aspen for their spinach crêpes—large crêpes made-to-order with a thick, hearty spinach filling. Their dessert crêpes, four to choose from, were also popular.

The previous owners Josie and Mark Butzier had to move their tiny eatery in the summer of '86 when the Brand Building was renovated. They found their new home in the Aspen Square Building. Poppycock's is now a contemporary café with table service. The new owners Bee and Paul Poh have retained a counter to satisfy customers who are in a hurry.

The original menu remained, with the addition of breakfast and more lunch items. Breakfast includes: delicious French toast made from cinnamon bread and topped with fruit, five varieties of pancakes (customers adore their Macadamia Nut Oatmeal Pancakes) and four innovative egg dishes. Lunch now includes sandwiches on their homemade bread, a variety of lovely fresh salads with homemade dressings and three pasta meals (Linguine with Pesto, Pine Nuts and Fresh Goat Cheese is a favorite).

The new Poppycock's was an instant success. Word spread quickly of the fresh, wholesome and delicious food with grand specials that change daily.

Maple-Glazed Pork Roast

SERVES 4

1 lb Boneless lean pork shoulder butt
2 Cloves garlic, thinly sliced
2 t Lime juice
1 T Dark rum
1½ T Maple syrup
⅛ t Cayenne pepper

With a paring knife, pierce the pork all over. Insert the garlic slices into the gashes, then rub the lime juice onto the pork. Combine the rum, maple syrup & cayenne pepper in a bowl, add the pork and coat well. Cover and refrigerate about 8 hours. Turn the pork occasionally in the marinade.

■ Preheat the oven to 425 degrees. Line a shallow roasting pan with tin foil. Lift the pork from the marinade and place on a rack over the lined roasting pan. Roast uncovered and brush often with the marinade for 20 minutes. Lower the heat to 350 degrees and roast another 20 minutes, continuing to brush often with the remaining marinade. Let the roast stand for 10 minutes at room temperature before slicing.

The kicker: this is very easy and delicious.

Wine Suggestion: Sanford, Pinot Noir.

The Red Onion

THE RED ONION'S CHARM COMES FROM ITS HISTORY. Still in its original location, the Red Onion is one of the few famous old mining-day saloons still operating. Tom Latta had "The Brick Saloon" built in 1892. The original fixtures and furnishings were elegant for their day. The club rooms, where billiards and pool were played, were praised as the "handsomest in the West," by the *Aspen Daily News.*

"Sporting men" of the region patronized The Brick Saloon. Their interests were prize-fighting, wrestling, cycling and other sporting events popular during that era. Today, pictures of prize-fighters on the walls serve as evidence of the past. A separate entrance led upstairs in case a man was in need of a "good time with a lady." A back door was provided for a discreet departure!

After World War II, Jonny Litchfield bought The Brick Saloon and changed its name to the Red Onion which means "something out of the ordinary." Skiing became Aspen's claim to fame, and with it, the Onion became the most popular bar in town for après-ski.

Werner Kuster purchased the Onion in 1953 and turned it into an internationally famous night club and restaurant.

The Red Onion is now owned by Dave (Wabs) Walbert and Bud Nicholson. Although a third smaller in size than it was, "Wabs" stresses, "It's still one of the oldest bars in town. We've kept it up through the years to look like it did in the 1800's. It has that great Western flavor."

Look around at the historic old photographs on the walls of the Smuggler Mine, old Victorian homes and the Onion as it was in 1948, surrounded by empty lots and looking a bit lonesome.

The food the Onion now serves is Mexican and "good old" American. In the summer, outdoor patio dining is provided for your enjoyment!

Pollo Encanelado

SERVES 6

Six 8 oz Boneless, skinless chicken breasts

MARINADE
½ C Fresh lemon juice
2 T Cinnamon
1 T Garlic purée
1½ C Cooking sherry
Pinch salt
1½ C Honey

Mix the marinade ingredients together in a large mixing bowl. Marinate the chicken breasts overnight, refrigerated. Grill the chicken. Garnish with fresh cilantro and serve with rice and beans and a salad.

♥ *The kicker:* this is a very nutritious meal since there's no oil in the marinade and no extra fat on the chicken. The rice and beans provide added protein. If you can afford the calories, enjoy with a cold Corona beer.

Renaissance Restaurant

"THE ALCHEMY OF FOOD." THIS IS THE UNUSUAL phrase, coined by chef/owner Charles Dale, to describe Renaissance Restaurant. It refers to the combination of science and magic. Magic is the key, and the difference between a chef who simply cooks and one who is inspired from the heart.

Dale's highly acclaimed dishes are created by blending the knowledge of the classical French techniques with the lightness and distinct flavors of contemporary ingredients. He intuitively relies upon the basics to produce a totally unique taste. He often uses ethnic twists to liven up an entrée. Ultimately, Dale is able to present a dish that maintains its own integrity. Julie Van Pelt, Dale's partner explains, "Everything on the plate is meant to be eaten, including the herb garnish. We use only the most healthful, organic ingredients so that the real flavors of the food come through."

You can't expect to have a successful restaurant in Aspen without the combination of superb food and unsurpassed service. Renaissance has both. While Dale works his magic in the kitchen, Van Pelt sees to it that the diners' needs are met in every way. She wants their guests to receive five star service in a more relaxed environment. This attitude has helped them gain a loyal clientele with recognition on an international level.

The decor reflects the Renaissance era; a combination of the old and new. The softness of the peach stucco walls and the boldness of the rough granite bar, along with other touches, convey a sensual, romantic atmosphere—one that thoughtfully complements their innovative cuisine.

Dale, an enthusiastic young man, with a most impressive culinary background from France and the U.S., explains, "We're very in-line with what Aspen stands for; we're elegant but we're simple. There's a mysticism behind what we do. I have a very strong inner motivation for what I do. I believe in living your own truth. Your work has to reflect that. Our work is the perfect canvas for the kind of world we want to live in."

Fresh Water Striped Bass with Fennel-Tomato Marmalade

CREATED BY CHARLES DALE, CHEF/OWNER

SERVES 8

8 Filets of Striped bass, 5-6 oz each (or substitute halibut, black sea bass or brook trout)

MARINADE

¼ C Fennel tops (anise), chopped
¼ C Pure olive oil
4 Cloves garlic, chopped fine
Freshly ground black pepper from a mill

MARMALADE

6 Roma tomatoes, peeled, seeded and chopped (set aside 1 T)
1 White onion, diced fine
2 Cloves garlic, chopped
1 T Fresh thyme, chopped
Salt and pepper to taste
¼ C Olive oil
5 Star anise pods, found in the spice section of the grocery
6 Bulbs fennel, cored and sliced
2 Red onions, sliced
¼ C Pernod

SAUCE VIERGE

¼ C Extra virgin olive oil
Juice of 1 lemon
1 T of each: plucked Italian parsley, chervil and tarragon
1 T Tomato, chopped

Recipe continued on the following page

For the marinade, rub the olive oil and garlic over the fish. Sprinkle with the chopped fennel and pepper, cover with plastic wrap and refrigerate until ready to use. Make the marmalade: in a small saucepan, sweat the onions in olive oil until translucent. Add the garlic and tomatoes and cook for 20 minutes. Add the thyme and cook another 5 minutes and season to taste. Meanwhile, in a large sauté pan with straight sides, stir the star anise in hot oil for 2 minutes, then add the red onions. Stir for 1 minute, then add the fennel. Turn down the heat to medium/low and cook for 20 minutes, adding water as necessary to prevent sticking or burning. Add the tomato compote to the fennel mixture, splash in the Pernod and simmer for 30 minutes.

■ Mix the sauce vierge ingredients together gently. Season the fish with salt. Grill or sauté (flesh side down) for 1 minute in olive oil. Turn and repeat and remove to a baking sheet. When ready to serve, finish in the oven for 4-5 minutes, depending on the size of the filet and the type of fish used.

To serve: spoon the marmalade onto the plate and garnish the side with a sprig of fennel, top with the fish and one teaspoon of the sauce vierge. Serve immediately.

♥ *The kicker:* this recipe is low-cholesterol and yet delicious.

Wine Suggestion: 1988 Sonoma Cutrer, "Les Pierres."

Chocolate Soufflé Renaissance

SERVES 7

2 oz Butter
3 oz Semi-sweet chocolate
1 oz Bitter chocolate
3 Egg yolks
2 oz Warm water
7 Egg whites
2 oz Sugar

Grease seven, 7 ounce soufflé molds with extra butter, dust with granulated sugar and refrigerate until ready to use. Preheat the oven to 375 degrees. Melt the butter in a saucepan, add the chocolate and stir until melted. Remove from the heat. Whisk the yolks and warm water together with an electric beater until fluffy and cream-colored.

■ Whisk the egg whites and sugar together over a double boiler until the sugar dissolves. Remove from the heat and continue to whisk into peaks. Mix the chocolate mixture and egg yolk mixture thoroughly together. Mix in 1/3 of the egg whites and fold in the rest very gently, but thoroughly. Fill the soufflé molds to just under the top and refrigerate until ready to use. You can make this 1 day before. Cook in 375 degree oven 7-8 minutes, or until risen and not too runny when shaken. Remove, quickly dust with powdered sugar and serve immediately.

Dessert wine suggestion: 1990 Quady Elysuim Black Muscat.

Pan-Baked Sturgeon with Arugula and Shoe-String Potatoes Sauce à la Nage

SERVES 8

Eight 6 oz Sturgeon filets (or can substitute halibut)
Flour for dredging
⅓ C Olive oil
Two 12 inch, oven/proof sauté pans
½ lb Arugula, stemmed and washed (or substitute spinach)
4 Baking potatoes
2 C Canola oil, for frying
One 2 x 12 inch sauté pan
2 Cloves garlic, one minced, one whole

SAUCE À LA NAGE
1 White onion
4 Shallots, peeled
3 Celery stalks
1 Leek
1 Head garlic
1 Fennel bulb
3 Stems fresh thyme
2 T Olive oil
1 Bottle white wine (Sauvignon Blanc or Chardonnay)
1 C Water
6 Whole black peppercorns

TO FINISH THE SAUCE
¼ C Extra virgin olive oil
Juice of one fresh lemon
2 T Butter
2 Roma tomatoes, peeled, seeded and diced
¼ C Chives, chopped
Salt and pepper to taste

In a medium saucepan, combine all the Nage vegetables, peeled and diced (except for the garlic, which is sliced crosswise) with the olive oil, and sweat over low to medium heat for 15 minutes. Add the white wine, water, thyme and peppercorns and cook for one hour, simmering gently. Remove from the heat and strain.

■ Cut the potatoes to match-stick size, preferably on a mandolin and preserve, submerged in cold water. Heat 2 cups of canola oil in a heavy-bottomed, 2 x 12 inch sauté pan to medium heat (the oil should not be smoking). Carefully drain the potatoes and dry them on a towel. Cook them, one cup at a time in the oil. Remove to a dry paper towel and repeat until all the potatoes are crisp and golden in color. Keep warm.

■ Rub the fish filets on the whitest side with the whole garlic clove, sliced in half, lengthwise. Salt lightly and dredge in white flour, just enough to form a thin film over the fish. Sauté the filets in each pan over medium heat, flour side down, in ¼ cup olive oil for 1-2 minutes or until golden brown. Season with salt and fresh pepper and turn. Put pans in 400 degree oven and let bake for 5 minutes or until barely flaky (this will depend on the thickness of the filets).

■ Meanwhile, sauté the arugula in the remaining olive oil, season with salt and pepper, add the minced garlic and remove from the pan. Keep warm.

■ Finish the sauce: bring 2 cups of the Nage to a boil, add the olive oil and butter and emulsify in a blender for 30 seconds. Put back in the saucepan over very low heat, season to taste and add the tomatoes, chives and the fresh lemon juice.

To serve: place a small handful of potatoes at the top of the plate, the arugula in the center, the fish on top of the arugula and spoon the sauce around. Serve immediately.

Wine Suggestion: 1989 Chateau Montelena Chardonnay.

Risotto with Wild Mushrooms

SERVES 8

½ lb Arborio rice
1 White onion, finely diced
½ C Dry white wine
4 C Chicken stock
1 t salt, or to taste
2 T Sweet butter
2 T Heavy cream
¼ C Grated Reggiano Parmesan cheese
2 lbs Assorted mushrooms (shiitake, chanterelle, portobello, etc.), sliced
2 T Olive oil
2 Shallots, minced
1 Garlic clove, minced
1 T Rosemary and thyme, chopped
Dash white wine
¼ C Chicken stock
Salt and pepper, to taste

Reserve ¼ cup chicken stock. Sweat the onion over medium heat in one tablespoon of butter. Add the rice and stir to toast but not color. Add the white wine, stir until absorbed (about 1 minute) and immediately add chicken stock to barely cover, stirring constantly. When the first batch of stock is absorbed, add more, again to cover and now add the salt, but keep stirring. Repeat until all the liquid is absorbed or the rice is al dente (about 20-25 minutes). Set aside briefly while you sauté the mushrooms.

■ Sauté the mushrooms over high heat in olive oil and stir. Add the shallots, garlic and herbs and toss briefly. Add the wine and allow it to absorb, then add the stock, salt and pepper. Keep warm. Return the risotto to the heat and add the reserved ¼ cup chicken stock. Add the butter, cream and parmesan cheese and season with salt and pepper. Serve in a bowl with mushrooms on top. The risotto should have a creamy texture and each grain should be distinct. Serve optional freshly grated parmesan cheese.

♥ *The kicker:* Renaissance always has a risotto on their menu. This is their winter version. It's like what you'd expect to find in France with less fat. Make use of your seasonal mushrooms.

Wine Suggestion: 1990 Cakebread Sauvignon Blanc.

The Sardy House

THIS NEWLY RENOVATED BRICK VICTORIAN HOUSE ON Main Street is now a hotel. But it's more than that; it's quiet, it's homey, the rooms are individually decorated, the views are magnificent, elegant dinners are served and the staff is friendly. It rather reminds me of one of those wonderful guest houses on the Island of Nantucket, filled with nostalgia and romance. The Sardy House also reminds me of Aspen as it was in the 1800's.

Originally built in 1895, it housed two families before Tom and Alice Rachel Sardy took up residence.

The parlour is very Victorian and lends itself to reading and relaxation. The dining room is beyond the parlour.

The public is invited to dine at The Sardy House for breakfast, brunch and dinner. You'll experience the splendor of eating in a country inn-type atmosphere. It's small and intimate, with fresh flowers on the tables. Classical music plays in the background. This lovely room is enhanced by bay windows that bring in light.

The breakfast menu allows you to choose from a special each morning: Brie omelettes, fruit bread, French toast made with their homemade cinnamon-raisin bread or oatmeal molasses waffles. Freshly brewed coffee adds just the right touch. Sunday brunch is relaxing. Sit outside by the pool with the paper and enjoy Sautéed Bay Scallops with roasted bell peppers and fresh greens; Baked Breast of Chicken, or Norwegian Salmon, baked on a bed of fresh spinach with fresh basil beurre-blanc sauce.

Todd Evan Olson, a creative young chef, has taken knowledge and style from each of the chefs he's trained with to produce a cuisine of his own. Olson explains, "The Sardy House is the perfect restaurant for me—it's quaint and I can give our patrons special attention to quality and detail."

Their dinners invite romance. For a special evening, The Sardy House is an experience you'll long remember.

Butternut Squash Soup with Maple Syrup

SERVES 4-6

1½ Onions, diced
1 Celery stalk, diced
1 Leek, diced
20 oz Water
16 oz Chicken stock, good quality
1 Sprig Fresh thyme
2 Butternut squashes, baked until just soft, cut in chunks
½ C Heavy cream
¼ C Maple syrup
1 t Nutmeg
Salt & pepper, to taste

Sauté the onions until golden. In a large pot, combine the sautéed onions with the next 6 ingredients and simmer for 25 minutes. Purée the mixture in a blender or Cuisinart. Add the cream, spices and maple syrup. Serve hot with homemade bread.

The kicker: this is a delicious soup. We made it several times in the fall while the squashes were plentiful. It makes a wonderful soup for Thanksgiving dinner.

Duck Confit with Marinated Grilled Duck Breasts

SERVES 6

3 Whole ducks
¾ C Kosher salt

MARINADE
½ C Oil
½ C Sugar
1½ T Cinnamon
1 t Pepper
½ t Salt

CONFIT
1 T Fresh thyme
3 Cloves garlic
2 Whole shallots
½ T Rosemary
½ t Pepper

FRESH RASPBERRY BRANDY SAUCE
1 Whole duck bone
1 C Sugar
2 Pints Fresh raspberries
2 C Red wine
6 Large basil leaves
1 T Fresh thyme
3 Whole shallots
2 Cloves garlic
¼ C Brandy
Pepper & salt
3 C Demiglaze

Have your local butcher separate the leg and breasts and skin them (save the skin). Pack the legs in kosher salt for 1½ hours. Take the breasts and place them in a bowl and marinate with the marinade ingredients for 2 hours. Meanwhile, render the fat by placing the skin in a saucepan and boil it down to liquid form. Strain the skin from the fat, then discard the skin. Keep the fat. Take the legs and wash the salt off. Place them in the duck fat in a baking dish. Totally covered with fat, add the garlic, thyme, shallots, rosemary and pepper. Bake at 225 degrees for approximately 3 to 3½ hours.

■ Grill the breasts medium rare. When the legs are cooked, pull the legs out of the duck fat and pat dry with a paper towel when you're ready to serve them. Make the sauce: brown the duck bones in the oven until dark brown. Then, put them in a medium size stock pot with the sugar and caramelize until dark brown. Add the raspberries, then the wine and the next 5 ingredients. Let reduce half-way on medium heat. Add the demiglaze and bring to a light boil. Add salt and pepper to taste. To serve: lay one leg on each plate with the sliced breast around it. Pour some sauce over the leg and garnish with fresh raspberries and basil leaves.

Wine Suggestion: Shafer, Napa 1987, Merlot.

Shlomo's

WHEN SHLOMO BEN-HAMOO MOVED TO ASPEN sixteen years ago from Israel, he saw a definite need for an authentic New York-style delicatessen. Having fallen in love with this area and knowing Aspen was the place he wanted to stay and raise a family, he set out to make this vision a reality. He went to New York City, the source, to study deli operations and to gain contacts for food distributors.

He found a perfect location in the Little Nell Hotel at the base of Aspen Mountain. Shlomo's became an immediate success. It's where the skiers meet in the mornings for a hearty breakfast before heading up the gondola for a day of skiing. The atmosphere is casual. Choose from a booth or their horseshoe counter. It has the flavor of a diner with friendly, fast-moving waitresses.

The food is exactly what you'd expect. Huge corned beef and pastrami sandwiches, reubens, kosher salami (blessed by Rabbi Goldman and Rabbi Leff) and lox and bagels are examples of Shlomo's fare. Their famous chicken soup, with an enormous matzo ball, has cured many a case of Aspen's flu. They are also known for serving the best milk shakes in town. Summer or winter, you'll find bikers and skiers sitting at the counter devouring a thick, delicious milk shake after a hard day's workout!

Shlomo, incredible as it may seem, is always there to greet you, making you feel at home (he speaks four languages) and making sure your meal was satisfactory. Tourists are always asking him to move to their hometown to open a deli. It's the ultimate compliment. Shlomo told me, "This place proves that you don't have to be Jewish to eat deli food! We get people from all walks of life and they all enjoy it here."

Shlomo, with his cheerfulness and sincere congeniality, complements Aspen. He reminds us that Aspen is still a town, and not just a glittery resort.

Shlomo's Chicken Soup with Matzo Balls

SERVES 4-6

SOUP ♥
1 Whole Chicken (2-3 lbs)
1 t Oregano
½ t Basil
½ t Sage
½ t Ground rosemary
3 Bay leaves
4 Carrots, sliced
4 Celery stalks, sliced
1 Large onion, diced

MATZO BALLS
6 Eggs
2 t Oil
2 t Salt
4 oz Club soda
1½ C Matzo meal

Add the chicken and spices to a large pot and cover with water and heat. Cut the vegetables and add to the soup. Cook the chicken for 90 minutes and remove from the soup. Pick the meat off the chicken and add back to the soup. Add salt and pepper to taste.

■ Make the matzo balls: mix all the ingredients together. Add more matzo meal if the mixture is very loose. Heat a large pot of water to a rolling boil. Dip your hands into cold water and roll the mixture into 3 inch balls. Drop the balls into boiling water and cook for 30 minutes. Occasionally, roll the balls with a spoon.

♥ *The kicker:* Shlomo's chicken soup has cured many a case of "the Aspen crud." It's like your grandmother used to make. If you remove all the skin from the chicken before making the stock and de-fat the broth, the soup (not the matzo balls) will be low in fat.

Smuggler Land Office

TIM COTTRELL IS THE PROUD OWNER OF THIS HISTORIC restaurant and bar. Its atmosphere takes you back to before the turn of the century when the Smuggler Mining Company was in operation. The actual Smuggler Mining Company office opened in July of 1879, and by 1888 was shipping 25 tons of silver ore per day to the smelter! As history goes, with the devaluation of silver, many of the mines in Aspen closed. The Smuggler Mining Company continued to operate, and in 1894, saw its success—the largest nugget of silver ever mined, 90% pure, and weighing almost one ton.

If you visited Aspen in the 70's, you'll remember the Smuggler Land Office to have been the Sub Shoppe, also owned by Cottrell. Now, after an intense restoration, the result is an elegant, three-leveled restaurant complete with stained glass, original U.S. Geographic Survey maps from the 1890's (of Smuggler and Aspen Mountains) and the two original vaults that have been beautifully repainted.

To complement this decor, Cottrell serves gourmet Cajun and Creole food. The credit goes to his chef Kenneth Botka who gained cooking experience working with great chefs around the country. The Smuggler uses their own spice mixtures. "Any O' Cajun Spice" has become so popular that they now offer it for sale; it's the perfect ingredient for the popular blackened fish recipes and in soups. Herbs grown in their garden are also used in cooking.

Their specialties include: Blackened Redfish or Salmon, Cajun Broiled Shrimp, Blackened New York Steak or Cajun Seafood Gumbo. Appetizers not to miss are: the Eggplant Boat, Creole Crab Cakes and the palate-pleasing Cajun Popcorn (wonderful on a Friday afternoon with an ice cold beer). Striving to be unique, Cottrell has the only wine bar in town. Customers can purchase vintage California and French wines by the glass, rather than ordering an entire bottle. This wine bar is run on a nitrogen-displacement system.

Cottrell has received the ultimate compliment from a Southern guest, "That's as good as my gumbo!"

Black Bean and Tasso Soup

SERVES 4-6

3 C Cooked black turtle beans in juice
4 C Chicken or duck stock
¼ C All-purpose flour
3 oz Spicy Tasso (can substitute smoked bacon or ham plus 1 t paprika, 1 t chili powder and ½ t dried thyme), finely diced
1 C Dry red wine
¼ C Tomato paste
2 T Roasted cumin seed
¼ t Cayenne pepper
1 Medium yellow onion
Salt & pepper to taste
1 T Honey
Sour cream and/or cheddar cheese for garnish

Roast the cumin seed: cook whole cumin seeds in a dry pan over high heat until the color darkens and they become aromatic. Turn into a mortar and crush or grind with a pestle. Chop and sauté the onion with the tasso (ham or bacon) until the onion is translucent. Add to the beans, stock, tomato paste, cumin and bring to a boil. Whisk the flour and red wine together until smooth. Add this to the boiling mixture to thicken. Season to taste with salt, pepper, cayenne and honey. Top with sour cream or grated cheddar cheese. Serve with warm cornbread muffins and a salad for a hearty meal.

Eggplant Boats

SERVES 4

2 Eggplants
Flour
Canola oil

BEER BATTER
1 C All-purpose flour
1 T "Any 'O Cajun"™ dry spice mix
6 oz Beer
1 Whole egg

SAUCE
6 oz Fresh sea scallops
4 oz Fresh shrimp
4 oz Crawfish meat (fresh when available), leave fat on
12 oz Heavy whipping cream
2 oz Clarified butter
2 Shallots, peeled & chopped
3 oz Cream sherry
3 T "Any 'O Cajun"™ dry spice mix
1 Bunch scallions

Add all the beer batter ingredients together and whisk. Adjust for thickness with water or flour. Peel and halve the eggplants widthwise. Carve out the insides of each half with a paring knife to form your boats. Discard the insides. Dredge the eggplants in flour, then through the beer batter and deep fry in Canola oil at 350 degrees until crispy brown. Set on paper towels and keep in a warm oven.

■ Make the sauce: sauté the scallops and shrimp in the hot clarified butter. Add the shallots and deglaze with the sherry. Add the cream and spice mix. Reduce to desired thickness, then add the crawfish last (so they do not dry out).

To assemble: place the boats on a plate and fill with the sauce. Garnish with fresh chopped scallions and serve.

The kicker: Tim Cottrell wants to stress that this recipe is definitely not low in fat but is so popular that he wanted to share it. Patrons say it's "to die for." See page 283 for information about ordering "Any 'O Cajun"™ spice.

The Steak Pit

ORIGINALLY, IN THE EARLY 60'S, THE STEAK PIT operated out of the Cooper St. Pier Building downstairs. The owners, Peter and Barbara Guy, came out from the East expecting to be in Aspen for a year and decided to stay. They say it was a combination of the feel of a small town, the mountains, the weather and more importantly, the people. "Back then, there wasn't a lot going on and there were very few restaurants."

The Steak Pit's original menu was small, offering mostly grilled steaks and beef kabobs. In 1968, they moved to the City Market Building and expanded their menu to include: Prime Rib, Teriyaki Chicken and Pork Chops, Australian Lobster Tails, Alaskan King Crab Legs and fresh fish.

They have the distinction of introducing the first salad bar on this continent. One of their waiters was from Hawaii (where the salad bar concept originated) and suggested trying it. Customers loved the idea of creating their own salads from a variety of fresh ingredients.

Thirty-three years later—and under the same ownership, the Steak Pit is still here, now in its new location at the Katie Reed Plaza.

Barbara, better known as "Mom," makes a hot fudge sauce you could die for! Many patrons become addicted to her sundaes. "Mom's" Mocha Pie and Cheese Cake are also available.

The decor is casual and the atmosphere is comfortable and relaxed. If you've ever been to The Steak Pit, you'll remember their large candle by the entrance. It was purchased at a pawn shop in Mexico City and has become quite a conversation piece—customers love it. The candle continues to grow by the year. Some things never change!

Albóndigas Soup

MEXICAN-STYLE MEATBALL SOUP

SERVES 10–12

3 Quarts regular strength beef broth
1 Large can (28 oz) crushed tomatoes, use the juice, too
1 Can (7 oz) diced green chilies
1 Large onion, chopped
1½ t Dried basil, crushed
1½ t Dried oregano, crushed
½ t Tabasco sauce, to taste
¾ C Long-grain white rice
½ C Fresh cilantro, minced
Salt & pepper

MEATBALLS
1 lb Ground lean beef
½ lb Bulk pork sausage
½ C Corn meal
¼ C Milk
1 Large egg
1 Small minced onion
1 Clove garlic, minced
½ t Dried basil, crushed

In a large pot (8 quarts or so) combine the first 7 ingredients. Bring to a boil over high heat. Add the rice, cover and simmer for 15 minutes.

■ Make the meatballs: in a large bowl, mix together the meatball ingredients until well blended. Shape them into ¾ inch balls. Add them to the soup, cover and simmer until the meatballs are not pink in the center—about 10-15 minutes longer. Stir in the cilantro and add salt and pepper to taste if necessary.

The kicker: this soup is very hearty and would be wonderful for a winter get-together. It freezes well so it can be made well in advance.

Peppermint Ice Cream

1 lb Peppermint stick candy
1 Pint milk
1 Pint heavy cream

DARK CHOCOLATE SAUCE
1 Bar (4 oz) Baker's German sweet chocolate
5 T Water
¼ C Sugar
Dash salt
1 T Butter
¼ t Vanilla

Soak the candy overnight in the milk. Whip the cream and add this before freezing. The candy sweetens, flavors and colors the cream pink! The Guys use an old wooden tub ice cream freezer (electric), but any ice cream machine should be fine. Freeze according to your machine's directions. Freeze to the consistency that you like, remove the paddle and place in your home freezer until ready to serve.

■ Make the sauce: combine the chocolate, water, sugar and salt in a saucepan. Cook and stir over low heat until the ingredients are blended and the sauce is smooth. Remove from the heat and stir in the butter and vanilla. Serve warm or chilled over the ice cream.

The kicker: this is a family favorite from the Guy family. It has a wonderful texture and a beautiful color. Sometimes Barbara is lucky enough to find giant candy canes (sticks that weigh 5¼ ounces). It makes unwrapping the small, round peppermint candies a little easier.

Syzygy

THE WORD SYZYGY (PRONOUNCED SIZ'·I·JE) IS AN astronomical term meaning the alignment of three or more heavenly bodies within a solar system that form a nearly straight line, as with the earth, sun & moon during a solar or lunar eclipse. You might think—what does that have to do with a restaurant? Owner Walt Harris wanted a name that would convey an earthly syzygy of expressive cuisine, fine service and elegant atmosphere.

The atmosphere is also romantic. Harris wanted each table to be special and intimate, so instead of one large room, he broke up the dining area with innovative "water walls" that have become quite the conversation piece. Soothing water flows down the glass which elicits the perception of rain.

Chef Alexander Kim is self-taught and loves to cook different cuisines. His Korean father and English/Irish mother were both excellent cooks who never used recipes. After twelve years working as a chef and running his own restaurant, Kim brings to Syzygy an eclectic style of cooking.

Interesting combinations of ingredients produce these appetizers: Pheasant Spring Rolls with shiitake mushrooms, fennel and napa cabbage; Caviar—3 heavenly spheres of beluga caviar in a thin crispy shell; and Red Curry Lamb.

Kim believes that presentation is as important as how the food tastes. He uses fruits and vegetables to provide visual stimulation. Everything on the plate is edible and meant to be eaten. He produces dishes that touch all of the palate senses.

Patrons' favorites include: Grilled Ahi, Rack of Lamb—roasted Colorado lamb presented with a sweet potato purée and juniper glaze and Roast Duckling served crispy with a tamarind chili glaze. Their sauces are essences of herb reductions. The true intense flavors come through without using cream—they're naturally lower in fat.

Harris has an impressive wine list and enjoys recommending wine to customers. Oftentimes, his guests are willing and open to explore—pairing the correct wine to a certain dish takes some expertise. Harris explains,

"When customers find the right match and break out of the mold, they're pleasantly surprised!"

Innovative cuisine, wonderful service and a romantic ambiance align together nicely at Syzygy.

Grilled Salmon Wrapped in Grape Leaves

CREATED BY
ALEXANDER KIM

SERVES 2

12 oz Filet of salmon
Extra virgin olive oil
Pinch salt
1 t Oregano
6 Grape leaves (found in most grocery stores)
1 Fresh lemon
Fresh cracked black pepper

Rub the salmon with olive oil and season lightly with the salt and oregano. Overlap the grape leaves in a triangle and place the filets across the small end. Fold over once, tuck in the edges and fold over again. Place the seam-side down on a hot grill. Cook for about 2 minutes. Keeping the same side down, turn 90 degrees and cook another minute or two. Turn to the other side and squeeze the lemon liberally over the fish. Cook for approximately 2 minutes more (depending on the thickness of the filet). Finish on the plates with more lemon and plenty of cracked pepper.

♥ *The kicker:* this recipe is so easy, but you'll be amazed at how tender the salmon is. All the flavor stays within the grape leaves. We grilled Vidalia onions and thinly-sliced vegetables (brushed with olive oil) along with the salmon for a wonderful meal.

Wine Suggestion: Jermann Vintage Tunina, an Italian white wine.

Steamed Mussels with Ancho Chile Crema

CREATED BY
ALEXANDER KIM

SERVES 4

2 lbs Prince Edward Island mussels (farm-raised), black mussels may be substituted, but make sure they're thoroughly cleaned
4 T Unsalted butter
⅓ C White wine
⅓ C Heavy cream

ANCHO CHILE PURÉE
4-6 Dried ancho chiles
1 t Lime juice
2 T Olive oil
Pinch salt

Make the chile purée: reconstitute the dried chiles in hot water for approximately 1 hour. When soft, drain and place all the ingredients in a blender or food processor. Run until it's smooth.
■ Place the butter, wine, cream and 3 tablespoons of the chile purée in a saucepan and heat until the butter is melted and it's all mixed together. Then, place the mussels in a pot with a tight fitting lid and pour the sauce over them, turn the heat to high and cook the mussels for 3-4 minutes. Shake the pan occasionally. Remove the lid and check. If all the mussels appear to be open, remove from heat immediately. Do not overcook.
■ Arrange the mussels over rice or angel hair pasta and divide the sauce evenly. Garnish with chopped cilantro and chives

The kicker: this dish makes a beautiful presentation. Be sure to get fresh mussels that have not opened yet; it will insure that this dish is successful.

Wine Suggestion: Spottswoode, Sauvignon Blanc.

Stilton & Watercress Salad

CREATED BY
ALEXANDER KIM

SERVES 4

6-8 oz Stilton cheese
2-3 Bunches Watercress
4 Large radicchio leaves
8 Slices (thick-cut) Sugar-cured bacon
2 oz Cabernet or red wine vinegar
4 oz Beaujolais wine
1 Asian or Chinese pear, sliced

Crumble the cheese and set aside. Wash and pick through the watercress and discard any damaged leaves and the thicker parts of the stem. Arrange the radicchio leaves at the top of the plates to form a loose cup. Fill with the watercress. Arrange the watercress so that it spills out and fills the plate. Slice the bacon crosswise into 1/16 inch strips or cubes. Sauté until almost crisp. Pour off only about 1/3 - 1/2 of the bacon drippings, add the vinegar and cook for 1 minute. Then add the wine and reduce the liquid by one third. Crumble the Stilton over the greens and ladle the warm dressing over the top. Arrange the pears around the plate.

Wine Suggestion: Etude, Pinot Noir.

Takah Sushi

THE *NEW YORK TIMES* STATES SIMPLY, "SOME OF THE BEST Japanese food between Manhattan and Malibu." Takah Sushi originated thirteen years ago and was Aspen's first Japanese restaurant. Owner Casey Coffman explains, "Japanese sushi bars and restaurants were very popular on the West Coast. Takah Sushi was the result of the feeling that Aspen needed something different. We took a chance." Locals and visitors alike are glad they did!

The restaurant is a combination of a sushi bar and a dining room that serves Japanese entrées. This appeals to non-sushi lovers.

Sushi, contrary to most people's belief, is not raw fish. Rather it is described as, "carefully prepared vinegared rice with something on top, most frequently raw, marinated or smoked fish or shellfish." California rolls, for example, contain no fish at all. The rice used is very difficult to make in order to achieve precisely the correct moisture content. It has a natural sweetness. Their sushi bar has mostly traditional items with some specials of their own. Casey boasts, "My Japanese chefs are perfectionists. Because of their techniques, our sushi bar has an exceptional level of quality." The sushi bar chefs dazzle you with their expertise and outstanding creations. It's a show worth watching with delicious results.

Sashimi, on the other hand, is something sliced and served without rice. The Japanese consider this to be one of the wonders of culinary delights. Casey told me, "The food has to be cut absolutely perfectly. If it's raw fish, it must be tender, tasty and very fresh. It must be the best!" Sashimi is always served with a garnish of daikon (a Japanese radish).

This whole concept of the Japanese style of presentation is much like their tea ceremonies—very simple and yet complex. They consider the look of the food to be just as important as how it tastes. Color, texture and design are combined to please you thoroughly.

If sushi is not to your liking, they also offer full-course Japanese dinners in the dining room. Favorites include: chicken, steak and salmon teriyaki, vegetable tempura and crispy duck.

Tanoshi Hitotokio!

Peppered Beef Sashimi

AN APPETIZER SERVING 6-8

One 4-5 lb Beef tenderloin, cleaned & trimmed

MARINADE
3 C Kikkoman soy sauce
1½ C Dry sherry
3 T Ground fresh ginger
3 T Ground fresh garlic

SEASONINGS
¼ C Table salt
1 C Szechuan peppercorns (found in Oriental markets)

GARNISH
1 Medium daikon, zested & placed in cold ice water (use a mandolin if available)
1 Large carrot, zested & mixed with daikon in water
1 Head red leaf lettuce

Take the cleaned beef and place in the marinade for 1 hour. While marinating, take the salt and peppercorns and dry roast in a sauté pan until the salt is browned (about 4-5 minutes). Take the salt mix and grind fine (a coffee grinder works well). After marinating, roll the tenderloin in the mixture. Use a grill and sear the beef until slightly black all the way around. Chill and slice into thin strips widthwise. Shingle in a circle over cleaned lettuce. Use the daikon-carrot garnish to fill in the middle. Mix the dipping sauce ingredients together. Serve the beef with the sauce.

♥ *The kicker:* this is a fabulous appetizer that can be made well ahead of time (keep the beef in the refrigerator and slice at the last minute). It's a real crowd-pleaser!

DIPPING SAUCE
1 C Lo Sodium Kikkoman soy sauce
4 Lemons, juiced
1 Bunch chives, chopped fine

Tuna Tataki

SERVES 4

1 lb Tuna or sashimi tuna
Shredded daikon (Chinese radishes)
Daikon sprouts, or other peppery sprouts

SAUCE
1 Whole lemon
5 T Rice vinegar
5 T Soy sauce
1 T Sugar or mirin (sweet sake)
Pinch Hon Dashi (optional)
½ t Grated fresh ginger
1 Pinch garlic
Scallions, chopped

Sear the tuna on the outside very quickly; seal it immediately. Stop the cooking by plunging it in cold water. Slice the tuna into ¼ - ½ inch slices. ■ Mix all the sauce ingredients together. Arrange the fish on shredded daikon, drizzle the sauce over the fish and garnish with daikon sprouts.

♥ *The kicker:* the ingredients for this dish are found in Japanese or Asian markets. This recipe is delicious and very low in fat.

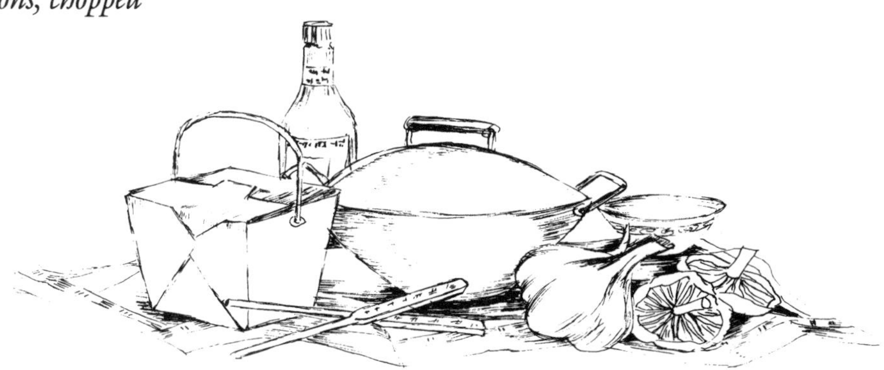

The Terrace Restaurant at The Ritz-Carlton, Aspen

THE RITZ-CARLTON, ASPEN OPENED IN DECEMBER 1992 with a traditional ribbon-cutting ceremony. Entering the hotel for the first time was like being invited into a magical Christmas scene. The gaiety and warmth immediately welcomed you. The Ritz opened in style and already has gained a reputation for being a landmark of elegance. Built with 800,000 Colorado red bricks, this luxurious year-round resort hotel was inspired by the spirit of the frontier.

Putting together a menu for The Terrace Restaurant was a challenging endeavor. Many months were spent researching cuisines that would be acceptable to their customers. Executive Chef, Xavier Salomon, who comes to the Ritz with an impressive background, describes the Terrace's cuisine as, "a mixture of California, Northern Italian and Mediterranean." Keeping in mind their customers' concern for health and fitness, they use very little cream or butter. The sauces are reductions of the juices. They rely primarily on using Colorado ingredients: farm-produced fruits, vegetables and herbs, trout, farm-raised bass, Colorado lamb and pheasant. They know that by using the best and freshest ingredients available, it takes experimenting with imaginative combinations of flavors to compose a memorable meal of gastronomic pleasure.

The Terrace Restaurant's menu changes twice a year in order to offer items indigenous to the particular season. The winter menu offers heartier cuisine—more meats and wild game specialties. Summer, with more of an emphasis on lighter foods, features an array of regional selections from pastas and risottos to their trademark dish: Oven-roasted Salmon in a Horseradish Crust. Each evening, the Chef adds three Market Selections that highlight exceptional meats or fish served with inventive sauces.

The Terrace's elegant, sophisticated dining room is decorated with refinement and a touch of class. It's enhanced with authentic European antiques. Stunning armoires display exceptional collectible treasures.

Original oil paintings of the dramatic Rocky Mountains tastefully adorn the walls. The decor complements the ultimate dining experience.

If you're a bit full after dinner but crave something sweet, stroll around their two-tiered courtyard and breathe some mountain air before choosing one of their sumptuous desserts. The soufflés, individually baked to perfection, are the Chef's signature.

Not to be ignored are breakfast and lunch; with the same attention to detail and the same care in menu-planning, these meals are anything but mundane. Banana Pecan French Toast or a Crisp Hazelnut Waffle with fresh peach compote and whipped cream will help anyone tackle the slopes of Aspen Mountain. After a long and grueling morning hike, enjoy a comforting lunch outdoors surrounded by the refreshing ambience of the Fountain Courtyard.

The Ritz's reputation worldwide for the finest food and wine coupled with outstanding service continues to prevail with the exquisite Ritz-Carlton, Aspen.

Bittersweet Chocolate Torte with Orange Ginger Chutney

AS PREPARED BY
EXECUTIVE CHEF
XAVIER SALOMON

SERVES 6

CHOCOLATE MIXTURE
1 oz Heavy cream
7 oz Dark bittersweet chocolate
1 Large egg
1 Egg yolk

SUGAR DOUGH
1¼ C Flour
8 oz Butter
⅔ C Powdered sugar
½ C Ground almonds
Pinch salt
1 Egg

Make the Orange-Ginger Chutney a day in advance. Boil the orange juice with the grated ginger and sugar. Reduce by half. Add the orange segments and chopped fresh mint. Allow to cool.

■ Make the dough: mix all the ingredients together in a mixer in the order of the recipe. Let the dough rest and then roll it out to fill 6 small tart molds or one 8 inch tart pan.

■ For the chocolate mixture: boil the cream and add the chopped chocolate until it melts. Whip the egg and the yolk. Add them to the cream/ chocolate mixture.

■ Par-bake the tarts in a 300 degree oven (until golden brown). Place the chocolate mixture in either the tarts or the tart pan and cook for 10 minutes in a 250 degree oven. Let cool to room temperature and serve with the Orange-Ginger Chutney.

The kicker: this is a fabulous dessert. The Orange-Ginger Chutney is a pleasant change from whipped cream!

ORANGE-GINGER
CHUTNEY
4 Large oranges, peeled
1 oz Fresh ginger, grated
1 Bunch fresh mint
2 C Orange juice
¼ C Granulated sugar
2 T Brown sugar

Salmon & Braised Leek Terrine with Balsamic Apple Shallot Vinaigrette

AS PREPARED BY
EXECUTIVE CHEF
XAVIER SALOMON

SERVES 8-10

TERRINE MOLD
8 oz Fresh salmon filet
10 Small leeks, using only the bottom part
1 Bunch fresh tarragon
2 oz Unflavored gelatin powder
Salt & pepper

For the terrine, line an 8 inch terrine mold with plastic film. Cut the leeks in half and rinse them well (to get any excess dirt out of the leaves). Blanch the leeks in boiling, salted water for 3 minutes, then place the leeks in iced cold water. ■ Start the terrine by sprinkling gelatin on the bottom, then line with half the leeks and season with salt and pepper. Add the tarragon and add thin slices of the salmon on top. Season with salt and pepper, then sprinkle some gelatin powder. Keep layering until the terrine mold is full. Make sure each layer has gelatin powder and seasonings. ■ Cook the terrine in a water bath in the oven at 350 degrees for about 20 minutes. Check the terrine with a thermometer. The inside should be 110 degrees. Put in the refrigerator immediately. Make the vinaigrette: combine the oil and vinegar. Add all the other ingredients together, add to the oil and vinegar and season to taste.

To serve: serve a slice of the terrine on a salad plate and pour some of the vinaigrette around it.

♥ *The kicker:* this dish is low in fat. Use less of the vinaigrette if you're watching your fat intake.

VINAIGRETTE
1½ C Extra virgin olive oil
2 T Balsamic vinegar
1 C Shallots, finely chopped
½ Apple, peeled, cored & finely diced
6 Lime segments, finely diced
3 Grapefruit segments, finely diced
4 Orange segments, finely diced
½ t Green peppercorns
1 T Tarragon, chopped
Salt & pepper

Ute City Banque

THE UTE CITY BANQUE IS A BEAUTIFULLY APPOINTED BAR and restaurant. It is named for the town of Aspen which was previously called Ute City.

This classic cut-stone building was erected in 1880 and was an operating bank from 1890-1963. Owner David Michael maintained the look with authentic teller windows and the original Victorian vault that sits behind the bar.

It's one of locals' and visitors' favorite restaurants—it has the Aspen feel. Plants, stained glass, a large oak bar, fans and windows that open to the Aspen scene all help to create a relaxed atmosphere. The bar is the hub of the downtown social scene. It's a wonderful place to meet friends and has a mix of Rugby players, locals with cowboy hats and couples dressed in their finest. They all seem to blend together and exchange conversation!

"The Ute's" menu combines items from the American West along with new cuisine. Head chef David Zumwinkle (D.Z.) serves fresh fish, steaks, lamb, veal and pasta. Old favorites include rack of lamb, herb-roasted chicken and their famous spinach and cheese casserole (served at lunch).

Owner David Michael explains, "Our food is in keeping with the energetic, rugged Rocky Mountains and the romantic history of the Days of Gold. Interests, activities and enthusiasms of every kind have a place in Aspen and in our restaurant. We want our service to be compatable with our customers' moods—knowledgeable or low-key, and always friendly." They have a well-chosen wine list to complement their hearty cuisine.

After skiing or after a concert, you'll often hear, "Meet you at The Ute." It's just that kind of place.

Madras Salad

SERVES 6

1 lb Carrots, julienne
6 Stalks celery, diced
4 Scallions, thinly sliced
½ Red bell pepper, diced
½ Green bell pepper, diced
3 T Lemon juice
2 t Worcestershire sauce
1½ C Low-fat yogurt
¼ C Mayonnaise
1½ t Madras curry powder
Salt & pepper, to taste
Lettuce (of your choice)
Grilled, sliced chicken breast
Toasted fresh coconut
Garnishes: Raisins, fresh pineapple slices, chutney

Blanch the carrots in boiling water for 2 minutes and shock in cold water. Combine with the next 10 ingredients. Serve on a bed of lettuce and top with the chicken breast and coconut. Garnish the plate beautifully and serve.

♥ *The kicker:* This makes a wonderful summer salad. It's already low- in-fat and you can use low-fat mayonnaise to lower it even more. If you're health-conscious, use range-free chicken and skin off the fatty top layer.

Wine Suggestion: Sanford, Sauvignon Blanc.

The Wienerstube Restaurant

THE WIENERSTUBE IS AN INSTITUTION IN ASPEN. IT'S one of the few restaurants from the past 30 years that's still here, and that says a lot.

Owners Gerhard Mayritsch and Helmut Schloffer were childhood friends in Austria. After chef-apprenticing for three years, they came to Aspen and worked at the famous Red Onion.

The owner of the Aspen Grove Building was so impressed by these two young Austrians and their talent for cooking that he talked them into opening their own restaurant. They opened in 1965 with eight tables and one waitress!

The name, Wienerstube, means "a Viennese living room." They wanted to create a homey European atmosphere. Today, after a few remodels and a move to the old Post Office Building, the Wienerstube remains a place to come and feel at home. Friendly waitresses in colorful dirndls, pine furniture, International flags and stained glass set a convivial mood. One of the unusual features of the "Stube" is the abundance of lush and beautiful plants. Helmut has used his "green thumb" to make the dining area feel like a garden even on the snowiest of days.

The "Stube" serves breakfast and lunch. They began with a simple menu and have expanded it many times. They pride themselves on using only the freshest ingredients. Everything is homemade. They have followed the trend of the 90's and offer many lower-fat items.

Popular at breakfast are the Oat Bran Pancakes, the German Apple Pancake and Huevos Rancheros. Many customers appreciate being able to choose the "Stube's" Egg Substitute, which consists of 99% egg whites and has no cholesterol. For the health-conscious, they're great scrambled or in omelettes.

The lunch menu is extensive but their daily specials allow the chefs to create and experiment. Ever-popular is the Hawaiian Mahi Mahi—a filet seasoned and grilled with olive oil and topped with a light citrus/caper sauce served with rice pilaf, fresh fruit skewers and fresh bread. For a wonderful low-fat alternative, try their Grain Salad Plate—grains from the regions of Pakistan, India, Turkey and Mexico. It's very close to cholesterol-free. On any given day you might find: Hungarian Veal Stew, Liver & Onions, Chinese Lobster Dumplings (with a light ginger/garlic sauce) or Chicken Fajitas.

You simply can't go into the Wienerstube without spotting their large glass pastry case filled with luscious and beautifully decorated desserts. There are always many European favorites like Black Forest Cake, Linzer Torte, Sacher Torte and Fürst Pückler (almond cake with pistachio raspberry nougat filling and chocolate icing). Few can resist; it's an impressive selection.

If you're dining alone, you've come to the right restaurant. The "Stube" has a "Stammtisch" which is a "local's table" where regular customers sit, eat and pontificate on a wide range of topics. You'll find ski instructors, patrolmen, lawyers, architects, realtors and others in (oftentimes) very heated discussions and arguments. It's one of the things that makes the "Stube" what it is.

Summer is always welcome in Aspen after a long winter. The "Stube" offers one of the nicest outside patios in town, surrounded by Helmut's splendid selection of plants and flowers.

Gerhard reflected on the past years and told me, "It's been a lot of hard work and we've seen the town go through a lot of changes, but owning the "Stube" has been very entertaining and has exposed us to a lot of wonderful people we wouldn't have otherwise met."

Chicken Vegetable Soup

SERVES 4-8

1 Large fresh whole chicken, 1-1½ lbs
3 Bay leaves
Crushed peppercorns
1 T Dry Italian seasoning (or use fresh herbs finely chopped: parsley, thyme, basil, oregano, marjoram & a sprig of rosemary)
1 Clove of garlic, crushed
1 C Scallions, diced (use the green part, too)
2 C Celery, diced to ¼ inch chunks
2 C Carrots, diced to ¼ inch chunks
Salt to taste

Use a large four-quart stock pot and fill it half full with cold water. Wash the chicken, place it in the water and under moderately high heat, bring it to a slow rolling boil. Add the crushed peppercorns and bay leaves and simmer for at least one hour until the chicken is done. Remove the chicken from the broth and let cool. Strain the stock through a strainer with a cheesecloth over it. Debone and skin the chicken, dice the meat into ½ inch cubes and set aside in the refrigerator. Continue to simmer the strained broth down to about a quart and a half of liquid. Then add the diced scallions, celery, carrots, fresh herbs and other spices and simmer until the vegetables are done but still firm. Add the diced chicken meat and adjust the seasonings.

♥ *The kicker:* this is one of Jill St. John and Robert Wagner's favorite soups! The soup can be made well ahead of time. Serve it piping hot with fresh crisp French or Austrian farmer's rye bread. If you remove the skin from the chicken before making the stock and de-fat the broth, this will be a low-fat soup.

Salzburger Nockerl

SERVES 4-6

2 Egg yolks
1 t Vanilla extract
½ t Grated lemon peel
1 T Flour or cornstarch
4 Egg whites
Pinch salt
2 T Sugar
Confectioners' sugar

Preheat your oven to 350 degrees. In a medium-sized mixing bowl, break the egg yolks with a wire whisk and stir in the lemon peel and vanilla extract. In another mixing bowl, using a clean wire whisk, rotary or electric beater, beat the egg whites with a pinch of salt until half firm. Add the sugar slowly and beat until the whites form a stiff, firm peak. Over-beating this meringue-type mixture will result in breaking the tiny air bubbles, resulting in failure to rise.

■ In a folding motion with a rubber spatula, fold the yolk mixture into the egg whites using under-cutting motion while turning the bowl with the other hand. Half-way through this process, sift or sprinkle the flour into the batter. Don't over-fold. In individual, fire-proof serving dishes or one large oblong 8 x 12 inch ceramic or decorative glass serving dish, brush with butter on the sides and bottom. Using a rubber spatula, make one mound of the mixture in the individual dishes. If you're using the large serving dish, make three large mounds of the mixture in the dish. Bake in the middle of the oven about 10 minutes for individual servings and about 15 minutes for the large serving until lightly brown but still soft on the inside. Sprinkle with confectioners' sugar and serve immediately. You may also serve this with a hot vanilla sauce or freshly made hot raspberry sauce.

The kicker: this soufflé of Salzburg is temperamental, like a prima donna, so take extra care in handling the ingredients. The baking and serving procedure should be followed explicitly.

Wiener Schnitzel (Breaded Veal Cutlets)

SERVES 4-8

2 lbs Leg of veal, cut into slices, ¼ inch thick (can substitute boneless turkey breast slices or skinless chicken breast slices)
Salt & freshly ground pepper
2 Eggs, beaten
½ C Flour, enough to coat the Schnitzel thoroughly on both sides
2 C Bread crumbs, homemade with dry French bread
1½ C Vegetable shortening
1 Lemon

Prepare the slices of veal by lightly pounding them with a meat mallet, or simply marinate them in a squeeze of fresh lemon juice for about an hour in the refrigerator to tenderize the meat. When marinated, pat them dry, then sprinkle them with salt and pepper. Dip them in flour and shake off the excess, then dip them in the beaten eggs and lay them flat in bread crumbs. Cover them well with more bread crumbs and press down lightly. Gently shake off any excess. You may prepare this ahead of time and refrigerate for no longer than 30 minutes.

■ Heat the shortening in an iron, 12 inch skillet until a light haze forms over it. Add the cutlets so they lay flat and do not crowd each other. Cook over medium heat, turning gently with tongs until they are crisp and golden brown. If you use thicker pieces or turkey or chicken, lower the heat so they cook without burning. Serve at once with lemon wedges, German potato salad and Lingonberry relish.

Wine Suggestion: Piesporter.

PART II

Snowmass Restaurants

Snowmass originated as a premier ski resort in 1967 and since then has developed its own identity. Skiers come to Snowmass from around the globe. Besides incredible skiing, they expect to dine in the very best restaurants. Snowmass offers a wide range of cuisines from French to Italian to American to Mexican. The Snowmass chefs invite you to enjoy and experiment with their most favorite recipes.

The Brothers' Grille

WITHIN THE LUXURIOUS COMPLEX OF THE SILVERTREE Hotel in Snowmass lives the Brothers' Grille—an all-American eatery right on the slopes.

Executive chef and manager Patrick Lowe turns out American grilled food: lots of fresh fish, Black Angus beef, elk, caribou and venison. Lowe's culinary background began at the young age of eight when he learned to cook from his mother, who was born and raised in the West Indies. But his father's Texan influence also prevailed, thus resulting in a wonderful combination of Caribbean and Southwestern cuisine.

Lowe explains, "My sauces are lighter and healthier; I use primarily fresh fruits and fresh herbs." An example is his papaya sauce with cilantro and coriander—wonderful served with mesquite grilled steak. He marinates often which enhances the flavors.

The exhibition grill, the mainstay of the Brothers' Grille, allows much experimentation with fantastic results. They grill squash, peppers, tomatoes and avocados, to name a few. The grilled vegetables are used in salsas and sauces.

They also compose their own herb and garlic-infused oils and vinegars which are always on hand to complement sauces.

Most popular is their grilled rack of lamb with a fresh rosemary and Merlot glaze. Fish lovers will enjoy the plantain-crusted grouper with a coconut buerre blanc served with a fresh papaya salsa.

Besides three different Eggs Benedict dishes, a natural foods buffet is featured for breakfast. Choose from homemade müesli and granola, fresh fruits and juices and breakfast breads and muffins. Serving a large hotel with many customers' tastes, the Brothers' Grille has something for everyone, including a full children's menu with alphabet soup and mouse-shaped pancakes.

Lunch satisfies hungry skiers with hearty deli sandwiches, soups, chiles and gumbo. But don't miss après-ski with live entertainment and complimentary buffalo wings with their secret sauce.

The Conservatory Café, a much smaller operation in the Hotel, satisfies Lowe's desire to create gourmet food. An International Chefs' Table changes nightly and features the exotic foods from Japan, Russia, Greece and Italy, complemented by an impressive wine selection.

Hotel owner Bill Burwell invites the public to dine at either the Brothers' Grille or the Conservatory Café and sample Lowe's superb and creative cuisine.

Southwestern Crab Cakes

SERVES 6-8

2 lbs Snow-crab meat, frozen in a can, lump crab meat
½ C White onion, chopped
1 C Red & green bell peppers, diced
1 T Cilantro, chopped
1 T Basil, chopped
½ lb Scallops
2 Egg whites
¼ C Cream
1 T Chef Paul Prudhomme's Seafood Cajun Magic

SAUCE
1 C Cream
¼ C Tomato, chopped
¼ C Green onion, chopped
¼ C White wine
1 t Cajun Magic

Thaw the crab meat. Then, drain the crab meat in a colander until dry. Combine the crab meat, onion, bell peppers, cilantro and Cajun Magic and mix with your hands. Combine the scallops, egg whites and cream in a food processor and whip into a mousse.

■ Blend all the ingredients together and form into patties and fry on each side until golden brown.

■ Combine the sauce ingredients in a saucepan and simmer until thick. Serve the sauce on the side with the crab cakes.

White Bean & Chicken Chili

Combine all the ingredients in a pot, bring to a boil and simmer for one hour, stirring often. Serve in bowls and top with sour cream and cheddar cheese.

SERVES 6-8

4 C Green chilies, diced
6 C Cooked Northern beans
2 lbs Boneless chicken breast, cooked & chopped
1 Large yellow onion, diced
¼ C Cumin
½ Gallon good quality chicken stock
½ C Cilantro, chopped
1 t Salt
1 t Pepper
½ C Cream

Chez Grandmère

A DREAM COME TRUE.

That's what Chez Grandmère was to Ruth and Bob Kevan. It all began when they retired and moved from Washington D.C. to Snowmass in 1972, with absolutely no experience in the food business. But, they had a strong vision.

After owning and operating The Stew Pot, The Wineskin, The Upstairs Place and The Pepper Mill, Chez Grandmère was born. It first opened on the Snowmass Mall. Two years later, the Kevans had an opportunity to restore the old, small Victorian-style Hoagland ranch farmhouse by the Snowmass Center. The old house is constructed of logs covered with narrow siding, which was the style in those days. The Kevans left a small section of the logs exposed so that their visitors can see the original method of construction. The farmhouse was built sometime between 1903 and 1905.

An addition was built to accommodate seven tables. Their dining format is a prix fixe, four-course dinner menu with only one seating each evening. It's a concept unique to any restaurant in Aspen or Snowmass.

Guests love the freedom of choosing their own arrival time, between the hours of six and nine o'clock. This ensures a leisurely and relaxed dining experience with plenty of time for that extra cup of coffee and liqueurs.

In 1989, the Kevans sold their much-loved restaurant to Chez Grandmère's Executive Chef Michel Poumay, knowing that he would carry on their legacy. Poumay, who was professionally trained in Belgium, was recently named one of the best chefs in Belgium, a most coveted award. He began his career in Aspen in 1972 as the chef at the Aspen Meadows.

Today, you'll find Poumay in Chez Grandmère's quaint and well-utilized kitchen. Constantly in motion, he does everything from baking the delicious homebaked bread to creating the desserts—an artist at his canvas!

Chez Grandmère's four-course dinner includes a choice of three appetizers; a fresh green salad with a homemade dressing which changes on a regular basis; fresh baked French bread; a choice among four entrées, always a fresh meat, a fowl and fresh fish served with three fresh vegetables; and a wide selection from a Continental-style dessert cart.

Chez Grandmère's patrons love Poumay's Scallop Mousse Mille Feuilles, a Napoleon-style appetizer. Their roasted rack of lamb with a mustard and tarragon crust on top, served with a rosemary sauce, is a favorite.

Poumay tells me, "Ninety-five per cent of my clientele come back year after year. They love the fact that they can truly relax and enjoy their meal for the entire evening. Not to be rushed, especially in a ski town, is a wonderful experience."

Grilled Maine Lobster with Café de Paris Butter

SERVES 1 WITH LOTS OF BUTTER LEFT OVER FOR OTHER USES

1½ lb Lobster
Olive oil
Chopped Chervil

CAFÉ DE PARIS BUTTER
1 lb Butter, soft when ready to use
1 oz Catsup
½ oz Prepared hot mustard
½ oz Capers
2 oz Shallots, roughly chopped
1 oz Parsley, roughly chopped
1 oz Chives
½ t Marjoram, dried
½ t Dill weed, dried
½ t Thyme, dried
10 Tarragon leaves
Pinch rosemary
1 Clove garlic
4 Anchovy filets
1 t Cognac
1 t Madeira
½ t Worcestershire sauce
½ t Paprika
1 t Curry powder
4 Grains black peppercorns
Juice of 1 lemon
Zest of ½ lemon
Zest of ½ orange
¼ t Salt

Combine the Café de Paris Butter ingredients (except the butter) into a bowl and let it stand in a warm place for 24 hours. Grind into a purée and fold into the soft butter.

■ Cut the lobster in half, lengthwise. Brush the meat with olive oil and sear, meat side down, on a hot grill. Remove and place into a 400 degree oven for 5 minutes. Spread the Café de Paris Butter from head to tail. Crack the claws and spread the butter in the claws. Bake for 10 minutes at 400 degrees. Remove and sprinkle with chopped chervil and serve immediately.

♥ *Lower fat suggestion:* To make a wonderful low-fat salad dressing using the Café de Paris spice base: combine all the Café de Paris ingredients except the butter and whisk in 3 T lime juice, 2 t sugar, 1½ T olive oil and 2 C no-fat yogurt.

Wine Suggestion: Newton, "Unfiltered" Chardonnay.

Four Corners Grill

BRUSH CREEK VALLEY'S FOUR LARGEST RANCHES WERE known in the early 1900's for their fields of vegetables, wheat and corn; their healthy cattle; their abundant trout streams and their wild game. Named for the spot where these four prosperous ranches meet, The Four Corners Grill is an elegant restaurant within the luxurious Snowmass Lodge & Club.

Not forgetting their heritage, the Four Corners Grill serves the "comfort" foods of Snowmass' early settlers. Executive Chef Scott Philip has researched these foods and developed his own culinary style. His Contemporary Ranchland Cooking blends indigenous ingredients with traditional cooking techniques.

Savory appetizers include: Smoked Duck and Wild Mushroom Turnover with sun-dried cranberry sauce, Asparagus Salad and Smoked Mountain Trout on griddled jicama cakes with curried apple/onion compote.

Innovative entrées reflect Philip's style: Herb Crusted Mountain Bass with Seafood Risotto and Lobster Sauce, Maple Glazed Porkloin on Oatcakes and Acorn Squash and Grilled Sirloin topped with Hunter's Sauce. In addition, guests with special dietary needs can order items created with lower sodium, fat and cholesterol.

Overlooking the golf course, Mount Daly and the surrounding mountains, the Four Corners Grill serves breakfast, lunch and dinner to guests, club members and the general public.

Blanketed by snow in the winter, the lush golf course is transposed into a cross-country skiers' paradise. A real treat after a good workout is to enjoy a hearty lunch at the Four Corners Grill.

Peach Fritters with Almond Sauce

SERVES 6

FRITTERS
1 lb Firm peaches, blanched, peeled, pitted & diced
3 Eggs
2 oz Milk
1½ C All-purpose flour
½ C Blanched almonds, finely ground
1½ t Baking powder
1 T Sugar
¼ t Salt
1 t Cinnamon

ALMOND SAUCE
1 Quart Heavy cream
12 Egg yolks
8 oz Sugar
2 oz Amaretto
¼ t Almond extract

Mix all the dry, fritter ingredients together in a mixing bowl. Whip the eggs and milk together, then add to dry ingredients and mix at a low speed for 2 minutes and at a medium speed for 2 minutes. Fold in the peaches that have been drained. With a 1/8 - 1/4 ounce scoop, place the fritter batter in a deep fryer with 3 inches of olive oil at 350 degrees until golden brown. Using a candy thermometer is helpful.

■ Make the almond sauce: whip the egg yolks and sugar until frothy. Bring the cream to a boil slowly and temper the egg mixture into the cream, cooking until a sauce consistency is achieved. Remove from the heat and add Amaretto and almond extract to taste.

The kicker: we served these delicious fritters at a recipe tasting. It makes quite a bit of sauce, but when the fritters are gone (in seconds), the sauce would be wonderful over fruit.

Roast Cumin Seed Chicken in Paper Bread

AN APPETIZER SERVING 6 PEOPLE

10 oz Boneless chicken breast, seasoned, charbroiled, chilled and diced small
1 Large yam, boiled and pressed through a sieve
3 T Onion, diced small
2 T Red pepper, diced small
2 T Green pepper, diced small
2 t Cumin seed, roasted and freshly ground
1 t Curry
¼ t Ground red pepper
Salt and freshly ground pepper to taste
1 Package filo dough
3 oz Olive oil

Preheat your oven to 400 degrees. In a skillet, sauté the onion and peppers until tender, then cool. Place the cooked and diced chicken, yam purée, pepper mix and spices in a mixing bowl and combine. Lay out the filo dough one sheet at a time, brushing each one with olive oil until four layers thick. Cut the sheet lengthwise in half, then strips about two inches wide from top to bottom. Place about one ounce of the chicken mix at the bottom of each strip, folding them into triangles, making sure all the edges are sealed. Arrange on a sheet pan and bake until golden brown. Serve hot.

♥ *The kicker:* This appetizer is already fairly low in fat, using oil instead of butter. To lower it even more, mix 1 large egg white with 2 tablespoons of extra virgin olive oil to spread on the filo sheets.

il Poggio

THE LITERAL TRANSLATION MEANS "LITTLE MOUNTAIN top." il Poggio is also a term used by vintners to describe the upper terrace of a vineyard. Since Snowmass is terraced like many towns in Italy, il Poggio seemed to capture the spirit of this Italian Caffē and Ristorante.

Jack Schuss, the first mayor of Snowmass, owned the restaurant upon conception. For a period of time, the current owners Christopher Blachly and Michael Gillenwater both worked at Charlemagne in Aspen. Each gaining experience independently, they came together once again when the opportunity presented itself to own and operate il Poggio in the spring of 1990. These two energetic young men complement each other well—Blachly is the chef and Gillenwater handles everything else.

il Poggio specializes in the rustic, traditional style of food from the small towns of Italy. They serve simple foods made with the best-quality ingredients that enhance and delight their devotees. For example, Blachly takes half a chicken, marinates it in garlic, olive oil, and herbs, then finishes it off on the grill. Something simple turns into something outstanding. They grow fresh herbs in the summer and have them flown in daily during the winter months.

The pastas are homemade and they use three varieties of olive oil—only the best to ensure flavorful results. Patrons love dipping il Poggio's delicious homemade breads into extra virgin olive oil as a starter. Since they make all their dishes "to order," they can eliminate or reduce fats and oils for customers on special diets.

Another staple food from Italy is polenta. il Poggio prepares it traditionally in a loaf pan and then onto the grill for a wonderful, satisfying accompaniment. They also serve Broschetta—a crusted bread with tomatoes, olive oil, basil, garlic and lemon juice. The key to duplicating it at home is to use all fresh ingredients.

Americans love pizza. il Poggio makes their pizza with a thin crust and bakes them in a traditional wood-burning, high temperature brick oven.

Customers who've been to Italy appreciate its authenticity. The simple secret, once again, is using the highest quality ingredients.

il Poggio has two entirely different dining areas available with somewhat different menus. The Caffè is more casual and faster-paced. It's a great spot for families. The Ristorante offers a more elegant, leisurely dining experience complete with tablecloths and opera music.

The wine list consists of Italian and California wines. Gillenwater explains, "The joy of Italian wines is that you can get a fantastic bottle for under $20.00." If you're willing to experiment, Gillenwater will be more than happy to suggest an Italian wine to complement whatever dish you choose.

Self-indulge with an Italian espresso and a piece of their sinful Tira Misu for dessert. You'll not be disappointed.

Before an outdoor evening concert in the summer or after an exhilarating day on the slopes, il Poggio, with its authentic Italian cuisine and friendly atmosphere, is where you'll want to dine more than just once.

Caponata

4 C Eggplant, diced ½ inch
Olive oil
2 C Red onion, diced ½ inch
¼ C Celery, finely diced
½ C Black olives, sliced
¼ C Green olives, sliced
⅓ C Raisins, cover with balsamic vinegar and soak overnight
2 t Capers
2 Anchovies, finely chopped
½ t Chili flakes
1 t Garlic
2 T Fresh basil, chopped
½ C Ground pear tomatoes
Salt & pepper

Lightly salt the eggplant and press it overnight in a colander or perforated pan; this removes the bitter juice. Sauté small batches of the eggplant (just enough to cover the bottom of the pan) in olive oil until soft and golden. Remove to a strainer and allow the excess oil to drain. Sauté the onions and celery until cooked, but not soft. ■ Add the garlic and anchovies and sauté briefly. Add the remaining ingredients and simmer for 2 minutes. Add the eggplant again, stir well, remove from the heat and refrigerate overnight. This relish is great on grilled bread that has been brushed with extra virgin olive oil and garlic. Some find it highly addictive!

The kicker: this was a hit at our recipe-testing party. We served it as an appetizer. Because of the various stages of prep work, allow 3 days before you can enjoy this delicious relish.

Tira Misu

SERVES 8

500 gram Tub of mascarpone, Italian cream cheese found in specialty stores, expect it to be expensive
1 C Heavy cream
¼ C Sugar
½ T Vanilla extract
½ -1 C Espresso
¼ C Dark rum
½ C Chopped bittersweet chocolate
1½ Packages "Savoiardi" lady fingers, enough to cover a 6 x 10 x 4 inch pan twice, found at some grocery stores (Clark's in Aspen) or at specialty stores

Combine the first 4 ingredients in a mixing bowl; whip by hand or with an electric mixer on high until stiff. Do not over-mix or it will become grainy.

■ Place a layer of lady fingers in the bottom of the pan. Sprinkle with half the espresso and half the rum. Spread half of the mascarpone mixture evenly over the lady fingers. Cover with chopped chocolate.

■ Place a second layer of lady fingers and sprinkle the remaining espresso and rum. Spread the remaining mascarpone mixture, cover and refrigerate overnight. Dust the top with cocoa powder or shaven chocolate. Cut and carefully remove with a small spatula.

The kicker: this was a very easy dessert to make. It's very rich and delicious, a small piece goes a long way!

La Piñata

A NEW MENU; A NEW LOOK. OWNERS DAN KLOSTER AND Bill Schneider were so excited about recently changing La Piñata's menu that they were inspired to do a complete renovation. The result is a warm fiesta atmosphere with three enormous fireplaces.

They've added Santa Fe-style cuisine. Many seafood items are featured; their focus nowadays is on healthier, less fattening dishes. They fry as little as possible and use only canola and extra virgin olive oil.

Kloster told me, "I've traveled Mexico for 10 years and I've eaten more Northern Mexican food than most Mexicans! I've also traveled in Europe and eaten at the top ten restaurants in the world. I know what I like."

Kloster credits his chef Rich Backe, who, although trained in the French classics, is very excited about cooking Southwestern and California cuisine. Backe still uses French preparation but incorporates Southwestern ingredients. White wine and homemade stocks are the basis for most of their sauces.

Kloster explains, "We make everything from scratch using fresh herbs and we smoke our fish and meats with hickory wood to add an incredible amount of flavor."

Since Kloster and Backe were on low-fat, low-cholesterol diets, they sought out the "Dine to Your Heart's Delight" program. "We send them our recipes, they test them and report back to us if they meet approval for being heart-healthy. We're proud to serve nine of their approved dishes on our menu." This program is endorsed by the American Heart Association.

Smoked seafood enchiladas, chicken fajitas, ahi fajitas and lobster ravioli are a few of the favorites that keep patrons coming back. Meat lovers appreciate their Steak Empenadas—Southwestern Beef Wellington with a luscious morel sauce. Appetizers vary from grilled oysters on blue corn cakes to baked Brie with a chili cranberry chutney to steamed artichokes with a red bell pepper garlic dip. These dishes are more complex yet satisfying.

Mexican restaurants are typically "fun" places and La Piñata is no exception. The white oak bar is a great place to hang out and enjoy a frosty margarita. Locals and visitors flock to their sunny deck for après-ski—never a dull time.

Kloster pays his restaurant the supreme compliment, "If I didn't own the place, I'd be there all the time."

Ahi Fajitas

SERVES 4

FAJITAS

2 lbs Ahi (yellow fin tuna), cut into ½ inch strips
3 Oranges, juiced
½ Lime, juiced
1 Sprig fresh tarragon, chopped course
1 T Cilantro, chopped
2 T Fresh garlic, puréed
½ Red pepper, julienne ½ inch thick
½ Yellow pepper, julienne ½ inch thick
½ Medium red onion, julienne ½ inch thick
½ Yellow onion, julienne ½ inch thick
8 Flour tortillas
2 T Canola or olive oil
Optional: Guacamole, sour cream, fresh salsa

Place first 10 fajita ingredients in a large mixing bowl and toss lightly from time to time. Marinate for at least 4 hours, refrigerated. Heat a large skillet to "smoking hot," add the oil and cook until the fish and vegetables are cooked but still tender, approximately 4-5 minutes.

■ Make the Melon Salsa by mixing all the ingredients together.

■ Serve the ahi-vegetable mix in warmed tortillas with the optional condiments and the Melon Salsa.

♥ *The kicker:* this is a wonderful recipe. It's low-in-fat, health hearty and approved by the "Dine to Your Heart's Delight" program as long as you limit each serving to 1 tablespoon of guacamole and omit the sour cream. Serve it with the Melon Salsa and some healthy brown rice.

Wine Suggestion: Fischer, Chardonnay.

MELON SALSA

½ Cantaloupe, ¼ inch dice
1 Ripe tomato, ¼ inch dice
½ Red onion, diced fine
½ Red pepper, diced fine
1 Jalapeño pepper (or less), minced
½ Lime, juiced
1 Orange, juiced
1 Sprig tarragon, chopped

La Piñata's Carne Asada

SERVES 4

Eight 3-4 oz Tenderloin filets, trimmed of any fat
20 Sun-dried tomatoes, julienne very small

TOMATILLA SALSA
¾ C Green chiles, fresh/frozen, diced
½ C Fresh tomatillas
½ Onion, chopped
1 Bunch cilantro, chopped
4 oz Beer
1 Garlic clove, minced (not out of a jar)
Salt & pepper

Make the tomatilla salsa: purée all the ingredients in a blender. Then, simmer them for 5 minutes. Add the sun-dried tomatoes into the salsa (you can poach the sun-dried tomatoes in white wine if you prefer first). Grill the tenderloin (to your liking) and slice thinly. Place the meat in warmed tortillas with the salsa and roll up. Serve with your choice of condiments (shredded lettuce, guacamole, sour cream, etc.) and rice. You can also serve with the Melon Salsa (see page 157).

♥ *The kicker:* This dish is approved by the "Dine to Your Heart's Delight" program as long as you limit the meat to 6-7 ounces per serving, omit the sour cream and limit each serving to 1 tablespoon of guacamole and 3 ounces of rice. It's great with an ice cold Mexican beer.

The Stew Pot

FROM THE MOMENT YOU WALK IN THE DOOR OF THE STEW Pot restaurant, you immediately feel at home. Its casual, relaxed atmosphere is complemented by the savory aromas coming from the kitchen. It's no wonder that when visitors arrive in Snowmass, the first thing they want to do is go to this tiny eatery on the mall for a home-cooked meal.

Originally owned by Bob and Ruth Kevan, the basic concept remains—to appeal to skiers' hearty appetites. James "Rob" Robinson has owned and operated The Stew Pot for 19 years and has fed hungry skiers, hikers, rafters and balloonists in a style befitting to their athletic endeavors.

They serve two homemade soups and two-three stews each day. Rob explains, "Our most popular soups are New England Clam Chowder and Tomato Soup topped with grated cheese. Our Belgium beef stew, in beer gravy sauce with mushrooms and potatoes, is also a favorite." Rob is very proud of his head chef and his innovative cooking skills. Rob still oversees the day-to-day operations.

Their honey wheat bread is a constant source of enjoyment to their patrons. They bake bread twice daily and the divine sniffs elicit praise from passersby and delight customers already seated.

The winter menu now includes a variety of fresh salads and sandwiches, and the summer menu offers a lovely fresh fruit plate that's refreshing on a hot day.

To satisfy the constant flow of people demanding their ice cream, Rob consented and built a take-out window. After a long winter, locals and visitors enjoy dining on their large outdoor patio, surrounded by flowers.

Cajun Stew

SERVES 6-8

2 lb Lean stew beef
1 lb Italian sausage
1 T Crushed garlic
½ C Flour
3 Ribs celery, chopped large
4 Carrots, chopped small
½ t Pepper
½ t Cayenne
1 Dash Worcestershire
1 Green pepper, diced
1 Red pepper, diced
½ Chicken, de-boned, cut into chunks
16 oz Can kidney beans
16 oz Diced tomatoes, canned or fresh

Brown the beef and sausage with the garlic. Add the next 6 ingredients and add water to cover. Cook for 2 hours at a simmer. Add the peppers and the chicken and cook for another ½ hour. Add the beans and tomatoes. Serve over your choice of rice.

The kicker: this is a spicy, hearty stew that would be wonderful served on a winter's evening with a loaf of bread and a salad.

Wine Suggestion: Raymond, Cabernet Sauvignon.

Fresh Spinach and Strawberry Salad

SERVES 8

½ lb Fresh spinach, torn into bite-size pieces
1 pint Strawberries, hulled, rinsed, cut in half
Bleu cheese

DRESSING
1 T Onion, chopped
¼ C Cider vinegar
¼ C Vegetable oil
¼ C Honey
Dash Worcestershire
2 T Sesame seeds
2 T Poppy seeds

Combine the dressing ingredients in a blender. Add the spinach and strawberries in a large salad bowl and toss with the dressing. Serve with crumbled blue cheese on the side.

♥ *The kicker:* To make the recipe lower in fat, use a small amount of bleu cheese and dressing. This delicious salad was enjoyed at our recipe tasting.

PART III

Mountain Restaurants

We are fortunate to be surrounded by four of the best ski mountains in the world: Aspen Mountain, Aspen Highlands, Tiehack and Snowmass. Known for a variety of terrain and incredible views, our ski mountains offer vast possibilities. Skiers possess hearty appetites and appreciate a satisfying and delicious meal. You'll not be disappointed with our mountain restaurants; each one has a unique charm of its own. The recipes in this section are indicative of the pride and commitment of the restaurant owners.

The Avalanche Ranch

IMAGINE THE PERFECT GETAWAY: A ROMANTIC COUNTRY inn with the most spectacular mountain views surrounded by blooming apple trees in the spring and blanketed by snow in the winter.

Avalanche Ranch is only 45 minutes away from the Aspen-Snowmass area. You can't miss their bright red 1913 ranch house as you travel Route 133 toward the quaint and historic town of Redstone.

Owners Jim and Sharon Mollica found a little piece of heaven when they purchased and renovated this 45-acre ranch. Guests who stay in the main house will never forget it. Upstairs are four rooms, each uniquely decorated by Sharon who truly has a special touch. Fourteen rustic, but charming, cabins accommodate families or groups of friends.

The wonderful aroma of freshly-brewed coffee welcomes you in the morning. Whether it be a day of cross-country skiing in the winter, hiking in the summer, or simply curling up with a good book by the fireplace, guests love their hearty and delicious breakfasts. Highly addictive homemade granola, muffins, fresh fruit, coffeecakes, cinnamon rolls and fruit-filled pancakes are immensely satisfying. The perfect spot to enjoy breakfast is in their sunshiny, antique-filled dining area that invites conversation and relaxation.

Avalanche Ranch is the ideal spot for weddings, family reunions and business conferences. They will cater breakfast, lunch and dinner to these groups. Sharon told me, "Jim and I eat very healthy foods and I like to pass this way of eating on to my guests, although we accommodate all requests. My staff and I love to experiment. Guests are often delighted and surprised that a meal is low-fat and yet incredibly delicious."

The Mollicas welcome you for whatever reason you decide to choose their wonderful ranch. They mean it when they say, "The ornaments of our house are the friends who frequent it."

Avalanche Griddle Cakes

MAKES 14 MEDIUM-SIZED CAKES

1 C Whole wheat flour
1½ C Rolled oats
½ C Unbleached flour
½ C Cornmeal
¼ C Oat bran
1 T Baking powder
1 t Salt
¼ - ½ C Sunflower seeds
2 Large eggs
2¼ C Low-fat Milk
¼ C Honey
¼ C Oil

Combine the dry ingredients, including the sunflower seeds, in a large bowl. Toss to mix. In a separate bowl, beat the eggs lightly, then blend in the remaining liquids.

■ Make a well in the dry ingredients and add the liquids all at once. Blend to mix with a few strokes. Let this mixture sit for 10 minutes. Then spray a medium-hot griddle with a no-cholesterol, non-stick cooking spray and cook.

■ The surface of these pancakes will show fewer air bubbles than normal. Serve with chopped walnuts, sautéed fruit and warm Vermont maple syrup.

Note: "At Avalanche Ranch, we serve these griddle cakes with our own sautéed apples from our orchard. They always taste best in our dining room, overlooking the Avalanche Ranch garden, apple orchard and watching the animals. Enjoy!"

♥ *The kicker:* These griddle cakes were delicious—-healthy and hearty, but not heavy. Surprisingly light, we served them with applesauce for a wonderful breakfast.

Blueberry Corn Bran Muffins

MAKES 9 MUFFINS

1 C White flour
1 C Corn bran, oat bran or wheat bran
½ C Sugar
1 T Baking powder
1 C Skim milk
¼ C Corn or canola oil
2 Egg whites plus 1 egg
¾ C Frozen blueberries

Mix the dry ingredients together. Then mix the wet ingredients. Add them together and do not beat. Bake in a preheated 400 degree oven for 15-20 minutes (ovens vary).

♥ *The kicker:* Sharon provided me with the nutritional value for these muffins: protein, 6 grams; fat, 9 grams; carbohydrates, 35 grams; fiber, 3 grams; sodium, 154 mg; cholesterol, .5 mg; calories, 221. These muffins are yummy and very light.

Bonnie's

THE DECK OF BONNIE'S ON A SUNNY WARM DAY, FILLED with skiers clad in a spectrum of colors, reminds you of many ocean-side California restaurants. It has that relaxed, "let's have a bottle of wine and enjoy ourselves" feeling. Everyone is smiling and joking.

Located two-thirds of the way up Aspen Mountain, Bonnie's is at the base of Tourtlelotte Park. Bonnie, along with partners Mary Anne and Peter Greene, has owned the restaurant since 1980. It was previously Gretl's. Their goal, when they took over ownership, was to make it even better. Bonnie explains, "Gretl is a dear friend and she was a tough act to follow!" They have continued her tradition of serving only fresh foods, using the best ingredients and starting from scratch.

Locals and tourists flock to Bonnie's for her homemade desserts, including strudl (her own variation), apple dumplings, cakes and pies—all topped with freshly whipped cream, if you desire. One of their most popular items is their pizza. They pride themselves on never making the same pizza twice. Choose from either a meat or a vegetarian pizza with generous and imaginative toppings.

Bonnie allows her chefs and bakers the freedom to show their creativity in order for them to stay fresh and enthusiastic throughout the ski season. They serve a chicken chowder and chili daily along with a soup of the day. Their homemade French bread as an accompaniment is a must. Although the Caesar and spinach salads are most popular, they also offer other varieties to satisfy their steady clientele.

To complement Bonnie's food is an extensive wine list. Skiers are a hearty bunch who are known to have a good time. What better way to spend a lunch hour than to eat a fine meal with a great bottle of wine and people-watch! After all, Bonnie's is *the* place to be on Aspen Mountain.

Lemon Raspberry Soufflé Tart

1 Pâte Sucré crust
3 Eggs, separated
6 T Sugar
1½ T Grated lemon zest
6 T Fresh lemon juice
1 Pint fresh raspberries, or blueberries

Roll out the dough 1/8 inch thick and place in an 8 inch tart pan with removable sides. Cut off 1/4 inch above the sides. Pinch crust with fork and chill for 1 hour. Line the shell with foil and fill with rice or pastry stones. Bake in a 400 degree oven for 8 minutes. Remove the rice and foil and bake 8-10 minutes more, until pale golden. Let cool on rack.

■ Beat the egg yolks with 4 tablespoons of sugar using an electric mixer, until the mixture is thick and pale yellow and forms ribbons when the beaters are lifted. Beat in the zest and lemon juice and transfer the mixture to a heavy sauce pan and cook over low heat, stirring constantly until the mixture just starts boiling and is thick. Transfer the mixture to a bowl and let it cool. Cover with a buttered, round piece of waxed paper until lukewarm.

■ In a bowl, beat the egg whites with a pinch of salt until soft peaks form. Slowly add 2 tablespoons of sugar and beat until it holds stiff peaks. Stir 1/4 of the meringue into the lemon mixture and fold in the remaining meringue gently and thoroughly. Put into the tart shell mounding slightly. Bake in the middle of the oven at 350 degrees, 12-15 minutes until the top is golden and puffed. Transfer to a rack and let it cool. Decorate the top with the fruit and serve with a dollop of whipped cream.

Mixed Greens with Ginger-Chili Macadamia Dressing & Smoked Trout

DRESSING
2 Egg yolks
3 T Ginger, finely chopped
1 T Soy sauce
1 T Rice wine vinegar
½ t Dark sesame oil
6 T Honey
½ t Salt
½ T Dijon mustard
1 Jalapeño Chili pepper, seeded and diced
¾ C Vegetable oil (Bonnie uses Mazola oil)
1 T Water
Juice of ½ large lemon

Make the dressing: in a blender, mix the yolks, ginger and soy sauce for 10 seconds. Add the next 6 ingredients. Blend at low speed and slowly add the oil. As the dressing thickens, add the water and lemon juice. Refrigerate for at least 10 minutes.

■ In a medium-hot skillet, heat the sugar until golden. Add the nuts and the water. Cook until the nuts are sugar-coated and the water is gone; cool to room temperature.

■ Mix the greens with the dressing, top with the trout and sprinkle the nuts on top.

The kicker: this is a delicious and unusual dressing. It could also be used as a sauce for fish.

CARAMELIZED MACADAMIA NUTS
¾ C Macadamia nuts, diced
2 T Raw sugar
2 T Water

SALAD
1 lb Seasonal mix of lettuces and greens
⅓ lb Smoked trout (optional)

Smoked Chicken Pesto Quesadillas

AN APPETIZER SERVING 8-12 OR CAN BE SERVED AS A MAIN COURSE

One 8-10 oz Smoked chicken breast (or turkey), pulled into thin shreds
8 Large flour tortillas, 8 inch size
8 oz Pesto, homemade or a good quality brand
¾ lb Provolone, or combine Provolone and Mozzarella, grated
Mazola oil

Spread 3 heaping tablespoons of pesto on each tortilla (use more if you love pesto). Divide the chicken breast shreds over the pesto on each tortilla. Sprinkle 1/3 - 1/2 cup of cheese over the chicken. Place another tortilla on top. Heat 1/8 inch of oil in a black iron frying pan and heat each side until golden brown and the cheese is melted.

The kicker: if you really want to dazzle your friends, make this as an appetizer. The flavors meld beautifully. Be sure to make enough because it goes quickly.

Café Suzanne

CAFÉ SUZANNE IS LOCATED TWO CHAIRLIFTS UP ELK Camp, in the Snowmass ski area. Serving only lunch, they cater to both downhill and cross-country skiers—as the Government Trail ends just below the restaurant.

Owners Susan and Doug McPherson have created a French country atmosphere to complement their primarily French menu. Susan is a collector and has decorated the restaurant with things she's picked up all over Europe. "Since I spend so much of my time here, I like to be surrounded by things I'm fond of. I mostly shop at street markets and thrift shops, where I often find incredible treasures."

Unique among the mountain restaurants in this area, Café Suzanne offers a variety of heart-healthy choices approved by the American Heart Association. "I got into this realm," Susan explains, "because of my concern for my family's health. It was a natural step to take." She serves extra-lean, doubly-trimmed meats and cooks exclusively with olive and canola oils.

Café Suzanne offers French-style crêpes, which customers enjoy as a change from the ordinary. Choose from three luncheon crêpes with heart-healthy fillings: spinach, ratatouille or chicken, and four dessert crêpes: Grand Marnier, raspberry, apples & cinnamon and Nutella (with hazelnut and chocolate). The batter is made from buckwheat flour like the traditional crêpe from Normandy, France. They're made fresh daily.

Two other French items are the Croque Monsieurs—a French sandwich of grilled ham and Gruyère cheese with Dijon mustard and a Parisian hot dog—an all-beef, extra lean hot dog served on a baguette with Dijon mustard and grated, melted Gruyère cheese.

Their menu also includes homemade soups, low-fat chile, many salads and specials. Susan explains,"It's nice to be able to change our specials daily. I trust my employees' creativity. Stuffed Cornish game hens and Pierre Lapin are examples of their choices."

Beside the dessert crêpes, Susan satisfies her customers with ravishing sweets. Her cheesecake, brownies, carrot cake, fudge cake, cookies and bread pudding are incredibly delicious.

The McPhersons' talents complement each other. Susan works culinary magic and Doug handles the wines. Wine is his love and he chooses mostly French wines at affordable prices. Wine with crêpes is a lovely traditional combination.

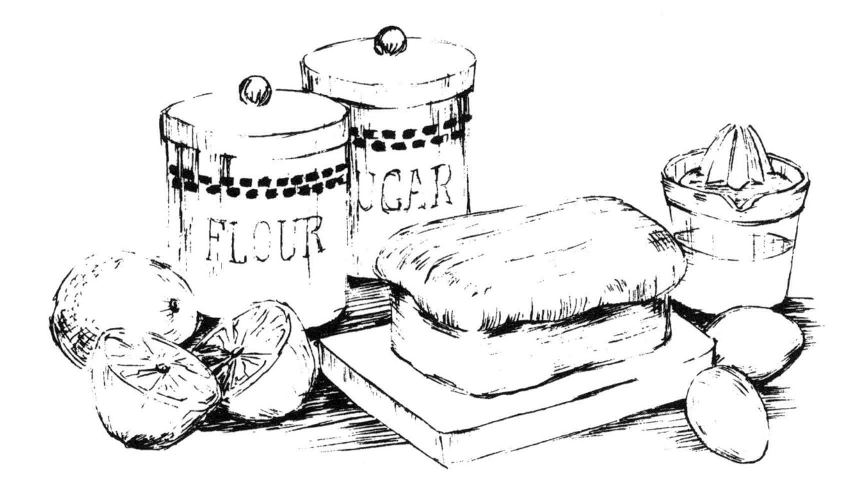

Bread Pudding with Brandy Sauce

SERVES 8

PUDDING

1 Loaf French bread (day-old is best), torn into bite-sized pieces
1 Quart Whole milk–or you can use ½ & ½ for a very rich pudding
8 Large eggs
1 C Sugar
2 t Vanilla
2 t Cinnamon
1 t Nutmeg
1 C Raisins, soak in approximately ¼ cup of brandy

SAUCE

1 Stick butter
1 C Sugar
1 C Brandy

Mix all pudding ingredients (except bread) in a large bowl until well mixed. Add the bread and let sit until the milk mixture is all absorbed, at least 10 minutes. Pour the mixture into a buttered, 9 x 11 inch, deep-dish baking pan. Bake at 325 degrees until a stainless steel knife inserted into the center comes out clean (approximately 45 minutes). Mix the sauce ingredients together in a heavy saucepan and cook slowly until all the sugar is dissolved. Serve the pudding hot with the sauce spooned over the top. If desired, add a dollop of freshly whipped cream.

The kicker: this dessert is wonderful on a chilly evening served with rich, dark coffee or espresso.

♥ *Health hearty suggestions:* the liquor in the sauce may be replaced with orange juice and you can substitute margarine instead of butter. You can substitute 1% low-fat milk for the whole milk, use "Egg Beaters" for the eggs, and cut the sugar in half.

Garbanzo and Couscous Soup

SERVES 8-10

2 t Olive oil
1 Medium yellow onion, diced
1 Clove garlic, minced
2 Stalks celery, diced small
1 Large carrot, diced medium
1 C Zucchini, diced
1 Bay leaf
½ t Basil
½ t Thyme
2 C Cooked garbanzo beans (1 can), drained
2 Tomatoes (1 can), diced
1 Box "Near East" brand couscous
8 C Chicken stock, homemade or canned, always defatted (have some extra on hand in case the soup is too thick)

In a soup pot, sauté the onion and garlic in the olive oil over medium heat until both are soft, not browned. Add the carrot, celery and zucchini and sauté for 3-4 minutes, stirring together to keep from browning. Add the herbs and broth, beans, tomatoes and couscous to the pot and simmer, covered, for about 30-40 minutes or until the veggies are tender and the grain is soft. If you're cooking at sea level, expect the veggies to be cooked sooner.

♥ This soup is low-fat and a little different from the usual bean soups one is served. If you prefer your soups a little chunkier, add more of any, or all, of the vegetables. The couscous and the beans will sink to the bottom of the pot, so be sure to stir well before serving.

■ Serve the soup with pita toasts. Cut pita bread in quarters and split each in half on the exterior. Rub each with a cut garlic clove and brush with a little olive oil. Place on a cookie sheet and put in a 350 degree oven for approximately 5 minutes or until lightly brown.

Tester's notes: this soup was a real hit at our recipe testing party! It's healthy and hearty and would be great served at a cross-country ski party.

♥ *The kicker:* This recipe is low in fat and approved by the "Dine to Your Heart's Delight" program.

Mucho Bean Salad

SERVES 20

BEAN SALAD

1 Regular sized can of each: green beans, great Northern beans, garbanzos, kidney beans, black beans, black-eyed peas, all drained

1 C Green onions, use the green part, chopped small

½ C Parsley, chopped

1 Red bell pepper, diced medium

1 Green bell pepper, diced medium

2 Medium tomatoes, seeded and diced

GARLIC DRESSING

Equivalent of 1 egg of "Egg Beaters"

⅓ C Red wine vinegar

1 T Garlic, chopped

1 t each: salt, pepper and sugar

¼-½ C Olive oil

Mix all ingredients for bean salad together. Meanwhile, make the Garlic Dressing: put all dressing ingredients (except oil) in a Cuisinart and blend. Slowly add ¼ - ½ cup olive oil as the motor continues to run. Cover until ready to use. Toss the bean salad with the dressing and let sit for at least one hour before serving.

♥ *The kicker:* this makes quite a bit, but is wonderful for a large pot luck dinner party. It gets better by the day and is delicious in a green salad.

Dudley's on Sam's Knob

AFTER RUNNING THE EVER-POPULAR DUDLEY'S DINER for 11 years, Paul and Patti Dudley seized the opportunity to operate and run the Sam's Knob Restaurant at the Snowmass ski area.

This hard-working couple oversees every facet of the restaurant from baking and cooking, to hauling the food and supplies to the top of the "Knob" each day. The Dudleys actually live at the restaurant for the entire winter. Since their day starts at 6:30 a.m. and ends at 6 p.m., it makes perfect sense. Patti tells me, "We love living at the top of a mountain and having it to ourselves. Often, we take evening walks up the Big Burn. It's incredibly quiet and the sunsets are spectacular. After a hectic day, it makes it worthwhile."

Their downstairs cafeteria features a 30-item salad bar, several soups, two kinds of chili, stew, pizzas, burgers, sandwiches and a different special daily. Not many can pass up their tempting desserts: fruit cobblers, carrot cake, Swedish creme, banana coconut pecan cake and their popular three-layer chocolate cake. All the food is homemade at the restaurant including scones, breads, and muffins baked fresh each morning. Drooling ski patrolmen come all the way from Elk Camp for Patti's hot cinnamon rolls with cream cheese frosting. Their menu is suited to the skiers' appetite.

If a more relaxed lunch is desired, they offer sit-down, waitress service at "The Top of the Knob." If you've been craving Dudley's Diner's Mexican cuisine, you'll find many of their favorites now on the menu. Also on the menu are: pastas, sandwiches, salads, fish and burgers. Moderately priced wines accompany a well-deserved meal. Luscious desserts and coffee drinks are a must. The views of Mt. Daly and the Big Burn are breathtaking. What a perfect environment to enjoy a delicious lunch.

Next time you're at Snowmass, come to Sam's Knob and look for "Shadow," Paul and Patti's friendly dog who waits in the snow outside the restaurant to greet his guests!

Carrot Cake

MAKES ONE 9" x 13" CAKE

CAKE

3 Eggs
¾ C Canola oil
¾ C Buttermilk
½ C Sugar
½ C Brown sugar
¾ C Pineapple juice
1 C Shredded coconut
1 C Chopped walnuts
2 C Carrots, grated
2 ½ C White flour
2 t Baking soda
½ t Salt
2 t Cinnamon

CREAM CHEESE FROSTING

½ lb Cream cheese, softened
½ lb Butter, softened
2 C Powdered sugar
1 t Vanilla
Half and Half

Preheat your oven to 350 degrees. Mix the first 6 cake ingredients with an electric mixer. Stir in the rest of the cake ingredients. Pour into a greased pan and bake about 45 minutes or until it tests done. Cool completely before frosting. Make the frosting: cream the cream cheese and the butter together, then add the powdered sugar and the vanilla. If it's too thick, add a little Half and Half. (We didn't need to add anything when we tested it!)

Swordfish with Tomatillo-Pineapple Relish

SERVES 6

3 lbs. Swordfish
(½ lb per person)

MARINADE
¼ C Light soy sauce
2 T Brown sugar
3 T Pineapple juice
½ t Fresh ginger, grated

TOMATILLO SAUCE
½ lb Fresh tomatillos
½ Small can (about 1 cup) crushed pineapple, in syrup
1 T Fresh cilantro, chopped
1 T Green chilies, diced (canned, frozen or fresh)
Juice of 1 lime

Look for fresh tomatillos in the produce section of the grocery or you can use one five-ounce can of drained tomatillos. Mix marinade ingredients together and marinate swordfish for several hours or overnight. Purée all ingredients for tomatillo sauce in a Cuisinart and serve over broiled or grilled swordfish. This sauce can be made 2 days in advance.

♥ *The kicker:* the Tomatilla sauce has no fat, nor does the marinade. This dish is marvelous on any occasion.

Wine Suggestion: Columbia Crest Chardonnay.

Vegetarian Chili

SERVES 8

16 oz Can diced tomatoes, in juice
16 oz Can pinto beans
16 oz Can kidney beans
16 oz Can black beans
½ C Onions, chopped
½ C Green pepper, chopped
½ C Celery, chopped
½ t Tabasco sauce
1 T Chili powder
1 T Cumin
1 t Black pepper
2 t each: Garlic salt, oregano, parsley
1 t Coriander

Place everything in a large pot and simmer 1-2 hours. Serve with fresh bread or corn bread and a tossed salad for a complete and healthy meal.

♥ *The kicker:* this chili is non-fat. When we had a testing party, we served the chili with Cache Cache's Polenta Pound Cake (p.18). This would also be delicious in tortillas with lettuce, cheese and tomatoes.

Gretl's

THIS COOKBOOK COULD NOT BE COMPLETE WITHOUT including Gretl, her world-famous restaurant and three of her favorite recipes.

I'm sitting in Gretl's homey kitchen sipping tea and reminiscing of days past, as the intense aroma of apple strudl permeates the air. How can anyone forget Gretl's apple strudl, made from scratch and served piping hot with a clump of whipped cream. It's legendary! It was served at her restaurant, Gretl's, perched halfway up Aspen Mountain.

It all began in December of 1966, when Gretl's dream of owning her own restaurant came true. Gretl had observed over the years the need for a European-style restaurant that would cater to those who loved to eat great food. Her family had owned and operated such a restaurant in Garmisch-Partenkirchen, Germany.

Gretl was appalled at the restaurants that were serving canned soups and packaged foods. "I wanted to serve my customers only the best—everything fresh." Gretl's became unique; people responded to her home cooking and Gretl's popularity made it *the* place to go for the best food anywhere. Gretl developed her own recipe for apple strudl and it was an instant hit. People loved it, they stood in long lines for it, they dreamt about it, they reserved it and they ordered it from such faraway places as Washington, D.C. This delicious concoction of homemade pastry, wrapped around apples (cored and peeled by hand), had customers dazzled. The recipe remains a secret. Gretl's other desserts that had customers drooling were: cream puffs, trifle, apple cake and streussl.

Her other specialties should not be overlooked. Her soups changed daily and on any given day you might find: butter or liver dumpling, cauliflower, tomato, broccoli or zucchini. "I do not believe in mystery soups," Gretl explains, "you should be able to taste the main vegetable." Gretl tells us her secret to the success of her soups. "Just before serving the soup, blend two egg yolks with ½ pint of heavy cream (for eight servings of soup) and add to the soup mixture. Do not boil. This will make the soup thick and delicious."

Each dish looked better than the next because Gretl believes, "You eat with your eyes."

Gretl's last year on Aspen Mountain was the spring of 1980. Now, she does consultation for the Merry Go Round restaurant on Aspen Highlands. You'll be happy to know you can still get Gretl's strudl and many of her other delights at the Highlands.

Gretl has wonderful memories of her restaurant on Aspen Mountain, and we have many fond memories of her.

Cream of Zucchini Soup

SERVES 6

1½ lb Zucchini, washed and sliced
1 C Water
½ t Salt
½ t Basil
2 T Onion, finely chopped
3 T Butter
2 C Chicken broth
Fresh ground pepper
½ C Heavy cream
2 Egg yolks
¼ C Milk

Bring first 4 ingredient to a boil and simmer for 15 minutes. In a saucepan, sauté the onion in butter until tender. Add the chicken broth, put through a blender and season to taste. Whip the egg yolks, cream and milk at the very last minute and add to the simmering soup, stirring constantly. Sprinkle with parsley or chives.

Gretl's Crumb Cake

2 Sticks butter
1 C Sugar
6 Egg yolks
1 C All-purpose flour
1 C Cake flour
2 Small squares Baker's semi-sweet chocolate, grated
1 C Hazelnuts, walnuts or pecans, ground up
1 t Baking powder
6 Egg whites
2 C Heavy whipping cream
1 t Vanilla
2 T Rum (more if desired!)
Confectioners' sugar

Beat the butter, sugar and egg yolks until creamy. Add the flours, the grated chocolate, the nuts and the baking powder. Beat the egg whites and fold gently into the mixture. Grease parchment paper or waxed paper and place around a 10 inch springform pan. Bake at 350 degrees for approximately 50-60 minutes (or until a toothpick comes out clean). Let cool.

■ Whip the heavy cream with a little confectioners' sugar and the vanilla until stiff.

■ When the cake is cooled (not warm at all), take a long knife and cut approximately 1 inch off the top of the cake, all the way around. Place that piece into a bowl (don't worry about keeping it all together because you'll be making it into crumbs). Then scoop approximately 2 inches out of the cake so that you leave the sides and the bottom—you'll end up with a cake shell.

■ Take all the scooped-out cake and make it into crumbs. Reserve approximately 1 cup of these crumbs. Take the large amount of crumbs and mix them with the whipped cream. Take the rum and sprinkle it over the bottom of the cake shell. Then take the whipped cream and crumb mixture and fill it back into the cake shell, scatter the reserved crumbs on top and lightly sprinkle with confectioners' sugar.

The kicker: Gretl says to make this cake one day, pour the rum over it and fill it the second day and serve it the third day. We made it in the morning and watched Gretl fill it in the evening of the same day. Of course, we couldn't resist eating it. It's absolutely delicious. This cake could also be used as a coffee cake if you left it alone!

Ham Dumpling Soup

SERVES 8

8 C Chicken broth
¾ Loaf white or rye bread
4 Eggs
¾ C Milk
1-2 t Salt
Pinch Italian seasoning
½ lb Cooked ham, sliced and cut into tiny pieces
½ C Butter
2 T Butter

Dice the bread. Beat the eggs, milk, ham, salt and ½ cup of melted butter and pour over the bread. Cover and let stand at least 1 hour. Butter the center of a large, cloth napkin and form into a ball with the mixture. Tie the corners tightly and submerge into a large pot of boiling, salted water. Let simmer for 1 hour and remove from the napkin and cut into bite-size pieces. Add to the heated chicken broth.

The kicker: Gretl uses half the loaf for the soup, and the other half she cuts into half inch slices and fries with an egg for breakfast.

Gwyn's

LOCATED WITHIN THE HIGH ALPINE RESTAURANT IS A charming, European-style sit-down restaurant complete with linen tablecloths, china place settings and flowers.

Skiers who come to Gwyn's treat themselves to an unforgettable experience. The service is friendly and professional. Their creative menu offers a wide variety of items, complemented by an extensive wine list.

It's quite amazing when you take into consideration the fact that all the supplies must come up to the restaurant's 10,000 foot elevation by snowcat.

Everything is homemade from the soups to the desserts. Only the freshest of ingredients are used to assure the highest quality.

Maybe that's why customers, during the height of the season, are willing to wait hours to eat at Gwyn's!

They're open for breakfast and lunch. Breakfast begins at 9 am and is a great way to start the day and beat the crowds. Sit down to a hot cup of Kona coffee and a basket of freshly baked muffins. The most popular items on the breakfast menu are: fresh fruit pancakes, Alpine Potatoes, Eggs Neptune and Huevos.

Lunch offers, in addition to their regular menu, a daily special list that allows the chefs to be creative. The fresh fish varies daily and the sauces change with the chefs' whims. Following are examples of the special list: grilled Hawaiian Ahi with papaya chive butter, poached Norwegian Salmon with a fresh raspberry cream sauce, swordfish with wild mushroom fettuccine and New Zealand Emerald Mussels.

Not many can pass up Gwyn's dessert tray, beautifully garnished with flowers. A selection may include: Poppyseed Torte, Chocolate Mousse Tart, White Chocolate and Chocolate Chip Ice Cream with linzer stars, Fresh Fruit Tart with kiwis, star fruit and raspberries and Chocolate Gâteau.

Ski Magazine boasts that Gwyn's is "...one of the handful of U.S. mountain restaurants on a par with the better European ones."

Grilled Ahi with Pineapple Jalapeño Salsa

SERVES 6

1½ lb Fresh ahi
1 T Olive oil
Salt & pepper

SALSA
1½ C Fresh pineapple chunks
1 T Jalapeño peppers, seeded
1 T Red peppers
3 T Orange marmalade
2 t Fresh lime juice
½ t Kosher salt
1 T Fresh cilantro, chopped

Finely chop the pineapple, jalapeño peppers and red peppers. Mix in the remaining salsa ingredients and refrigerate. Rub the ahi steaks with the olive oil and salt & pepper to taste. Grill the ahi medium-rare, do not overcook. Top the ahi with the salsa.

♥ *The kicker:* this is an incredibly simple meal to prepare. Make it easy on yourself—make the salsa a day in advance, then all you need to do is grill the ahi, make a mixed green salad and dinner is ready! This dish is low in fat and makes a beautiful presentation!

Wine Suggestion: Acacia Chardonnay.

Smoked Turkey, Spinach & Feta Salad

SERVES 4

8 oz Smoked turkey, cut in strips
10 oz Fresh spinach leaves
1 Bunch bok choy
½ C Extra virgin olive oil
2 Cloves garlic, minced
½ C Scallions, chopped
⅓ C Pine nuts
6 T Dijon mustard
3 T Red wine vinegar
2 T Water
6 oz Feta cheese, crumbled
Fresh ground pepper

Toss the turkey with large pieces of spinach and bok choy. Sauté the garlic, scallions and pine nuts in 1 tablespoon of the olive oil. Blend in the mustard and vinegar. Whisk in the remaining oil, water and 4 ounces of the feta cheese until just blended. Toss the salad with the dressing and top with the remaining feta and fresh pepper.

♥ *The kicker:* this makes a healthy summer salad.

Wine Suggestion: McDowell, Syrah.

High Alpine Restaurant

UPON ENTERING THE HIGH ALPINE RESTAURANT, YOU may perceive it to be like any mountain restaurant—a gift shop, a bar and a cafeteria line. But after you've spent a few moments wandering around, you'll realize it's not quite like any restaurant you've ever visited. Hanging on the main level is a windsurfer. Go one level up and you'll find a sailboat; a 16-foot Fireball complete with sails. Hanging upside down and looking like it may have just completed a loop, is a full-size, 50 foot wing span, sailplane. Look a bit further and you'll find a racing bike and a hang glider!

The owners of this museum-like mountain restaurant are George and Gwyn Gordon. Having run the Highlands Merry-Go-Round and Base Restaurants for six years, the Gordons moved over to Snowmass in 1979. Their philosophy and the reason for their success is, "it must be the best!" They strive for perfection in everything they do and it shows.

The cafeteria serves nutritious, wholesome meals. Some examples of their fare include: Shrimp and Wild Rice Salad, Chicken Brunswick Stew and Fresh Teriyaki Burgers. Their desserts, on the other hand, are mouth-watering, naughty delights—some healthy, and some simply decadent. Try their carrot cake, chocolate Amaretto cheesecake, Bavarian apple torte, chocolate nougat bars or bread pudding with brandy sauce.

The employees at High Alpine are a cheerful, lively bunch. There's a definite camaraderie amongst them. The Gordons explain, "Our employees are the best in the valley. Most have just graduated from college or are taking a year off from grad school. They have decided they want to have the most fun year of their lives. They play and ski really hard and also bring the same enthusiasm for life to work with them. We really enjoy working with them!"

This personal enthusiasm, the food and the exciting atmosphere make High Alpine a definite place to stop for breakfast or lunch while skiing Snowmass.

Lemon Ginger Chicken Fettuccine

SERVES 4

8 oz Fettuccine (udon noodles work well, too)
3 Chicken breasts
2 T Peanut oil
2 Garlic cloves, minced
½ C Scallions
½ Red pepper, cut in strips
½ Green pepper, cut in strips
½ C Carrots, sliced thin
½ C Celery, sliced on an angle
⅓ C Shiitake mushrooms, sliced
2 T Fresh ginger, grated
⅓ C Fresh lemon juice
2 T Soy sauce
Pinch cayenne
3 T Chicken stock
2 t Cornstarch

Cook the fettuccine or udon al dente. Bone, skin and cut the chicken into bite-size strips. Sauté in the oil and set aside. Sauté the vegetables in oil and add the seasonings. Simmer for 2 minutes. ■ Dissolve the cornstarch in the chicken stock. Toss with the vegetable mixture and the noodles. Let it thicken slightly in order to coat the noodles.

The kicker: this dish has a nice flavor—its zingy taste comes from the fresh ginger.

Wine Suggestion: Trefethen, Sauvignon Blanc.

Praline Apple Pie

FILLING
2 lb Tart apples
1 T Butter
2 T Brown sugar
1 T Lemon juice
½ t Nutmeg

CRUST
1¼ C White flour
½ t Sugar
¼ t Salt
½ C Butter, cut into pieces
¼ t Lemon extract
¼ C Ice water

TOPPING
2 Large eggs, beaten
⅜ C Brown sugar
¾ C Light corn syrup
½ t Vanilla extract
¼ t Maple flavoring
1 C Pecans, chopped

Peel, core and thinly slice the apples. In a skillet, stir the butter and sugar until dissolved. Add the apples, lemon juice and nutmeg. Simmer for 10 minutes and cool.

■ Make the crust: cut the flour, sugar, salt and butter together until they resemble coarse sand. Add the lemon and water slowly with a food processor running. Form into a ball. Refrigerate for 30 minutes. Roll out to fill a 9 inch pie pan. Preheat the oven to 375 degrees.

■ Mix the topping ingredients together. Pour the apples into the shell. Pour the praline over the apples and bake for 50-60 minutes or until golden brown and set when shaken. Cool.

The kicker: this pie is also great using peaches or pears.

Krabloonik

IF IT'S ADVENTURE AND ROMANCE YOU'RE SEEKING, Krabloonik is where you'll find it. It all began when Dan MacEachen took over the enormous task of training and taking care of Stuart Mace's Husky dogs. After an apprenticeship with Mace, MacEachen found a new home for the dogs near the slopes of the Snowmass ski area.

The dogs are born and bred for running and MacEachen trains them to pull dog sleds. The kennel hosts over 240 Huskies who willingly take people on two-hour rides through the pristine wilderness. The happy howls of these special canines delight Snowmass skiers daily.

MacEachen knew the dogs alone wouldn't make ends meet, so he built a rustic log cabin restaurant to supplement his income. The idea was to be unique in this most unusual setting. They serve many items not found anywhere in this area—specifically wild game and game birds. Their Head Chef prepares classic French sauces that he embellishes with fresh herbs and spices. They grow their own herbs and use fresh fruits for sauces and desserts. The menu changes weekly with imaginative and harmonious combinations. They offer four to six wild game items each evening. Not many experience the opportunity to try wild boar, moose, elk or caribou. Game birds are popular with such favorites as pheasant, duck and quail prepared in an appealing manner. For those not "wild" about game, you can choose from an array of fresh fish which the kitchen handles with a delicate touch. Beef entrées are also available. The most popular dishes are wild boar and caribou (which has a naturally sweet flavor and is more delicate than beef).

The desserts are presented on a tray after the meal, and not many can pass up these tempting delights.

The wine list is carefully selected by manager Gary Watts with over 250 wines from California and France. He changes the list twice a year and keeps it moderately priced. He enjoys making suggestions to customers who are often baffled with their entrée choice. His efforts have paid off—they have won the Award of Excellence (for four years) from *Wine Spectator* magazine for featuring a superb wine list.

Krabloonik's patrons enjoy a totally different experience. By the time they've walked down the long stairway, seen the dogs and feasted their eyes on the splendid view of Mt. Daly, they're usually hooked! They're willing to explore and experiment in this unpretentious environment.

Most people inquire about the name, Krabloonik. MacEachen named the restaurant after his first lead dog. The term in Alaskan means, "Big Eye Brows." MacEachen has put his work to the ultimate test and has participated in the famous Iditarod race seven times. It's a grueling 1,200 mile dog sled race from Anchorage to Nome, Alaska. The restaurant exhibits many photographs of this daring, exciting endeavor.

Boneless Breast of Pheasant with Apple-Blackberry Relish

SERVES 4

Olive oil
4 Boneless pheasant breasts (or substitute chicken)
1 Apple (with skin on), ¼ inch dice
½ C Fresh blackberries
½ Small red onion, diced
¼ C Red bell pepper, diced
¼ C Toasted pecan halves
1 T Honey
1 T Rice wine vinegar
1 T white wine

Preheat oven to 450 degrees. Sauté the onions until slightly transparent, yet crisp. Add the pecans, red pepper and apples. Sauté for 2 minutes. Add the honey, vinegar and wine. Bring to a boil and remove from the heat. Add the blackberries. Keep at room temperature. Dust the pheasant in flour. Sauté in a hot pan, skin side down until the skin is golden brown. Turn over and place in the oven (skin side up). Roast for approximately 8-10 minutes until no pink is left in the middle. Slice the pheasant on a bias and fan on four plates. Serve the relish over the top.

Wine Suggestion: Grgich Hills, Chardonnay.

Pesto Marinated Ahi

SERVES 4

4 Ahi steaks, approximately 6 oz each

PESTO
¼ lb Fresh basil
¼ C Pine nuts
6 Cloves garlic
½ Bunch parsley
¼ C Parmesan cheese
¼ C Olive oil

MARINADE
½ C Olive oil
Juice of 1 lemon
¼ C White wine
Salt & pepper to taste

In a Cuisinart, combine and purée the pesto ingredients. Take ½ of this mixture and add the marinade ingredients. Marinate the steaks for 30 minutes at room temperature or 1 hour refrigerated. Grill the steaks on a hot grill for approximately 2-3 minutes per side. The fish should still have a thin line of pink through the middle when properly cooked. Do not overcook. Heat the remaining pesto with ½ cup of white wine and salt and pepper to taste. Serve over the fish.

Wine suggestion: Silverado, Sauvignon Blanc.

Roast Loin of Elk with Wild Mushroom Cream Sauce

SERVES 4

2 lbs Boneless elk loin, all fat and silver skin removed, or substitute beef tenderloin
¼ lb Tree oyster mushrooms, chopped (found at most grocery stores)
½ Small yellow onion, diced fine
1 t Garlic, chopped
1 C White wine
1 Pint Heavy cream

Preheat oven to 450 degrees. Sauté the onions until transparent. Add the garlic and mushrooms and sauté 1 minute longer. Add the wine and bring to a boil. Reduce the heat to maintain a simmer. Simmer until all liquid is evaporated. Add the heavy cream and bring to a boil. Reduce the heat to maintain a simmer. Simmer until the sauce reduces in volume by one third. Season to taste with salt and pepper. Dust the loin of elk with flour. Sauté in a very hot frying pan to brown on all sides. Remove to a cookie sheet and place in a hot oven. Cook approximately 8-10 minutes turning once. Don't overcook the meat, it should be medium rare. Remove from the oven and cool, 5-7 minutes. Slice and serve with the sauce.

Wine Suggestion: Newton, Merlot.

The Main Buttermilk Restaurant

IT'S YOUR FIRST DAY SKIING. YOU'RE HEADED OUT TO Buttermilk Mountain because you heard it's a haven for rank beginners. And that's exactly what you are!

You forgot your goggles, gloves and scarf rushing out the door. A good cup of coffee would ease your ever-present nervousness.

You've come to the right spot. Located at the base of this non-threatening mountain is the Main Buttermilk Restaurant. They have a well-stocked gift shop, a bar with a cheerful bartenderess named Ellyn and a cafeteria which serves breakfast, lunch and snacks. Try Eggs Buttermilk, a variation of Eggs Benedict. It's the perfect choice for skiers who crave early-morning nourishment. They also serve homemade muffins, delicious cinnamon rolls, and great hot coffee.

Bob Olenick, the manager for the last four years, explains, "Our menu has evolved over the years just as people's eating habits have changed. We've gradually added more organic and healthier items. Our customers have responded positively."

Lunch features the standard fare of burgers and hot dogs, but they also cater to those who are more health conscious. They have an extensive salad bar, garden and black bean burgers, fajitas and a variety of homemade gourmet pizzas. They offer 2-3 soups a day made with lower-fat ingredients. There is always a daily special. Look for satisfying, ethnic creations such as: Mexican, Oriental, West Indies or Italian. Finish the meal with one of their scrumptious, homemade desserts.

Olenick told me, "I feel the service we provide to the beginner skier is wonderful. We realize that they're in new territory and we try to simplify and ease this situation."

Buttermilk's Vegetarian Chili

SERVES 10-12

¼ C Olive oil
3 Cloves garlic, minced
2 Large onions, diced
¼ C Flour
½ Bunch celery, diced
6 oz Tomato paste
24 oz Can diced tomatoes (in juice)
⅓ C Chili powder
2 t Ground cumin
1 t Oregano
½ t Black pepper
½ t Salt
¼ C Cider vinegar
1 Bell pepper, diced
24 oz Can red kidney beans, drained
24 oz Can pinto beans, with the gravy
⅓ C Bulghur wheat
½ C Tomato juice
Olive oil for sautéing
½ C Carrots, sliced
¾ C Mushrooms, sliced
⅓ C Cut corn

Brown the onions and garlic in the olive oil, cover them and sweat them over low heat for 5 minutes, sprinkle the flour over the onions and cook for 1 minute. Add the next 9 ingredients and place over medium-low heat. Stir thoroughly and cook for 1½ hours, stirring often so it doesn't stick to the bottom. Add water to thin. Add the green peppers and cook for an additional 15 minutes. At the end, add all the beans and gravy. Soak the bulghur wheat in ½ cup of tomato juice brought to a boil, then add the mixture to the chili.
■ Sauté the carrots and mushrooms in some olive oil. Add to the chili along with the corn. Serve hot with garnishes of shredded cheddar and sour cream if desired.

♥ *The kicker:* this is a wonderful, hearty chili that was enjoyed by all the ladies at our recipe testing. If you garnish the chili with chopped chives or scallions instead of the cheese and sour cream, this dish is low in fat and very nutritious.

The Merry-Go-Round Restaurant

THE MERRY-GO-ROUND WAS NAMED BY HIGHLANDS' owner, Whip Jones—the significance being that it is located at the center of the ski area and all activity flows around it.

George Schermerhorn and Robert Cronenberg have co-owned the restaurant since 1982. They brought Gretl Uhl with them as their food consultant. Gretl had just retired from her tiny restaurant on Aspen Mountain and wanted to pass on her knowledge to others. Schermerhorn and Cronenberg benefited from this arrangement because Gretl had such a wonderful reputation and skiers missed her style of cooking.

Gretl's strudl was once again baking and emitting those wondrous aromas—-to the enjoyment of hundreds of skiers daily. She taught these two young owners how to make strudl her way—only using the best ingredients and peeling and coring the apples by hand. They sell frozen strudl to anyone on request. It comes with baking instructions so that people can now enjoy this famous dessert at home!

Many of the dishes served at the Merry-Go-Round are Gretl's recipes, but each year, as Schermerhorn and Cronenberg felt more confident, they have expanded and added many of their own creations, which have turned out to be successes in their own right.

The appearance of their cafeteria line looks as appealing as Gretl's did—one dish looks better than the next. Perhaps it's because of this extra care and labor-intensive preparation that constant praises are elicited from hungry skiers. The desserts, which are presented first, are impossible to pass up. In addition to the strudl, the most popular items are Maui rum cake (it's authentic!), trifle and banana cream pie. Their creative and colorful salads change often depending on fresh produce. Favorites are: pasta salad, tomatoes stuffed with shrimp and Crab Louis, stuffed avocado and Gretl's spinach salad. There are two soups made fresh daily, chili, ratatouille, Gretl's secret sauerkraut, and, of course, burgers and fresh sandwiches. An innovative daily special is featured for variety, and a full wine list is offered for accompaniment.

It's no small task to run a mountain restaurant. The owners' philosophy shows in everything they do. They don't think cafeteria food has to be dull, conversely, it can be very exciting. Schermerhorn explains, "We know that you can feed 2,000 people the same food you might serve 20. We're not limited in scope and we're not afraid to try new things. You just need to be willing to take a chance."

Banana Cream Pie

MAKES 1 PIE

PIE CRUST
1 C Flour
¼ C Sugar
1 Egg yolk
¼ lb Margarine

FILLING
2 C Vanilla pudding, homemade or packaged
1 Large banana
1 oz Grand Marnier
½ T Gelatin
½ C Water
Whipped cream
Fresh strawberries or blueberries

Put all the pie crust ingredients in a mixing bowl in the above order, cutting the margarine into small slices. Mix until consistent and turn the dough out onto a floured table. Work into a ball with your hands, cover with film and chill for at least 1 hour. Then, generously flour the table and work the ball of dough into a flat circle, about 6 inches in diameter. Roll the dough into a circle, about 2 inches larger than the pie pan. Place in a pie pan and generously prick the dough with a fork. Bake in a 350 degree, preheated oven for about 8 minutes or until the crust begins to slightly brown on the edges. Check the crust at 4 minutes and if bubbles start to appear, poke with a fork.

■ Make the filling: heat the pudding in a double boiler until thin. In a separate sauce pan, heat the water and gelatin and stir continuously, until thin and clear. Add the gelatin and Grand Marnier to the pudding and mix well. Pour a thin layer of pudding in the bottom of the pie shell. Cut the banana in 1/8 inch slices, place on the pudding layer, then pour the remaining pudding on top of the bananas. Allow to cool in the refrigerator for at least 2 hours. Top with fresh whipped cream and garnish each piece with a strawberry half or a handful of blueberries.

Zucchini Pie

SERVES 8

4 C Zucchini, finely diced
1 Medium onion, finely diced
½ C Vegetable oil
½ C Grated parmesan
4 Eggs
½ T Oregano
½ T Garlic powder
1 T Dried parsley, or 3 T finely chopped fresh parsley
1 C Bisquick

Combine the first 3 ingredients and mix lightly. Stir in the parmesan and eggs, spices and bisquick and mix well. Pour the mixture into a 9 x 9 inch greased pan. Bake at 350 degrees for 50 minutes -1 hour. The pie should be firm when done, do not overcook. Sprinkle with parmesan and serve.

The kicker: this pie is a nice substitute for a vegetable with dinner and would make a nice brunch dish.

The Pine Creek Cookhouse

NESTLED HIGH ABOVE ASPEN, IN THE EXQUISITE Ashcroft Valley, is a quaint Alpine restaurant. The Pine Creek Cookhouse is situated in the heart of the Ashcroft Ski Touring area. Dine for lunch and dinner on Hungarian and European cuisine with the most breathtaking view of the Elk Mountain range. Winter access to the Cookhouse is either by cross-country skiing or by horse-drawn sleigh.

An evening at the Cookhouse is a wonderful experience. Ski in with miners' headlamps for a fantastic dinner "away from it all." It's relaxing and fun. After a chilly ski, warm up with a hot drink by the pot belly stove and enjoy Krisi's Hungarian cheese dip and a glass of wine. Dinners feature predominately French cuisine. The menu changes often depending on the chef's whims and the availability of fresh ingredients.

Ashcroft Ski Touring offers 30 kilometers of set cross-country ski tracks in this pristine valley. Stop for a nutritious, wholesome lunch at the Cookhouse. There are hearty winter soups, homemade breads, an unusual salad bar (with Tabouli, Quinoa, pasta salads, etc.), sandwiches, spinach crêpes and a daily hot pasta.

Summer at Ashcroft holds its own beauty. You can drive or bike from Aspen, or horseback ride from a nearby ranch.

Lunch and dinner are once again served. The lunch menu is basically the same with cold salads and iced cherry soup to complement the warm days. For dinner, fish, chicken and duck are prepared on a mesquite grill.

Formerly owned by Ruthie and Ted Ryan, the land is now owned by filmmaker John Wilcox. Greg and Krisi Mace ran the ski touring area and the restaurant for 12 years. After Greg Mace's tragic death in a climbing accident, Krisi is once again the magic force behind the Pine Creek Cookhouse's success.

Krisi's love of the area, her delicious creative Hungarian cooking and her desire to have others share in this mountain experience, make the Pine Creek Cookhouse an idyllic place to dine.

Grilled Quail Salad

SERVES 4

8-10 Quails, thawed & boned
Champagne vinaigrette (see page 207)
1 lb Mixed field greens
Fruit in season: summer cherries, peaches, blueberries, grapes, strawberries, winter pears, oranges, apples, star fruit
1 Bunch Enoke mushrooms
1 Bunch Belgian endive

SUN-DRIED CHERRY VINAIGRETTE

½ C Sun-dried cherries
1 Serano chile
1 T Dijon mustard
3 T Toasted sesame oil
½ C Cooking sherry
¼ C Fresh basil, chopped
1 T Mayonnaise
½ C Champagne vinegar (found at specialty stores)
2 C Olive oil
Salt & pepper

Marinate the quails in the champagne vinaigrette. Make the cherry vinaigrette: add the mustard and mayonnaise in a bowl with a whisk. Slowly mix and add ½ of the vinegar and a bit of the olive oil. Add the rest of the vinegar and slowly whisk in the rest of the olive oil and sesame oil. Add the remaining ingredients and whisk again until incorporated.

■ Grill the quail for approximately 4-5 minutes on each side (broiling works, too). Either on a large serving platter or individual plates, arrange the field greens, the fruit, mushrooms and endive around the edges. After the quail is cooked, cut them in half and arrange on the greens. Pour some of the cherry vinaigrette on top.

The kicker: this is a lovely summer dish. It's very low in calories and yummy!

Wine Suggestion: Duck Horn, Sauvignon Blanc.

Oriental Soba Noodle Salad

A SIDE DISH SERVING 4

1 lb Soba noodles (available in the health food section)
1 C Yellow & red bell peppers, chopped
1 C Broccoli florets, blanched
½ C Sugar snap peas
½ C Green onions, chopped
½ C Frozen corn, thawed
½ C Red cabbage, chopped
¼ C Toasted sesame seeds
Pinch red pepper flakes
Salt & pepper, to taste
2 T Fresh ginger, grated
⅓ C Olive oil
2 T Toasted sesame seed oil
⅓ C Rice vinegar
1 T Dijon mustard

Bring water to a boil with a pinch of salt and a tablespoon of olive oil. Cook the noodles—it takes only 5 minutes. Check for doneness—do not overcook. Drain and rinse with cold water. Put into a big bowl, pour in the olive oil (until the noodles are well-coated), add the other ingredients and mix well. Add the seasonings to taste. If you like your food a bit spicier, add a dash of hot chili oil.

♥ *The kicker:* this is a wonderful dish with incredible flavor. It's healthy and is a great accompaniment to any meal. The colors from the vegetables are beautiful.

Pan Fried Trout

SERVES 4

4 Trout (purchase the freshest you can find)
2 T Olive oil
Lemon pepper
Fresh basil
½ C Cornmeal (blue and yellow mixed works nicely)
Fresh lemon juice

Clean and rinse the trout. If you want, you can cut away the fins and inside bone structure. Otherwise, it comes away easily after cooking. Leave the trout slightly damp and cover with the cornmeal mixture. Place the olive oil in a sauté pan and wait until it is nice and hot and add the trout with the skin down. Sprinkle with the lemon pepper and basil. Allow to cook for another 2-3 minutes. It would make a lovely presentation to serve it on a bed of steamed fresh greens such as: spinach, arugula or mustard greens. Steam them with a bit of vegetable broth.

♥ *The kicker:* this low-cholesterol dish was enjoyed at our recipe testing. John Smollen caught the trout in a nearby stream.

Wine Suggestion: Saintsbury, Chardonnay.

Quinoa Salad

A SIDE DISH
SERVING 6-8

2 C Quinoa
3 C Vegetable broth (Knorr is a good brand)
¼ C Toasted pine nuts
¼ C Fresh chopped chives
1 C Red peppers, chopped
Salt & pepper, to taste

CHAMPAGNE VINAIGRETTE
1 T Dijon mustard
1 T Mayonnaise
Pinch salt & pepper
1 t Italian seasoning
1 T Honey
½ C Champagne vinegar (found at specialty food stores or substitute a good quality white wine vinegar)
2 C Olive oil

Wash the quinoa, drain and add a tablespoon of olive oil to a pan. Pour in the quinoa and stir until the kernels are coated with olive oil. Add the vegetable broth. Quinoa takes about 15-20 minutes to cook. When done, remove from the pot and place into a bowl, let cool and add the chives and peppers. Toast the pine nuts in a 400 degree oven for 10 minutes—be careful, they burn quickly. Add to the quinoa mixture. ■ Make the vinaigrette: add the mustard and mayonnaise in a bowl with a whisk. Slowly mix and add ½ of the vinegar and a bit of olive oil. Add the rest of the vinegar and slowly whisk in the olive oil. Add the spices and whisk again. Add approximately ½ of a cup (or more) of the vinaigrette to the quinoa mixture and serve.

♥ *The kicker:* This is an extremely healthy dish. Using a small amount of dressing makes this dish low in cholesterol.

The Ullrhoff Restaurant

THE ULLRHOFF RESTAURANT, LOCATED AT THE BASE OF the infamous Big Burn at the Snowmass ski area, has come a long way from the early 70's. Since then, owners John and Pat Drake have remodeled over eight times.

In the beginning, the Drakes (who also owned Greuter's Deli in the Aspen Square Building), made the hot food in town and transported it to the mountain. L.J. Erspamer, the Drakes' first manager, remembers skiing down Max Park with a bucket of soup in one hand and a bucket of chili in the other. "It was challenging to say the least. My goal was not to spill anything," L.J. told me. They had 5 tables then.

Ten years later, the Drakes added onto their kitchen and finally had the opportunity to cook with an oven! Pat, along with Barbara Isakson, happily made the transition into cooking homemade food. Together, they worked on recipe development; starting with a basic recipe (from a variety of sources) and changing it to suit their tastes.

They no longer had to ski the food to the restaurant—now it's transported by way of a modern snowcat. Instead of one soup and one chili, you can now choose from a varied menu: four wonderful soups, beef stew (served in homemade boules), many kinds of wonderful and satisfying salads, burgers and a daily special. Skiers enjoy having a complete meal such as veggie lasagna with a salad and garlic bread. A favorite is meatloaf, complete with mashed potatoes and gravy.

"Early birds" can expect a full breakfast featuring fruit muffins and warm cinnamon rolls.

A large deck outside is always crowded on sunny days with skiers trying to "soak in the rays" on a gorgeous Colorado day. It's become a great meeting spot.

Fresh flowers, homemade quilts on the walls, an antique hutch displaying holiday decorations and European copper engravings come together to create a homey environment. Since Pat and John spend so much of their time at the restaurant, they wanted to feel comfortable and "like" being there. The patrons appreciate the effort.

Grilled Chicken Breast Salad

SERVES 6

BALSAMIC VINAIGRETTE
4 Large Garlic cloves, chopped fine
6 T Balsamic vinegar
1 C Extra-virgin olive oil
Salt and freshly ground black pepper, to taste

2 Large whole boneless, skinless chicken breasts plus 1 - ½ lb of chicken meat, cooked & cubed
¾ C Ripe olive wedges
2 Scallions (green & white parts), sliced
One 7 oz Can Artichoke hearts in brine, drained & quartered
1 C Fresh mushrooms, sliced
2 Large Tomatoes, diced
½ C Fresh parsley, chopped
1 C Water chestnuts, sliced
Mixed greens

Make the dressing: combine all the ingredients in a jar with a tight-fitting cover. Set aside at room temperature for 30 minutes or as long as one week. Shake well before using.
■ Marinate the chicken breasts in the salad dressing for at least one hour. Grill or broil until done. Refrigerate until cool.
■ Pour enough salad dressing over the cubed meat to moisten and flavor it while you're putting the rest of the salad together. Toss the next 7 ingredients together with enough salad dressing to coat the mixture.
■ Line 8 chilled plates with torn mixed greens. Divide the salad mixture evenly amongst the plates. Thinly slice the cooled breasts and fan the slices over the salad. Garnish the plate with a dollop of guacamole (if desired).

♥ *The kicker:* this salad is a full meal and is wonderful served with a crusty peasant bread.

Wine Suggestion: Knocti Sauvignon Blanc.

Zucchini Nut Muffins

MAKES 2 DOZEN MUFFINS OR 2 LOAVES OF BREAD

3¾ C All-purpose flour
1½ t Cinnamon
1 t Baking soda
1 t Salt
¼ t Baking powder
3 Large eggs
2 C Granulated sugar
1½ t Vanilla
1 C Vegetable oil
2 C Grated zucchini
½ C Chopped nuts
1 t Flour

CINNAMON-SUGAR MUFFIN MIXTURE
½ C Packed brown sugar
1 T Margarine, melted
1 T Flour
2 t Cinnamon
½ C Finely chopped nuts

Pre-heat oven to 375 degrees and line a muffin tin with cupcake liners or grease 2 bread pans. Combine the first 5 ingredients and set aside. Beat the eggs well in a large bowl. Gradually add the next 3 ingredients and mix well with a mixer. Add the dry ingredients to the egg mixture and stir just until moistened. Stir in the grated zucchini. Combine the chopped nuts with 1 teaspoon of flour and add to the batter. The batter should be stiff.

■ Divide the batter amongst the muffin cups or the bread pans. Make the topping: blend the first 4 ingredients to make a dry and crumbly mixture. Mix in the nuts. (This mixture may be kept covered in the refrigerator for about a week.) Sprinkle the tops of the muffins with some of the Cinnamon-Sugar mixture. Bake the muffins for 20-25 minutes or the bread for 50-60 minutes or until a cake tester comes out clean. Let the muffins or the bread cool for 10 minutes before removing from the pans. Serve the muffins warm.

PART V

Caterers

There was a time when Aspenites entertained and prepared all the food themselves. A new era is here and with it are different life styles and less time. Catering has become an ever-growing business. With the influx of wealthy homeowners, many caterers are busy year-round. They are incredibly flexible, creative and willing to please their clients. Within this section, you'll meet some very special caterers who shared their most popular recipes.

Condra of Aspen

"IT ALL STARTED WHEN I WAS A CHILD WITH MY KENNER Easy Bake Oven," laughs Condra Easley as she describes her first experiences making pastry!

When she grew up, her career path led to an architectural firm in Chicago where she worked doing interior design and space-planning. Later, she married and moved back home to Mason City, Iowa where she owned and operated an Italian Bakery-deli. She learned to make authentic hard-crusted Italian bread from an old Italian baker in Chicago. Patrons traveled miles for that bread.

In 1981, Condra moved to Aspen where she baked the breads for Pour La France and made pastries for Abetone. At that point, she realized an overwhelming desire to learn more—she traveled to New York to gain experience at Le Cirque and to San Francisco where she trained at Masas. "My desire to learn kept growing until I knew that I had to go to Paris, to the source, to experience pastry-making their way." She landed a job at Fauchon, the world-renowned pastry-gourmet shop. She explains, "That's where I learned Nouvelle French—pastries made lighter and more creative." She also went to La Maison de Chocolat to learn about chocolate and attended a school devoted especially to baking with chocolate.

From Paris, she went to London and worked at a Nouvelle pastry shop and finally back to Aspen. She worked at Piñons as their pastry chef before opening a wholesale bakery outlet at the Airport Business Center. Now, she works beside her sister, Debby, turning out exquisite artful creations specializing in chocolate. She's a self-acclaimed chocolate addict. It's no surprise to see her numerous "Annual Chocolate Classic" awards displayed.

She sells to some of Aspen's best restaurants and, of course, to individual customers. Her wedding cakes are truly works of art—many incorporate ribbons and fresh flowers. She made Don Johnson and Melanie Griffith's wedding cake—the best cake actor Johnson had ever tasted. It was a three-tiered chocolate cake with white chocolate butter cream frosting crowned with a white orchid.

Watching Condra buzz around her kitchen blending, mixing and folding ingredients for four different desserts, it's more than apparent that she has come full circle—back to what she loved doing as a child.

Flour-less Chocolate Cake

NOT FOR THE WEAK OF HEART!

5 oz (10 T) Unsalted butter
½ C Sugar
12 oz High-quality semi-sweet chocolate
4 Eggs, separated
¼ t Salt

Melt the butter, ¼ cup of sugar and the chocolate over hot (not boiling) water. Or melt in a microwave for 30 seconds at a time, stirring after each melting. Cool a little. Whisk in the egg yolks. Whip the egg whites and salt until peaks form and then add the rest of the sugar. Fold into the chocolate mixture.

■ Turn into a 9-inch round pan that has been lined with parchment paper. Bake in a 350 degree oven just until the sides set, approximately 8-10 minutes. The middle will be loose. Remove and let sit on a cooling rack for 10 minutes and put in the freezer to set up for at least 8 hours. This is best done the day before.

■ To remove, dip the bottom of the pan in hot water to loosen it. Invert onto a plate or cake circle and remove the parchment paper. Refrigerate again. Before serving, sprinkle with confectioners' sugar. You may serve with flavored and sweetened whip cream and berries. Cut with a hot knife.

The kicker: if you truly are a chocolate lover, this cake is for you!

Spiced Pear Cake

5 Ripe pears, peeled, cored & chopped fine
1 ¾ C Dark brown sugar
1 ¼ C Pecan pieces
½ t Allspice
2 t Cinnamon
2½ C Plus 2 T All-purpose flour
4 t Baking powder
8 oz Canola oil
3 Eggs, slightly beaten

ORANGE GLAZE
½ C Freshly squeezed orange juice
⅓ C Fine sugar

Combine the first 5 ingredients in a mixing bowl and let them sit for 30 minutes to let the flavors meld together. Meanwhile, sift together the flour and baking powder. Carefully fold the flour mixture, the oil and eggs into the pear mixture.
■ Turn into a 10 inch teflon bundt pan and bake at 350 degrees for approximately 1 hour and 10 minutes and invert onto a cooling rack.
■ In a small sauce pan, heat the orange juice and the sugar together. Bring to a boil, reduce the heat and cook until the sugar is dissolved. Pour the glaze immediately onto the cake.

The kicker: this is an incredibly rich, moist and flavorful cake. Everyone enjoyed it at our recipe tasting. Be creative with nuts or fruits for decoration.

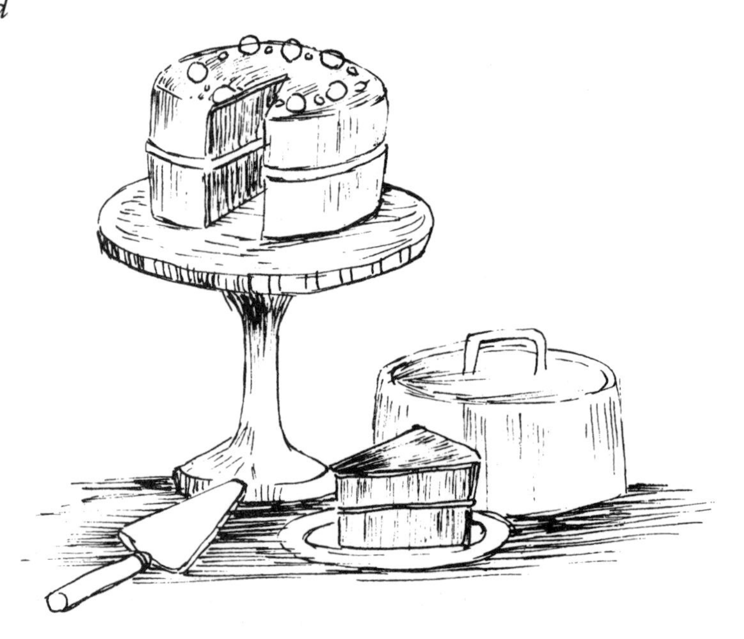

Jackie Kasabach
Mom's Catering

JACKIE ORIGINALLY RAN "MOM'S TRUCKED-UP-FOODS," which was a catering truck that served homemade sandwiches and desserts to hungry construction workers, a well-appreciated alternative to junk food. After her trusty truck blew up, she decided to stay in the food business. Word spread about her wonderful dishes which led to catering private parties and other affairs.

She clinched the Design Conference account in 1974. Designers from all over the world converge in Aspen every June to learn from each other. Jackie has fed them homemade breakfast breads, salads, sandwiches and has become famous for her authentic Tabbouleh.

Jackie is Armenian and has a strong ethnic background. Her family kept up many of the Middle Eastern traditions and enjoyed eating dishes such as Plaki and Jajik. They're tasty, low in fat and a nice change from the ordinary. She uses many of these Middle Eastern recipes when catering.

Jackie also works at The Gant in their Food and Beverage Department organizing and catering a variety of different events. With an eclectic cookbook library as her background, Jackie can plan any kind of party, complete with entertainment and decorations.

"I was bored to tears as a librarian in Chicago. The Aspen community has given me the flexibility and freedom to do what I love. I get such satisfaction when it all comes together."

Jajïk (A Cucumber and Yogurt Salad)

SERVES 4

3 Medium cucumbers
¼ T Salt
1 Clove garlic
1 T Vinegar
1 T Dry dill or 6 T fresh dill
16 oz Low or non-fat yogurt
2 T Olive oil (optional)
½ T Dry mint leaves or 1 T fresh mint
½ C Cooked barley

Peel the cucumbers, quarter lengthwise and slice about 1/8 inch thick. Place in bowl and sprinkle lightly with salt. Rub another bowl with garlic and swish vinegar around to collect flavors, then add dill and yogurt.

■ Stir until the mixture is the consistency of a thick soup, if necessary, add cold water. Pour over cucumbers, add barley and stir. Pour into individual serving dishes, add one ice cube to make it very cold (or refrigerate), and sprinkle with olive oil and garnish with mint.

♥ *The kicker:* this is a Middle Eastern dish, typically served as a first course. We served it with Jackie's Tabbouleh recipe and a salad for an incredibly healthy meal.

Tabbouleh

SERVES 6

1 C Large grain bulghur wheat, preferably bought at a Middle Eastern grocery store or a health food store
2 C Hot water
1 Bunch chopped green onions (use the green part, too)
1 Bunch parsley, chopped
⅔ C Fresh mint or 3 T dried (best with fresh)
1 Tomato, cubed
1 Cucumber, peeled & chopped
¼ C Olive oil, or to taste
Juice of 1 ½ lemons, or to taste
Allspice
Garlic salt
Salt & pepper
Romaine lettuce leaves
Pita bread, cut in wedges

Soak the bulghur in water for at least ½ hour. Drain well. Mix the bulghur with the onions, pressing and squeezing with your hands to combine flavors. Add the parsley, mint and a dash of allspice. Add the salt, pepper and garlic salt to taste. Dress with olive oil and lemon juice. Continue to toss and squeeze with your hands. Cover and chill. Before serving, add the chopped tomatoes and cucumbers. Line a serving platter with romaine lettuce leaves and arrange the tabbouleh in a mound on the leaves. Use the smaller leaves as "dippers." You can also decorate the platter with olives, cucumbers or lemon wedges.

♥ *The kicker:* this Middle Eastern dish is very healthy and naturally low in fat.

White Bean Plaki

CAN BE AN APPETIZER OR A VEGETABLE SIDE DISH

SERVES 10

One 15 oz Can of Great Northern Beans, not drained
3 C Water
¼ C Olive oil
½ t Salt
2 Celery stalks with leaves, sliced
2 Carrots, sliced
1 Green onion
1 Medium white onion
1 T Dill (dry), or 6 T fresh dill
2 Minced garlic cloves
2 Chopped tomatoes
2 T Tomato paste
Small bunch of parsley, chopped
Lemon wedges
Lettuce leaves

Make this dish a day in advance. Do not drain the beans. Put them in a saucepan with the water, oil and salt and heat. Add the next 8 ingredients and cook over medium flame for 1 hour or until thick. It should be thick enough to eat with a fork. Add the parsley right at the end. Chill overnight in order for the flavors to blend. Serve on lettuce leaves with lemon wedges as an appetizer, or serve as a side dish.

♥ *The kicker:* this recipe is low in fat. We enjoyed it at a summer recipe testing and it was very refreshing.

Peter O'Grady's Creative Catering

IT'S NOT UNCOMMON. PETER O'GRADY CAME TO ASPEN AS a ski bum and decided to stay. However, O'Grady is one of the lucky ones—he started his own catering business and was able to survive in a town where the "ski bum" is a term of the past.

He gained experience at Shannon's Galley, where he apprenticed under Michael Shannon. He soon became their head chef and ran the kitchen. After various and assorted jobs, O'Grady, along with Julie Murad, started their own catering business. Their timing was perfect. It was during a period when several caterers quit. Julie and Peter filled a niche in Aspen for catering with a creative touch.

"We started out catering mostly private dinner parties until we built up a reputation." From there, O'Grady explains, "we started catering large events like the Aspen Club Celebrity Tennis Tournament, parties for the various arts and culture groups and large corporate functions." O'Grady bought out his partner and is now on his own. "Catering is a real challenge for me. My clients expect me to create something really special." And that he does. His services run the gamut; he provides flower arranging, costumes, decorations, music, varied menus and wine suggestions.

He cooks with the freshest of everything that is available. He buys outstanding herbs and produce from a local grower. When asked what cuisine he prefers, O'Grady replies, "I have a French cooking background, which is the basis for everything I do, but I'm extremely flexible. You have to be in this business whether it be a down-home picnic, an intimate French dinner or a Mexican feast. There is always much research to be done to obtain the right look and the right taste of the cuisine for my clients. It's exciting to be given the chance to test myself constantly."

O'Grady's newest venture is food styling. Jill St. John contracted him in the summer of '86 when she decided to photograph her cookbook in Aspen. O'Grady describes food styling as, "the preparation of food for photographing." The project became quite a challenge and required much experimentation. He enjoyed it. Food styling is a realm O'Grady intends to pursue further.

He continues to read, travel and take classes in order to stay current in the food business. O'Grady says with a grin, "I feel like I've only just begun. So much more is open to me than before which is a function of being happy with my work."

Cold Salmon with Niçoise Tomato Coulis

SERVES 6

2 lbs Salmon filet
¼ C Dry white wine
2 Sprigs parsley
¼ Lemon, squeezed
¼ t Sea salt
1 T Balsamic vinegar

TOMATO COULIS
2 lbs Fresh tomatoes
¼ C Olive oil
1 Medium onion
2 Cloves garlic
2 T Green olives, chopped
2 T Black olives, chopped
1 T Capers
1 T Parsley, chopped
½ t Sea salt
¾ t Freshly ground pepper
2 T Fresh basil, shredded

Make the tomato coulis: core each tomato and slash the opposite end. Skin the tomatoes by placing them in boiling water until their skin loosens, approximately 30 seconds. Remove to a colander and peel the skin off. Split them in two and squeeze the seeds out. Slice the onion thinly in half-rounds. Chop the garlic. Heat the olive oil in a medium skillet and add the onions. Sweat for 5 minutes over medium heat. Add the garlic and continue to sweat for 5 more minutes. Add the tomatoes and the rest of the coulis ingredients (except for the basil) and cook over medium-low heat for 15-20 minutes or until a soft moist consistency is achieved. Remove from the heat and add the basil. Set aside at room temperature. *Note:* the tomato coulis can be prepared a day ahead, if desired.

■ Place the salmon filet in a glass baking dish. Add the white wine, parsley, lemon and salt. Cover and bake at 350 degrees for 12-15 minutes (ovens vary). Do not overcook. Remove from the oven and drain the cooking liquid. Sprinkle the salmon with the tablespoon of balsamic vinegar.

■ Place the warm tomato coulis over the salmon, cover and refrigerate for several hours or overnight. Remove from the refrigerator and allow to warm at room temperature for 20 minutes before serving.

♥ *The kicker:* this is a low-fat, low cholesterol recipe. Since you prepare it the day before, it's perfect for a summer's evening after an active, fun-filled day!

Wine Suggestion: Cakebread Cellars, Sauvignon Blanc.

Warm Balsamic Marinated Salmon with Orange Ginger Sauce

SERVES 6

2 lbs Salmon filet

MARINADE
4 T Balsamic vinegar
4 T Pure olive oil
1 T Fresh rosemary sprigs, chopped rough

ORANGE SAUCE
1½ C Orange juice, fresh squeezed
1 inch Fresh ginger, grated
1 T Lemon juice
1 T Orange zest, chopped
⅓ C Dry white wine
½ t White pepper, freshly ground
½ t Sugar
⅛ t Sea salt

Place the salmon in a stainless or glass dish. Add the marinating ingredients and allow to marinate for at least 6 hours, preferably overnight. Combine the orange sauce ingredients in a stainless pan. Bring to a boil and simmer for ½ hour or until it's reduced to the consistency of cream. Set aside. ■ Grill or broil the salmon and cook medium-rare; do not overcook the fish. Divide the fish into 6 servings and spoon the warmed orange sauce on top.

♥ *The kicker:* this is a very easy recipe. If you marinate the fish and make the sauce a day in advance, all you need to do the evening you're serving it, is to cook the salmon, make a wonderful salad and perhaps some pasta. This dish is low-in-fat and cholesterol.

Wine Suggestion: Edna Valley, Chardonnay.

Silver City Gourmets

ROBERT WIESER'S A PRETTY LUCKY GUY. HE'S CATERED parties for the likes of Oprah Winfrey, Cher, Robert Wagner, Kate Capshaw and other celebrities. Not bad for a native Aspenite who fell in love with cooking while still in high school.

After apprenticing at the Ute City Banque, Wieser was the chef at the Golden Barrel and, most recently, at the Sardy House. He was written up in *Food & Wine* magazine as "serving the best rack of lamb in town."

Having earned a reputation for innovative cuisine, Wieser began his own catering/concierge business. These services complement each other. Beside cooking an elegant meal, accompanied by classical music, he can provide such amenities as: hair styling, massage, manicures and ski, golf and tennis instruction. He's listened to the requests of his clients.

"I'm considered the best dressed chef in town," Wieser proudly told me. "I always wear a tuxedo—it makes a statement. I want to show my clients I care and that I offer the best in service and style."

Wieser feels that to be a chef in the 90's, you need to be versatile, creative and responsive. You need to meet a variety of dietary needs. He has catered Spa Weeks. "It was a real challenge to cook for two weeks with no fat, no cholesterol, no butter and no cream. Basically, I served carbohydrates, starches and protein. My clients lost 10 pounds in two weeks and no one went hungry!" The trick, Wieser divulges, is adding a lot of fresh herbs (in the correct combinations) so that the flavors come out. At the Spa Weeks, fish was served often. Rich in natural oils, fish is a superior source of protein and can be prepared in numerous appealing styles.

Salads were enjoyed thoroughly and enhanced with fresh lemon juice and fresh herbs. Grain salads, such as Tabbouleh, were well-appreciated after 6-8 hours of exercise! Fresh fruit, in season, finished off a no-fat meal.

If you're not into Spa Cuisine, Wieser is pleased to concoct Smoked Salmon Caviar Rosettes, Lobster Thermadour and Crème Brûlée. Either way, his goal is to satisfy his clients.

"Cooking is the best part of my life; it's my religion. Cooking is truly the way to someone's heart!"

Danish Yogurt Apple Pie

1 Unbaked 9 inch pie pastry
¼ C Firmly packed brown sugar
¼ C Sugar
2 T Cornstarch
¼ t Salt
4 C Baking apples, peeled and thinly sliced
Few drops of lemon juice
1 C yogurt
1 Egg
½ -1 t Vanilla

TOPPING
½ C Toasted almonds
½ C Packed brown sugar
1 t Cinnamon

Preheat oven to 400 degrees. Combine the sugars, cornstarch and salt. Mix with the apples. Place in the shell and sprinkle with lemon juice. Bake for 20-25 minutes. Blend the yogurt, egg and vanilla. Reduce oven to 350 degrees and pour the mixture over the apples. Bake 30 more minutes until the custard is set. After 15 minutes, coat with mixed topping.

Grilled Salmon and Shrimp with Orange-Basil Vinaigrette

SERVES 8

4 lbs Salmon filets or steaks (if using filets, leave the skin on)
2 lbs Medium-large shrimp
Freshly grated zest of 2 oranges
4 C Orange juice
Garnishes: watercress, lime slices, cherry tomatoes

BASIL OIL
(make a day in advance)
1 C Packed basil leaves, blanched and rinsed in cold water for brilliant color
2 C Olive oil

Make the basil oil: mix ¼ cup oil in food processor with the basil and mix until blended. Add the rest of the oil and cover for 24 hours for flavor. In a nonreactive saucepan, cook the zest and orange juice. Reduce to ¼ - ½ cup (approximately 20 minutes). Strain and let cool. Blend in ½ cup of the basil oil by whisking. Add salt and pepper to taste. Grill the salmon and the shrimp basting with the orange-basil vinaigrette (do not overcook). Serve with extra vinaigrette and garnishes.

Wine Suggestion: Puligny Montrachet.

Honey Baked Chicken

SERVES 2

- *1 Whole chicken, or boneless breasts*
- *2 T Butter*
- *4 T Flour*
- *½ C Honey*
- *¼ C Prepared dry mustard*
- *1 t Salt*
- *1 t Cinnamon*
- *1 C Yogurt, plain or vanilla*
- *⅓ C White wine*

Wash the chicken and dry. Melt the butter in a saucepan. Add the flour until bubbling. Stir in the next 4 ingredients, remove from heat and let cool. Slowly add this mixture to the yogurt. Coat the chicken and marinate 2-3 hours. Spoon on extra marinade and pour some wine around the dish. Bake at 350 degrees for an hour or until the chicken is done (less for breasts) and browned.

Wine Suggestion: Cakebread Cellars, Sauvignon Blanc.

Hungarian Cherry Soup

SERVES 8

A VERY SIMPLE, REFRESHING SUMMER SOUP, A BEAUTIFUL PASTEL COLOR

3 lb Fresh cherries, can also use frozen or canned, pitted
½ -1 C Sugar, depending on sweetness of cherries
5 C Cold water
2 C Beaujolais, or a light, fruity wine
1 qt Your choice: light cream (sweeter result), sour cream (for a crisp, sharp taste), yogurt, or a mixture of sour cream and yogurt (for a full-bodied taste)

Bring the first 3 ingredients to a boil for 30 minutes until the cherries are tender, still with lots of color. Don't overcook. Cool for 30 minutes-1 hour. Add the wine and cool completely for at least 2 hours. Then, add your choice of cream or yogurt and mix thoroughly.

Salmon Mousse

AN APPETIZER THAT WILL SERVE 20

2 C Flaked salmon, left-over salmon or canned
1½ C Yogurt
½ C Mayonnaise
½ C Celery, minced
¼ C Cucumber, minced
2 T Shallots, minced
2 T Parsley, minced
4 t Fresh lemon juice
¾ t Salt
½ t Prepared horseradish
½ t Fresh dill
2 T Unflavored gelatin
½ C Dry vermouth

LEMON DRESSING
⅓ C Yogurt
1 T Lemon juice
½ -1 t Dry mustard
½ C Cream, whipped

Combine the salmon, yogurt and mayonnaise. Flake while mixing. Add the next 8 ingredients and mix well. Mix the gelatin and the vermouth together and heat gently to dissolve. Add the gelatin/vermouth mixture to the rest of the ingredients and pour into an oiled fish mold. Chill until set. Make the dressing by combining the first 3 ingredients and folding in the cream. For those who are watching their fat intake, serve with lemon dressing on the side.

The kicker: this is a great appetizer especially nice served in the summer and wonderful made with fresh, poached salmon.

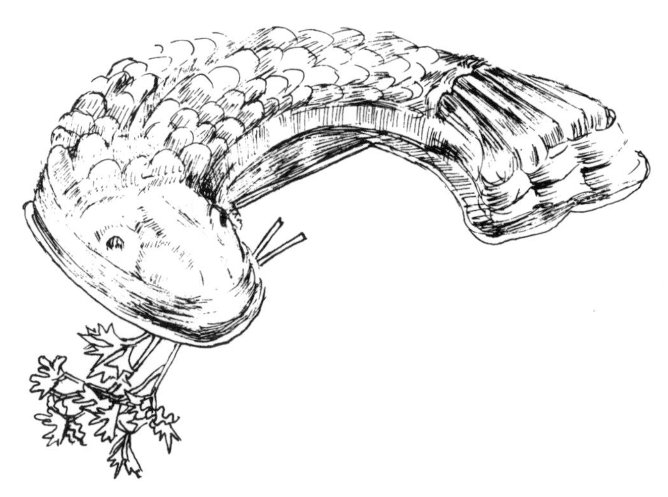

PART IV

Aspen Specialty Foods

Nothing is more satisfying than to produce a recipe for friends and family who truly appreciate the effort and adore the results. They may, however, bug you for months for another jar or bottle! The next giant step is to manufacture and market this special recipe. The Aspen area is home to many successful entrepreneurs. The recipes in this section come from local specialty food producers. They've created a variety of ways to use their products and invite you to experiment and enjoy!

Aspen Specialty Foods

THESE WONDERFUL FOOD ITEMS WERE ORIGINATED AND marketed by Aspen locals. They're all well worth trying. Following is a brief history about each item:

■ *Any O' Cajun Spice™*. Tim Cottrell, owner of the Smuggler Land Office, credits his former chef, Peter Soto, with the creation of these spices. They decided to bottle this wonderful combination of Cajun spices that they use nightly to create their famous blackened fish and beef entrées.

■ *Aspen Coffee Company.* Aspen's only coffee roaster features freshly-roasted coffees from around the world! Owners of this wonderful eatery and espresso bar, Sally Jo Mullen and Wendy Bishonden, invite you to come in and enjoy "a cup" of any one of their many varieties of coffee drinks.

■ *Aspen Mulling Spices.* An Aspen tradition that originated in 1971 as a gesture of hospitality at Wax & Wicks, Aspen's renowned gift shop. The many requests for the recipe resulted in a carton of Aspen Mulling Spices. Today the spices enjoy both national and international popularity.

■ *Aspen Specialty Foods Mustard Sauce.* For thirty years, Marsha Brendlinger made mustard sauce from her grandmother's recipe and gave it as a holiday gift to Aspenites. The sweetness encourages the user to include it with a variety of fruits and cheeses. The tang enhances vegetables, meats, fish and pasta. It was so well liked that people requested that she make it year 'round. It is marketed in many states across the country.

■ *Crooked Spoke Barbecue Sauce.* Crooked Spoke is an original favorite from the Old Snowmass Food Company in the Old Snowmass Valley, near Aspen. Crooked Spoke is a Becker family tradition. Its unique flavor and versatility sets it apart from ordinary sauces. They hope it becomes a tradition in your family, too! The gourmet flavor will turn your grill into a Chef's Kitchen.

■ *Forever Pesto.* Forever Pesto comes to you from a cottage industry nestled in Colorado's finest ski country. Owned and operated by Jolee Henry, the pesto business began three years ago and has since become a popular "convenient gourmet" pleasure. If you find yourself in the Rockies,

Jolee invites you to call Forever Pesto and share her brand of Colorado hospitality with you. You'll learn why her pesto and commitment is Forever.

■ *Lydia's Gardens.* Lydia McIntyre developed her gourmet food line with great pride. Each product has been blended with the finest ingredients available to produce exceptional flavor combinations. The flavored vinegars, olive oils and seasoning blends create delicious salad dressings. The Italian salsa can be enjoyed many ways. She has created wonderful combinations of handmade pastas. Each product is guaranteed to be a culinary delight!

■ *Roaring Fork Sauces.* Kim Wille created her wonderful sauces while running her Last Stand restaurant in the summer at Iselin Field and operating her own catering business. Everyone kept asking for her recipes, so she finally decided to market four of her favorite sauces.

■ *Standing Ovation Pizza Sauce.* This low-fat classic sauce is robust enough for a traditional cheese pizza, yet subtle enough to complement your favorite toppings. Now a pizzeria-style pizza can be created at home! Standing Ovation Pizza Sauce was created by Lori Kasabian and Elaine Bonds who love to make pizzas for their families and friends.

Any O' Cajun Spice™ Pan-Blackened Salmon

SERVES 6

Six 8 oz Salmon fillets,
1½ inches thick
Oil or butter
Any O' Cajun Spice™

Heat a large cast iron skillet over very high heat. You must use iron (no other metal can take the heat). Rub the salmon fillets with oil or butter and coat both sides with Any O' Cajun Spice™. Sear the salmon in the hot skillet for about 2 minutes. Warning: Blackening is very smokey! The cooked side should be dark brown, almost charred. Cook the flip side another 1½-2 minutes (thickness of fillets determines the cooking time). Remove from skillet. The texture should be crispy black on the outer crust and wonderfully moist and tender on the inside. Experiment with your favorite meats and fish. You'll love it!

Any O' Cajun Spice™ is a special blend of twelve herbs and spices. Use for blackening, grilling and baking with fish, meats, game or poultry. Add to salads, soups, sauces, vegetables, gumbo, jambalaya, pasta and Bloody Marys.

Aspen Coffee Company Aspen Latté

Hot espresso
2 T Aspen Coffee Company's Aspen Spices
Hot steamed milk

In a 16 ounce cup, fill with one third hot espresso, the two tablespoons of Aspen Coffee Company's Aspen Spices and two thirds of hot steamed milk. Mix together well and enjoy.

The Aspen Layered Drink

Hot espresso
Steamed whole milk
Foam
Optional: chocolate sprinkles, flavored syrups

Using a glass mug with a handle, pour one third of steamed milk for the first layer. Hold a soup spoon over the top of the mug, but close to one edge. For the second layer, very slowly pour the hot espresso so that it trickles over the spoon and fills two thirds of the cup. To finish, spoon foamed milk on top. If you want to add flavored syrups, add to the steamed milk and stir well. Top with chocolate sprinkles if desired.

Sally and Wendy suggest experimenting with flavors and liqueurs.

Aspen Mulling Spices

Wine

1½ liters Burgundy
½ part Water
1 package Aspen Mulling Spices

Cider

1 gallon Apple Cider
1 package Aspen Mulling Spices

Tea

1 gallon Tea
1 package Aspen Mulling Spices

To make the wine, cider and tea, mix together the ingredients and serve either hot or cold. For a variation with the tea, use three parts tea and one part orange juice.

■ *Some unique (and sometimes surprising) ideas* for serving Aspen Mulling Spices: *Beverages*—combine Aspen Mulling Spices with: combination of apple, cranberry and orange juices; mixture of ginger ale and orange and lemon juices; hot buttered rum; Southern Comfort, Sake, Apple Jack, Hiram Walker or Red Hot Schnapps. *Baked Goods*—generally, any sugar or spices that the recipe calls for can be substituted with equal amounts of Aspen Mulling Spices. Try it in: apple pie, pumpkin pie, nut breads or fruit breads, muffins, cookies—especially oatmeal, apple crisp, apple strudel, peach cobbler, spice cake, applesauce cake or carrot cake, coffee cake—use in the topping, too! *Breakfast Ideas*—sprinkle on granola or hot cereal, sprinkle on toast or French toast. Simmer apple juice with Mulling Spices, cornstarch and lemon juice to make a syrup; delicious on apple pancakes. *Snacks and Desserts*—Jello squares, candied apples, sprinkled over ice cream or yogurt, chocolate fondue, apple or banana fritters, place Mulling Spices in the core of apples and bake. *Other Uses*—mulligatawny soup, brown sugar brandy sauce, sprinkle on apple sauce, mix with orange juice to baste ham, pork chops or pork roast, to spice Waldorf salad, in chilled fruit-base soups.

♥ The spices are all natural and are fat free.

Aspen Mustard Sauce Swordfish

Marinate the fish in the marinade. Refrigerate for 3-4 hours. Drain the fish and broil the steaks for 5-6 minutes per side. Brush with the marinade several times while cooking.

4 Large swordfish steaks

MARINADE
2-3 T Aspen Mustard Sauce
4 T Lemon juice
1/3 C Light soy sauce
1/2 C Peanut oil
2 Green onions, finely chopped
1 Clove garlic, minced

Chicken Salad

Mix the first 6 ingredients together. Whisk the last 5 ingredients and pour over the salad.

2 C Cooked, cubed chicken
1 C Pineapple chunks
1/2 C Water chestnuts, chopped
1/2 C Celery, chopped
1/3 C Toasted almonds
1/4 C Carrots, grated
2 T Aspen Mustard Sauce
1 T Soy sauce
1 t Toasted sesame oil
2 T Rice vinegar
1/3 C Mayonnaise

Vinaigrette

Combine all the ingredients by whisking together. Use it as a salad dressing or over cooked vegetables.

2 T Aspen Mustard Sauce
3 T Balsamic vinegar
4 T Olive oil
1 T Lemon juice
Salt & pepper, to taste

Crooked Spoke Barbecue Sauce Ribs

Baby Back Ribs
Crooked Spoke Barbecue Sauce

Marinate the ribs in Crooked Spoke for 1-2 hours before grilling on moderate heat.

Pork Chops

Pork Chops
Crooked Spoke Barbecue Sauce

Apply the Crooked Spoke sauce liberally while grilling the pork chops. Crooked Spoke has a special blend of ingredients which allows you to cook with less chance of "BBQ burn."

Swordfish or Halibut

Swordfish or Halibut
Crooked Spoke Barbecue Sauce

Apply the Crooked Spoke Barbecue Sauce lightly to Swordfish or Halibut steaks. The light covering will provide a delicious flavor enhancement to these healthy foods!

■ An all-time favorite is barbecue chicken: parboil the chicken for 15-20 minutes prior to grilling; then brush on Crooked Spoke from start to finish!
Experiment with Crooked Spoke Barbecue Sauce on your own and let us know what your favorites are!

Forever Pesto

Walnut/Basil
Sun-Dried Tomato
Jalapeño
Garlic/Tomato (non-dairy)
Traditional (non-dairy)

■ To make sauces, there is no need to heat the pesto. Simply mix with the following already-warmed foods: pastas, rice, quiches, omelettes, vegetables, baked potatoes, mushroom caps.
■ Forever Pesto is wonderful for spreads and for basting. Try it on the following: chicken, bread, tortillas, fish, sandwiches and pizza.
■ For salad dressings, add extra virgin olive oil to Forever Pesto until you reach the desired consistency.
■ "Covenient Gourmet" hors d'oeuvres—combine Forever Pesto with cream cheese or goat cheese and spread on crackers, melba toast or French bread.
Forever Pesto contains all natural ingredients with no added preservatives.

Lydia's Gardens Garlic Basil Vinaigrette Dressing

1/3 C Lydia's Garlic/ Basil Vinegar
2 T Lydia's Garlic/ Basil Seasonings
1 C Lydia's Red Chile Olive Oil

Blend Lydia's Vinegar, Seasonings and Olive oil together to make a wonderful salad dressing. To make antipasto, combine: 2 cups broccoli tops, 2 cups cauliflower tops, 1 red pepper (seeded & cubed), one 2-ounce jar green pimento olives, one 3¼-ounce can black pitted olives, 6-8 pepperoncini, 8-10 whole baby corns, one 8½-ounce can quartered artichoke hearts, 1 cup cherry tomatoes, 2 cups fresh green beans (cubed into 1" pieces). Pour the dressing over the vegetables and toss. Let it marinate in the refrigerator at least 5 hours or overnight. Serve on a bed of Romaine lettuce. This is a versatile combination which can be served traditionally as an antipasto or heated and served over pasta.
The combinations of this gourmet food line are endless and new sauces will soon be available.

Roaring Fork Sauces Sumi Salad

SERVES 4

2-3 C Main item: poultry, meat, seafood, vegetables, tofu, etc., cut in bite-size pieces
⅓ C So Sumi Sauce
3 C Napa cabbage, thinly sliced
8 Green onions, thinly sliced
1 C Mandarin oranges
¼ C Sesame seeds
½ C Almonds, slivered
One 3 oz package Ramen Noodles
Optional items: 1 C red cabbage, ⅓ C medium red bell pepper, thinly sliced

Marinate the main items in the *So Sumi Sauce.* Toast the sesame seeds and almonds on a baking sheet at 400 degrees. Heat for 3 minutes, stir, then toast for 3 more minutes. Crush the Ramen Noodles (still in the package) to small pieces using the heel of your hand on a counter. Discard the flavor packet, then mix together with the toasted sesame seeds and almonds. Heat a wok or heavy skillet to hot, then add and coat the pan with 1 tablespoon oil or non-stick spray. Add the prepared main item and stir until almost done. Then add the prepared cabbage, green onions and optional vegetables. Cook and stir for approximately 1 minute. Add ⅓ cup *So Sumi Sauce*, or to taste. Toss all the ingredients together in a serving bowl and decorate with red pepper rings.

♥ *Kim Wille's Roaring Fork Sauces* are low in sodium, low in fat, contain no cholesterol, no MSG and are preservative-free! Choose from: *Curry Lime, So Sumi, My Thai* or *Mexicali Blues* to make 30-minute meals!

Standing Ovation Pizza Sauce Tri-Color Hors D'Oeuvres

Prepared pizza dough
Standing Ovation Pizza Sauce
Low-fat, part-skim mozzarella cheese, grated
1 Green bell pepper, diced
1 Red sweet pepper, diced
1 Yellow banana pepper, diced

Preheat your oven to 400 degrees. Sprinkle the prepared crust lightly with half of the mozzarella cheese. Bake until the cheese is melted (which seals the crust). Remove from the oven and cover with Standing Ovation Pizza Sauce. Add the second half of the mozzarella cheese and top with the peppers. For an extra zip, sprinkle with grated parmesan cheese. Bake for an additional 10-15 minutes—time will vary with different ovens. Cut into small pieces and serve.

♥ This recipe is colorful and very tasty! If you're concerned with your fat intake, use a very small amount of cheese. Standing Ovation Pizza Sauce is prepared without oils or preservatives.

■ Hints for using Standing Ovation Pizza Sauce: Sprinkle your pizza crust with cheese and bake slightly before applying sauce. This will seal the crust and prevent sogginess. Crusts can vary from basic pizza dough to bagels.

■ Try serving Standing Ovation Gourmet Pizza Sauce on the following: French bread, sourdough bread, English muffins, flour tortilla shells, pita bread and focaccia bread.

■ *Experiment with* a combination of fresh cheeses. Top with your usual pizza toppings or try some of our favorites: fresh tomato slices, eggplant, spinach, green onions, broccoli, sun-dried tomatoes, fresh basil, roasted garlic and green chilies. Be adventurous and enjoy!

PART VI

Old Favorites

When friends and clients knew that *Lighter Tastes of Aspen* was in the works, they suggested that I include the most popular recipes from my first cookbook, *Tastes of Aspen*. Travel the pages in this final section to find some very special and most-loved "old favorites." Although a few of the restaurants they originated from have currently left Aspen, it is to their credit that these wonderful recipes live on.

Aspen Mine Company's Bloody Mary Mix

Combine the first 8 ingredients in a blender. Add the desired amount of vodka per glass, fill with ice and garnish each with a celery stalk. This is a wonderful drink served for brunches or before a light supper.

32 oz Tomato juice
Juice of 2 lemons and 2 limes
½ -1 T Pepper, depending on your preference
½ T Celery salt
2 T Horseradish
¼ t Tabasco
1 T Grey Poupon mustard
1 T Worcestershire sauce
Vodka

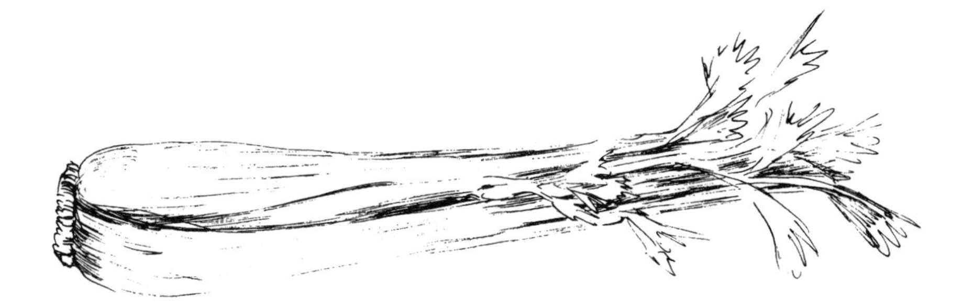

Aspen Mine Company's Gaspacho Soup

SERVES 4-6

2 Cucumbers, ¼ inch diced
5 Tomatoes, diced
20 oz Tomato juice
2 Onions, finely chopped
3 Carrots, diced to ¼ inch
½ C White wine
½ Bunch chopped fresh cilantro
½ Bunch chopped green onions
½ lb Jicama, diced
½ Fresh jalapeño, diced
1 Green pepper, diced
1 T Pepper
2 T Lemon juice
Avocado slices for garnish

Combine all the ingredients (except the avocado) and refrigerate until ready to serve. Garnish with the avocado slices and serve either as a main course with a green salad and French bread, or as a soup course.

♥ *The kicker:* Gaspacho is a very healthy dish—low in fat. Garnish with fresh parsley instead of avocado if you're watching your fat intake.

Aspen Mine Company's Grilled Chicken Caesar

SERVES 4-6

2 Heads Romaine lettuce, crisp and freshly torn
2 oz Fresh parmesan cheese
Croutons
Freshly ground pepper
6 oz Grilled chicken breast, julienne

CAESAR DRESSING
4 Cloves fresh garlic
4 Anchovy fillets
1 T Dijon mustard
1 Egg yolk
1 Whole egg
2 T Red wine vinegar
Juice of 1 lemon
1 T Worcestershire
4-6 oz Extra virgin olive oil

Mince the garlic and anchovies together to make a paste. Make the dressing: use a wooden bowl and whisk together the ingredients in the order they are listed. Toss the dressing with the lettuce. Add the parmesan, croutons, pepper and top with the grilled chicken.

Bonnie's Caesar Salad Dressing

In a Mixmaster, not a blender or Cuisinart, mix first 4 ingredients. Dissolve it with the egg yolks and slowly add the 4 oils. Turn mixer off and add the last 7 ingredients all together. Use Romaine lettuce with homemade garlic croutons.

MAKES MORE THAN
1 QUART

2 T Sugar
2 T Salt
3 T Dry Mustard
4 T Good quality red wine vinegar
2 Egg yolks
1 Pint Wesson oil
1 C Garlic oil (keep on hand in your refrigerator-vegetable oil with lots of garlic cloves) or 1 C Wesson oil mixed with 4 pressed garlic cloves
2 C Olive oil
½ C Wesson oil
¾ C Wine vinegar
1 T Tabasco
1 T Worcestershire
2 T Coarsely ground black pepper
6 T Lemon juice
1 Can chopped anchovies
1 C Parmesan, freshly grated

Charlemagne Salad with Hot Brie Dressing

SERVES 8

1 Medium head curly endive
1 Medium head iceberg lettuce
1 Medium head romaine lettuce
Garlic croutons (preferably homemade)
½ C Olive oil
4 t Minced shallot
2 t Minced garlic
½ C Sherry wine vinegar
2 T Fresh lemon juice
4 t Dijon mustard
10 oz Ripe French Brie cheese (rind remains), cut into small pieces, room temperature
Freshly ground pepper

Tear lettuce into bite-size pieces. Toss with garlic croutons in large bowl. Warm olive oil in heavy large skillet over low heat for 10 minutes. Add shallot and garlic and cook until translucent, stirring occasionally, about 5 minutes. Blend in vinegar, lemon juice and mustard. Add cheese and stir until smooth. Season with pepper. Toss hot dressing with lettuce and serve.

The kicker: do not use high heat. Charlemagne used a sterno heater and prepared this salad table-side. The aromas are wonderful!

Chart House Mud Pie

½ Package Nabisco chocolate wafers
½ Stick butter, melted
1 Gallon coffee ice cream
1½ C Fudge sauce
Whipped cream
Slivered almonds

Crush wafers and add butter, mix well. Press into 9" pie plate. Cover with soft ice cream. Put into freezer until ice cream is firm. Top with cold fudge sauce (it helps to place in freezer for some time to make spreading easier). Store in freezer approximately 10 hours. To serve, slice pie into 8 portions and serve on a chilled dessert plate with a chilled fork. Top with whipped cream and almonds.

Crystal Palace's Swedish Cream

Heat the first four ingredients until warm, whisking constantly. Do not boil. Remove from the heat and whisk in the sour cream. Pour into individual serving cups or wine glasses. The remainder can be refrigerated and reheated to be used later. Top with berries of your choice. Citrus and fresh fruits are not recommended.

SERVES 6–10

2 C Heavy cream
1 t Vanilla
1 t Gelatin
¼ C Sugar
1½ C Sour cream

Chez Grandmère Brittany Almond Cake

FILLING
2/3 C Almonds, preferably with skins on (for more flavor)
1/2 C Sugar
Egg white, enough to make a spreadable paste

CAKE
8 oz Butter
1 Whole egg
1 Extra yolk
1/2 C Sugar
2 t Orange flower water
1/4 t Almond extract
1 1/2 C Sifted flour
2 T Sifted cornstarch
1/3 t Baking powder
Pinch salt
1/3 C Ground almonds

Preheat oven to 350 degrees. Grease an 8½" springform pan. Grind almonds in food processor. Add sugar, a little egg white and water if necessary. Set filling aside. Cream butter well. Add egg and two-thirds of the extra yolk. Set the remainder aside in a small bowl with a teaspoon of water to use as a glaze. Add sugar and flavorings to cake batter and beat very well. Add dry ingredients. Turn half batter into cake pan. Cover with almond filling, then top with remaining batter. Beat glaze ingredients together with a fork. Paint top of cake lightly with glaze then make a crosshatch design in glaze with tines of fork. Bake for 30-35 minutes until firm and golden. Serve warm, with fresh crushed berries and heavy pouring cream.

This is an adaptation of a Madeleine Kamman recipe for a traditional cake made in Brittany. It is more suitable for preparing at home rather than in a restaurant because you can put it in the oven while you eat your dinner, then eat it at its best—warm and tender and aromatic, covered with crushed raspberries and a little heavy cream (not whipped).

Patti Dudley's Chocolate Dream Pie

CRUST

1½ C Chocolate wafer crumbs (preferably Nabisco's Famous Chocolate Wafers)

4 T Melted butter

FILLING

3 Eggs, separated

¾ C Sugar

4½ oz Unsweetened chocolate

5 T Butter

2 T Extra strong coffee

2 T Brandy

½ C Heavy whipping cream

TOPPING

½ C Heavy whipping cream

2 T Sugar

1 t Vanilla

To make the crust: melt the butter, stir in wafer crumbs and press into bottom and sides of a 8" pie tin. Set aside.

■ To make the filling: melt butter and chocolate together. Add coffee and set aside. Mix egg yolks, sugar and brandy in top of double boiler. Over medium heat, beat egg mixture for 8-10 minutes, until thick and pale yellow. Remove from heat. Add melted chocolate mixture. Beat egg whites until fairly stiff. Fold into chocolate. Beat whipping cream until stiff, then fold in. Fill pie shell and chill well.

■ To make the topping: beat whipping cream and sugar together until stiff. Add vanilla. Spread over pie. Can be garnished with chocolate curls if desired.

The kicker: this pie is like a very dense mousse. The recipe can be doubled or tripled or made in any size pan. The pie, without the topping, freezes well for several weeks.

Gordon's Lobster Lasagna

AN APPETIZER
SERVING 5

DOUGH
8 Egg yolks
1 C Flour

COURT BOUILLON
½ Orange, chopped
½ Lemon, chopped
½ Lime, chopped
1 Onion, chopped
Pinch thyme
1 Carrot, chopped
1 Celery stalk, chopped
1 Bay leaf
1 C White wine

FILLING
1 Lobster (1½ lbs)
8 oz Cream cheese
1 Shallot, chopped
Salt & pepper
3 Cloves garlic, minced
Fresh Parmesan cheese, grated
2 C Mushrooms
Olive oil
1 T Garlic, blanched and chopped
¼ C Red pepper, chopped and roasted
⅛ C Niçoise olives, remove stones and chop
⅛ C Sun-dried tomatoes, chopped
⅛ C Red onion, finely sliced
1 T Each: fresh thyme, marjoram, chives, Italian parsley, chopped
2 T Fresh basil
Whole milk Mozzarella cheese, grated
Chives (for garnish)

GOAT CHEESE SAUCE
1 Pint Heavy cream
4½ oz Montrachet goat cheese
1 t Garlic, chopped
1 t Shallot, chopped
Salt & pepper to taste

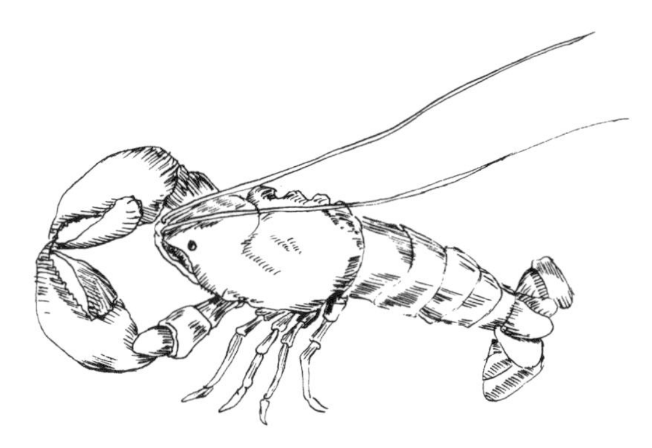

Recipe continued on following page

Make the dough: place the egg yolks in a mixing bowl with dough hook on medium speed. Add the flour and mix until it forms a ball. Remove and knead by hand until smooth. Roll through a hand pasta machine starting on 1 through 2,3,4 and twice on 5. Cut into five 6 inch squares and cook in boiling salted water until tender (about 3-4 minutes). Transfer to a bowl of ice water to stop cooking. Then take it to a work table and trim each into a neat square.

■ Mix court bouillon ingredients in a large stock pot (large enough for the lobster) filled with water. Boil. Poach lobster rare (3-4 minutes). Remove meat and cut into bite-size pieces.

■ Mix next 4 filling ingredients together and spread each square with ¼ inch of this mixture. Sprinkle with parmesan. Briefly sauté the mushrooms in olive oil, then cool. Mix the next 7 ingredients together with the mushrooms. On ½ of each square, place 4 tablespoons of the above mixture. Distribute the lobster meat evenly onto the squares. Fold each square over into a triangle and top with grated Mozzarella. Brown slowly under a salamander or in an oven to heat thoroughly.

■ Make the sauce: bring all sauce ingredients to a boil. Remove from heat and keep warm. To serve: place a very shallow pool of this sauce on 5 plates. Place 1 pasta square on each plate on the sauce. Top with chives.

The kicker: although this recipe is time-consuming and requires searching for special ingredients, it's well worth the effort. Each bite bursts with flavor!

Wine Suggestion: 1985 Domaine Michel, Chardonnay, Sonoma County.

Gretl's Apple Streussl

PASTRY
1½ C Unbleached flour
⅓ C Sugar
4 Egg yolks
½ C plus 2 T Unsalted butter
½ t Almond extract

FILLING
2 lbs Tart, crisp apples
1 T Lemon juice
1 T Brown sugar
1 t Cinnamon

TOPPING
1½ Sticks unsalted butter
1 C Flour
1 C Brown sugar
1 t Cinnamon
Powdered sugar

Preheat oven to 400 degrees. Mix all pastry ingredients and knead on a board. Roll out two-thirds of the dough. Take ring off 10" greased spring form pan and place dough on bottom of pan and bake 15 minutes. Form finger-thick rolls from rest of dough to place around the inside of the ring before filling.

■ Peel, core and slice apples. Toss apples with sugar and lemon juice. Add cinnamon. Fill prebaked shell. Make the topping: cut the butter into small slices. Place flour, sugar and cinnamon in a large bowl. Work quickly so butter does not melt. Use pastry cutter until mixed together, continue until all flour and sugar is incorporated into butter and streussl is loose and crumbly. Crumble over apple filling. Bake at 375 degrees for 50 minutes to 1 hour. Let cool. Dust with powdered sugar.

Gwyn's Seafood Puffs

AN APPETIZER
SERVING 4–6

FILLING
1 Clove garlic, minced
¼ C Green onions, chopped
¼ C Mushrooms, chopped
1 T Butter
½ lb Crab, cooked and chopped
½ lb Baby shrimp, cooked and chopped
12 oz Cream cheese
1 T Dry sherry
1 t Dill weed, dry
1 t Dijon mustard
Salt, pepper to taste
Egg White

PASTRY
½ Package puff pastry

SWEET HOT MUSTARD SAUCE
1 Egg
½ C Sugar
½ C Vinegar
½ C Dry mustard

Sauté the garlic and onions together in butter until tender. Add the mushrooms and sauté for a few more minutes. Whip the remaining filling ingredients together with the onion and mushroom mix. Cut puff pastry into 8 squares. Cut each square in half on the diagonal. Brush edges with egg white and place 2 teaspoons of seafood mixture in the center of the triangle. Fold in half, making a triangle and crimp the edges with a fork and seal with a brush of egg whites (if you bake them). Either bake in a preheated 375 degree oven for 15-20 minutes, or deep fry at 360 degrees for approximately 5 minutes.
■ Make the mustard sauce: beat the egg and add sugar. Add vinegar and dry mustard and mix fiercely. Heat in a double boiler, stirring constantly until thick. Serve the mustard sauce room temperature with the hot puffs.

Wine Suggestion: Silverado, Chardonnay.

Hibachi's Shabu Shabu

SERVES 2

JAPANESE-STYLE FONDUE. PAPER THIN SLICES OF CHICKEN, BEEF OR SEAFOOD SWISHED IN A POT OF BOILING BROTH THEN DIPPED INTO A SAUCE. USE CHOPSTICKS!

1 lb New York steak or other prime quality well-marbled beef or
1 lb Chicken breast or
1 lb Seafood (of your choice)
½ lb Napa cabbage
1 Bunch green onions
3 oz Bean threads
6 Shiitake mushrooms
½ C Bamboo shoots
½ Onion, sliced
½ Tofu cake, cut in rectangles
½ lb Fresh spinach
½ C Bean sprouts
1 Tomato
Chicken Broth (enough to fill the pot you use twice)

Thinly slice the meat or seafood you choose to use. Cut all vegetables into bite-size pieces. Give meticulous attention to arranging the vegetables on one platter and the meat onto another. Japanese presentation of dishes is very important. ■ Mix Ponzu sauce ingredients together. To make the sesame sauce, toast sesame seeds in a dry skillet. Grind them well and mix well with other ingredients. Serve these sauces in separate bowls. ■ Fill a heavy pot or electric wok with chicken broth. Start off with some vegetables (not all) in the pot. Swish meat in boiling broth (it takes only seconds) and dip in either of the 2 sauces. Towards the middle of the meal, ladle out this now-seasoned broth into bowls and enjoy as a soup. Add more broth and vegetables as needed. Sake complements this meal very well!

♥ *The kicker:* the secret to this dish is in the sauces. It's a very healthy way of eating.

PONZU SAUCE
½ C Lemon juice
½ C Light colored soy sauce

SESAME SAUCE
4 T White sesame seeds
3 T Sugar
2 T Soy sauce
1 T Shiro miso
1 T Sake
3 T Rice vinegar
½ T sesame oil

Krabloonik's Grand Marnier Mousse

SERVES 12

Melt chocolate with water and Grand Marnier. Whisk until smooth. Let cool. Whip the cream until soft peaks form. Fold whipped cream into chocolate mixture. Place into individual serving glasses and refrigerate, covered.

1 lb, 11 ounces White chocolate
½ C Water
¾ C Grand Marnier
4½ C Whipped cream

Wild Mushroom Soup

MAKES 12 CUPS

2 C Dried wild mushrooms (soaked), or 2 cups fresh wild mushrooms
1 Large onion
1 C Red wine
1 Pint Buttermilk
12 oz Sour cream
4 oz Plain yogurt
2 C Rich beef stock (Magi concentrate will work)
½ C Cornstarch
1½ Qt Water
Garlic to taste
Salt & pepper to taste

Strain liquid and save from dried mushrooms. Purée the mushrooms and onion. Add the strained liquid and all other ingredients except for cornstarch and save some sour cream for garnish. Bring to a low boil. Dissolve the cornstarch in lukewarm water, then whisk into the soup. Stir so it doesn't stick and scorch. Cook 3-5 minutes (or longer) until thickened. Garnish with a dollop of sour cream!

The kicker: a bowl of this soup from Krabloonik combined with a loaf of warm, homemade bread and a lovely salad makes a wonderful meal.

Wine Suggestion: Fumé Blanc. Chateau St. Jean, La Petite Etoile.

Maurice's Crêpes Suzette

SERVES 8-10

CRÊPES
1 C Flour
3 t Sugar
Pinch salt
7 Eggs
2 C Milk
1 t Remy Martin brandy
1 T Butter, melted

CUSTARD FILLING
2 C Milk
⅓ C Sugar
⅔ C Flour
6 Egg yolks
1 Stick butter
¼ C Triple sec
1 Orange, zested then squeezed

Whisk all the crêpe ingredients together. Strain to remove the lumps. Let rest for 2 hours, then make the crêpes. In a caste iron skillet, lightly butter the pan using a paper towel. When the pan is hot, use a cup with a spout to pour the batter into the pan. Swirl it all around and quickly pour any excess out. Whatever batter sticks to the pan will make a perfectly thin crêpe. Cook until just before the edges turn crispy.

■ Make the filling: scald the milk. In a bowl, whisk together the sugar, flour and egg yolks. Add the hot milk. Return all to a saucepan and bring to a boil, stirring constantly. Boil for 2 minutes, then remove from the heat. Gradually whisk in the butter, orange zest, juice and triple sec.

■ Fill each crêpe with a tablespoon of the custard. Spread it evenly. Fold the crêpe any way you prefer. The crêpes may be prepared to this point several hours in advance. When ready to serve, heat your oven to 350 degrees. Put the crêpes on a buttered baking sheet and bake about 8 minutes. Remove the crêpes to a serving dish or warm plates, allowing about 3 per person. Sprinkle with a little sugar. Gently warm ⅓ cup brandy. Pour over the crêpes. Averting your face, ignite the brandy with a match and serve.

Mezzaluna Bakery's Chocolate Tureen

CREATED BY ART SCHILDGEN

MAKES 1 LARGE LOAF PAN

10 oz Bittersweet chocolate (we use Callebaut)
6 oz Butter
2 T Cocoa powder
⅓ C Sugar
4 Egg yolks
4 Egg whites
1 C Heavy cream
Liqueur of your choice (see The Kicker)

Melt the chocolate, butter and cocoa powder together in a double boiler. Remove from the heat. Whisk in the sugar; the mixture might be granular. Whisk in the yolks until the mixture is smooth. The sugar granules should be dissolved. If you wish to flavor the tureen with a liqueur, it can be done at this point.

■ Whip the egg whites until stiff but not too dry. The bowl must be free of any oil or egg yolks in order for the whites to whip properly. This is best done with a mixer on medium-high speed. Fold in the meringue to the chocolate mixture gently—do not deflate them too much. The heavy cream can be whipped in the same fashion as the egg whites. The cream can now be folded into the chocolate mixture.

■ Pour the tureen mixture into a loaf pan and chill for at least 3 hours. Un-mold the tureen by placing it in a shallow pan of hot water and running a knife around the edge. Immediately turn it onto a serving tray and smooth with a palate knife.

The kicker: this chocolate tureen is best described as a fortified chocolate mousse that can be sliced. It is best if served with a fruit coulis such as raspberry or blackberry. The tureen is wonderful by itself or can be flavored with a liqueur such as Framboise, Grand Marnier or dark rum.

Mezzaluna Bakery's Green Salad Tropic

CREATED BY KATE FREEMAN

SERVES 8

SALAD
3 Heads Romaine, clean and chopped
1 Head red leaf lettuce, cleaned and left whole
4 Large chicken breasts, roasted and skinned, then diced
1 Small cantelope, skinned and diced into ½ inch pieces
2 Mangos, peeled and diced into ½ inch pieces
2 Papayas, peeled into ½ inch pieces
1 Red onion, sliced thin for garnish
4 oz Roquefort cheese, crumbled
4 oz Pine nuts, toasted

KIWI DRESSING
¼ C Raspberry vinegar
1 T Dijon mustard
2 T Honey
4 Kiwis, peeled
1 Lemon, juiced
2 C Extra Virgin Olive Oil

Make the dressing by combining the first 4 ingredients in a food processor and purée. Slowly add the olive oil to the kiwi mixture while processor is on, to emulsify. Add the lemon juice at the end. At this point, it's best to taste the dressing. Depending on the size of the kiwis and the lemon, more vinegar or mustard may need to be added. The dressing should be sweet and tangy at the same time.

■ Line a large salad bowl with whole leaves of red leaf lettuce. Add chopped Romaine lettuce. Mix the diced fruit around the edges of the bowl (you can mix the fruit in a separate bowl first). Arrange the chicken in the middle of the fruit ring. The dressing can be ladled over the salad or served on the side. Top the salad with the crumbled Roquefort cheese and pinenuts. Arrange the onion slices on top. This salad is best served cold and immediately after making it.

■ Best described as a summer salad with the right combination of fruit, chicken and a tangy dressing. Created on the island of St. Barts, it is best made in the summer with ripened fruits.

♥ *The kicker:* the Bakery served this salad as lunch along with their Italian-style bread. To make this meal low-cholesterol, substitute freshly-grated parmesan cheese for the Roquefort.

Krisi's Brownies with Hot Fudge Sauce from the Pine Creek Cookhouse

MAKES 24

BROWNIES

1 Stick plus 3 Tablespoons butter
2 oz Semi-sweet chocolate
4 oz Unsweetened chocolate
1 C Brown sugar, tightly packed
1 C Granulated sugar
1½ t Vanilla
1½ C Flour
1 t Salt
2 t Baking powder
4 Eggs
½ C Chopped nuts (your choice, we use almonds)

Preheat oven to 350 degrees. Use a 9" x 13" pan. Make the brownies: in a heavy medium sized saucepan, melt butter and chocolates over low heat, stirring occasionally. When all are melted, remove from heat and stir in sugars and vanilla. Add flour, salt and baking powder and mix well. Then add the eggs, stirring briefly after each addition. Sprinkle top with chopped nuts. Bake 25-30 minutes, more for a double batch. Toothpick should come out dry.

■ Make the sauce: in a small saucepan, melt butter. Remove from heat, add cocoa, whisk until smooth. Stir in chocolate, sugar and evaporated milk or whipping cream. Bring to boil over medium heat stirring constantly. Remove from heat. Stir in salt, cool and stir in vanilla.

■ Serve brownies with hot fudge sauce and whipped cream!

HOT FUDGE SAUCE

5 T Butter
¼ C Cocoa powder
2 Squares unsweetened chocolate
¾ C Granulated sugar
⅔ C Whipping cream or evaporated milk
Pinch salt
1 t Vanilla

Krisi's Korozott (Hungarian Cheese Spread) from the Pine Creek Cookhouse

MAKES 2 CUPS

1 lb Cream cheese
⅓ lb Butter
¾ C Sour cream
⅓ C Green onions, chopped
1 T Hungarian paprika
1 T Caraway seeds
1 T Dijon mustard
½ lb Cottage cheese
1 T Anchovy paste
1 T Capers

Bring the cream cheese to room temperature. Melt the butter. Put all ingredients into Cuisinart and blend well. Serve with cocktail bread or vegetables.

♥ *The kicker:* this is the dip that arrives at your table after skiing or biking to the Cookhouse. It's a well-deserved treat. It's incredibly easy to make. To lower the fat, omit the butter and use low-fat cream cheese, sour cream and cottage cheese.

Krisi's Spenot Palacsinta (Spinach Crêpes) from the Pine Creek Cookhouse

SERVES 6

CRÊPE BATTER
4 Eggs
1 C Milk
½ C White flour
½ C Whole wheat flour
2 T Oil
1 C Club soda water

SPINACH FILLING
4 T Margarine
¼ C Green onions, chopped
1 t Hungarian paprika (found in specialty stores)
Pinch garlic powder
¼ t White pepper
¼ C Flour
1 C Chicken broth
½ C Milk
1 C Mushrooms, chopped
½ C Cheddar cheese, shredded
2 C Cooked spinach, chopped
Pinch nutmeg
1 T Worcestershire sauce

TOPPING
1 C Sour Cream
1 C Buttermilk
Fresh Parmesan cheese, grated

To make the crêpes: put flour and milk into a large bowl and whisk until very smooth. Add oil, eggs and mix well. Add soda water and stir. Refrigerate overnight. Make the crêpes in any standard crêpe or omelette pan.

■ To make the filling: melt margarine in small saucepan, sauté green onions, add paprika, garlic and pepper. Whisk in flour and blend thoroughly. Remove from heat and whisk in chicken broth and milk. Cool, stirring constantly, until mixture is smooth. Add mushrooms and cheese. Heat and stir until cheese is melted. Add spinach, nutmeg and worcestershire sauce. Stir. Spoon filling into crêpes and wrap around.

■ To make the topping: whisk sour cream and buttermilk together. Spoon 3 or 4 tablespoons on each crêpe. Sprinkle with fresh Parmesan and place under broiler until Parmesan melts.

Wine Suggestion: Badacsoni Kéknyelï (a Hungarian Chenin Blanc!).

Windstar's Spinach Lasagna

CREATED BY DIANE STURGIS

SERVES 8

1 Recipe Italian sauce (recipe follows)
1½ lbs Fresh spinach
1 lb Firm tofu, drained well on paper towels
1 lb Creamed, low-fat cottage cheese
¼ C Grated Parmesan cheese
½ C Fresh chopped parsley
1 t Vege-sal or to taste
Pepper to taste
1 C Grated Monterey Jack cheese
¾ lb Sesame or spinach lasagna noodles
1 T Olive oil
¾ lb Grated Mozzarella cheese
Oregano

First make the sauce: sauté garlic and onions in heated oil for a few minutes until tender. Add bay leaves, basil and oregano. Lower heat and stir in tomato paste, blending well. Add next 7 ingredients. Simmer over low heat for about 30 minutes, stirring occasionally. Add sliced mushrooms and simmer for another 20 minutes. If sauce is too thick for your taste, thin with water. Adjust seasonings to taste.

■ Wash, stem and steam spinach. Do not overcook. Drain well. In a bowl, crumble tofu. Add cottage cheese and blend together. Add the next 5 ingredients and mix well. Cook lasagna noodles al dente in lightly salted water to which 1 tablespoon of oil has been added. Keep covered in cold water until ready to use.

ITALIAN SAUCE

¼ C Olive oil
4 Large cloves garlic, minced
1 Small onion, chopped
2 Small bay leaves
4 t Dried basil
1½ t Oregano
1 6 oz Can tomato paste
1 28 oz Can crushed tomatoes
1 14 oz Can diced tomatoes
2 T Fresh chopped parsley
½ t Sea salt or to taste
¼ t Pepper or to taste
½ t Honey
Dash tamari
½ lb Mushrooms, sliced

Recipe continued on following page

■ In a lasagna pan or large casserole dish, spread 1 cup of sauce. Arrange a flat layer of noodles on sauce, and spread another ¾ cup of sauce on noodles. Sprinkle cheese mixture on top and add a little Mozzarella cheese. Arrange spinach and cover with 1 cup sauce. Layer remaining noodles, smother with sauce and top with Mozzarella cheese. Sprinkle with oregano. Cover loosely with foil and bake in a pre-heated 350 degrees oven for 50 minutes. Uncover and bake another 10 minutes or until hot and bubbly. Remove from oven and let sit for about 5 minutes before serving.

The kicker: you can substitute 2 pounds of ricotta cheese for tofu and cottage cheese. You might want to double this recipe because it freezes so well. Although this recipe takes quite a bit of time to prepare, it's one of the best lasagnas I've ever served. Even men who love meat and potatoes love this recipe!

APPENDIX I

High Altitude and Low Altitude Cooking Conversions

These recipes have been prepared for high altitude (above 7,000 feet) cooking. However, contrary to popular belief, adjusting them to low altitude requires very little work. In fact, many of the recipes in this book will work perfectly when cooked at sea level. Many of these recipes were tested both in Aspen and at lower elevations to prove this theory. Breads, cakes and muffins are the few exceptions. The following hints will allow you to be successful:

YEAST DOUGH: Increase the flour. Plan on 15 minutes longer to rise at lower altitudes.

CAKES AND QUICK BREADS: Increase each teaspoon of baking powder or soda by ¼ teaspoon and increase the sweetener by ⅛ cup for each cup requested. Decrease liquids from 1 to 4 tablespoons per cup and lower the oven temperature 25 degrees.

MUFFINS: Increase the sweetener and baking powder by a fourth.

On the other hand, if this is your first attempt at cooking at high altitude, you'll want to know the following information:

☐ The air is thinner which causes less pressure.

☐ Liquids boil at lower temperatures than at sea level.

☐ If boiling anything, plan on a longer cooking time.

☐ Because the air is drier, plan on using extra liquids to prevent evaporation. Don't be surprised at how quickly yeast dough rises!

Abbreviations

C=cup t=teaspoon T=tablespoon oz=ounce lb=pound

APPENDIX II

Introduction

"Do you like wine? Would you like to have the confidence to choose a wine to serve with a new recipe or an old favorite? Do you want to know where to begin when selecting a wine that makes your food taste better and the meal more enjoyable?"

"It's not difficult; in fact, it's fun! Of course, the more you learn about wine, the easier it becomes. You can begin by asking the advice of your fine wine shop or reading the wine description, but ultimately, you must learn to taste for yourself and to trust your own judgement. *If it tastes good to you, it is good*!"

These suggestions were written by Karen Keehn and I could find no better person to write an introduction to wine and food than Karen. She and her husband, Rich, own McDowell Valley Vineyards, an estate winery in Mendocino County, in Northern California. They are frequent visitors to Aspen. It is said of the Keehn's, "They don't just grow grapes and make good wine, they create varietal wines in a style to complement food and they know just which foods enhance which wines best, because they are constantly trying different combinations." (Millie Howie, *The Review* 1986.)

I have asked Karen, as a great cook and wine expert, to write some facts linking wines to food; a wonderful combination when used to enhance each other.

The Interested Consumer's Guide to Wine and Food

WINE HAS FIVE PRIMARY STRUCTURAL COMPONENTS
THAT AFFECT THE WAY FOOD TASTES:

1. FLAVOR What flavor do I taste? Is it a fruit or berry, herb or spice (which are contributed from the grape itself) or vanilla, nut-like, oily or buttery (that comes from the way the wine was made)? How strong or how delicate is the flavor? Do I want to repeat a similar flavor in the food or use something that contrasts but does not compete with the wine?

2. ACIDITY What level of acidity does the wine have? Is it low (lacking "zing"), balanced, crisp or tart? Wine acids peak food flavors, and "cut" the fat content of foods. Try using citrus instead of vinegar to enhance wine acids.

3. SWEETNESS Is this a dry wine or does it have some level of sweetness? How much? Wines with sweetness tend to taste better with foods that have some sweetness, tartness, or saltiness. Dry wines tend to taste sour with sweet foods.

4. TANNIN What is the level of tannin? Tannin (usually in fine red wines) is recognized by a puckering, dry sensation in the mouth like very strong tea. Its presence is necessary for wine to age and will be more noticeable in younger wines. Strong tannins can detract from delicate foods or combine with salt or acids to taste metallic. However, when these same wines are paired with foods higher in fat content (lamb, beef, duck, butter, cheese, etc.), their tannins seem to "bind" with the fat and "release" the fruit flavors in the wine.

5. STYLE Style is the sum of flavor, acidity, sweetness, and tannin and is determined by the way the wine is made or processed. When

matching wines and foods, *style may be as important as the variety of grape used to make the wine.* A wine grape variety can be made in many styles. Chardonnay, for instance, can be made with a clear perception of fruit, crisp acidity, some sweetness, and no oak complexity. Or, that same grape can be fermented in barrels for oak complexity with balanced acidity and no sweetness to produce a Chardonnay of a completely different style. Both may be excellent wines but the different styles will complement different foods.

Karen has provided the following wine descriptions. She prefaces them with saying, "These descriptions reflect the most common style from premium wineries. We believe that seasoning can be the tie that binds the food to the wine."

CHARDONNAY. The Chardonnay grape makes the world's finest dry wines. The fruit often conveys complex flavors of melon, pear, fig, apple or grapefruit with touches of honey and clove. The style is most often dry with rich fruit flavors and good acid structure complexed by a toastiness from fermentation or aging in small oak barrels. Other styles can be less assertive in flavor with a more pronounced acid structure.

SAUVIGNON BLANC/FUMÉ BLANC. Sauvignon Blanc's taste characteristics are often described as melon, pear, gooseberry or grapefruit; it can sometimes have vegetal, spicy or herbal overtones. This versatile white wine is most frequently made in a dry style with balanced acidity, complex fruit flavors and a touch of oak. Sauvignon Blanc is sometimes made with a light sweetness and no oak complexity.

CHENIN BLANC. This delicate white wine's charm lies in its subtle melon and pear flavors. It can be fermented to dryness with a balanced acidity and a touch of oak complexity. Other styles may be sweeter or more acidic with no oak complexity.

RIESLING or COLOMBARD. The Colombard can be similar to a Riesling wine with fresh, lively but delicate apple aromas and flavors. It should have a crisp, refreshing acidity to balance the usual hint of sweetness.

ZINFANDEL BLANC/WHITE ZINFANDEL. This wine has an appealing pale rose color with lively fruit flavors reminiscent of watermelon and spice. It is usually enhanced by a slight sweetness and a refreshing tartness. This popular blush wine category can vary in levels of sweetness and acidity, and is popular as an apéritif.

GRENACHE. A beautiful ruby red-colored wine with complexed flavors similar to strawberry and cherry. A delicious wine when made with just a touch of sweetness and good acidity; it serves as one of the most versatile wines with food.

CABERNET SAUVIGNON. The world's most noble red wine having a deep ruby color with distinctive, pungent aromas of black currant, raspberry, cherry, with touches of cinnamon, cedar and pepper. Premium styles may be more tannic when young to provide the necessary structure for aging. Its complexities and elegance are enhanced with bottle age.

SYRAH. Syrah is a wine of deep purple color when young, intense aromas and rich flavors of plum, blackberry and currant. Tannins are balanced with rich fruit, showing great finesse and complexity with age. The Petite Sirah, a different but similar variety, has cherry-like flavors, heavier tannin and pepper spice.

ZINFANDEL. Zinfandel is a ruby red wine with appealing raspberry flavor complexed by spiciness and hints of bay leaf and herb. Usually made in a readily drinkable style, it is also made as a light Beaujolais, heavy red or even a port style depending on the winery.

THE DO'S AND THE DON'TS OF COMBINING FOOD AND WINE

The DO's—to make pairing more enjoyable and less traumatic, we suggest that you adhere to a few basic concepts:

1. Try to strike a balance between the wine and food so that they each taste better when tasted together. To do this remember:
   a. Stronger flavored wines seem to taste better when balanced with stronger flavored foods.
   b. Conversely, more delicately flavored wines are better appreciated when served with foods that are more delicately seasoned or textured.
   c. Wines with spicier aromas and flavors are often enhanced by similar spicy accents in foods; to carry this further, wines with bolder, coarser flavors are better matches for coarser, simpler fare.
2. When developing a recipe or deciding on a dish to pair with wine, it sometimes helps to think that most foods have little flavor of their own that enhances or competes with wine. Rather, foods serve as a base flavor or medium to carry other seasonings that can be matched to a wine variety or style. These seasonings can be the key to tying the wine & food flavors together.
3. Learn to use specific herbs, spices and seasonings to enhance certain wine varieties or styles. Examples: marjoram butter with fish & Fumé Blanc; beef with tarragon sauce and Cabernet Sauvignon, lamb with rosemary and Syrah.
4. Use the "beverage" wine as a cooking ingredient in sauces, etc. It really doesn't take much wine and it reinforces the same flavors in the food that are in the wine. If this sounds too inconvenient or expensive, you can use a wine of similar flavor, structure or style.
5. When serving more than one wine variety or style, we suggest that you progress from cold to room temperature, dry to sweet, white to rosé then red, delicate to bold, old to young.
6. Serve more simple foods with older wine vintages to better appreciate their complexities and elegance.

The DON'Ts—to avoid being disappointed, we advise a few words of caution when working with fine wine:

1. Wine that does not taste good enough to drink should not be considered good enough to cook with. The "off" flavors are often transferred to the dish.

2. Excessive use of some seasonings can overpower the taste & pleasure of wine. These include salt, garlic, vinegar, ginger, sugar, hot peppers & cilantro. Don't avoid using them altogether, just use with some restraint. Or combine with milder ingredients to "cut" their strength.

3. Vegetable acids can compete with wine. Many vegetables have acids that compete with the pleasures of wine, particularly artichokes, asparagus, spinach and sorrel. We suggest diminishing the competitive effect of their acids by using sweet spices or sauces containing cheese, cream, mayonnaise or other dairy products.

4. Cold temperatures subdue wine aromas & flavors. Temperatures that are too cold (below 55 degrees Fahrenheit) can subdue the aromas and flavors of more complex wines.

The pleasures of our palate are a complex interaction of flavors and aromas that are never perceived in isolation. Wine alone has over two hundred different aroma compounds. In this context we would like to suggest that it is a good practice to *serve the wine first* to savor its various flavors and impressions and *then* serve the food. In this way, each can be appreciated for its own enjoyment and then together. And, if you should choose a combination that delights all the senses together...Voila! Our heartiest thanks and congratulations.

Karen & Rich Keehn, PROPRIETORS
McDowell Valley Vineyards

RECIPE INDEX

SAUCES & SALSAS

SIDE DISHES

SOUPS, CHILIES & STEWS

NOTES

COOKBOOK ORDER FORM

To: Jill Sheeley, Box 845, Aspen, Colorado 81612
Please send me____copies of **"Lighter Tastes of Aspen"** at $19.95 per copy. ($19.95 plus $3.00 for shipping) Enclosed is my check for $ _________ made payable to Jill Sheeley. (970) 925-6025.

Name____

Street____

City__________________________State_______________Zip____________

☐ This is a gift. Please send directly to:

Name____

Street____

City__________________________State_______________Zip____________

☐ All books will come autographed by the author. Please specify if you'd like yours personalized.

- ✂

To: Jill Sheeley, Box 845, Aspen, Colorado 81612
Please send me____copies of **"Lighter Tastes of Aspen"** at $19.95 per copy. ($19.95 plus $3.00 for shipping) Enclosed is my check for $ _________ made payable to Jill Sheeley. (970) 925-6025.

Name____

Street____

City__________________________State_______________Zip____________

☐ This is a gift. Please send directly to:

Name____

Street____

City__________________________State_______________Zip____________

☐ All books will come autographed by the author. Please specify if you'd like yours personalized.